1,001 Accounting Practice Problems® FOR DUMMIES®

A Wiley Brand

1,001 Accounting Practice Problems® For Dummies®

A Wiley Brand

by Kate Mooney

For Dummies®
A Wiley Brand

1,001 Accounting Practice Problems® For Dummies®

Published by: **John Wiley & Sons, Inc.,** 111 River Street, Hoboken, NJ 07030-5774, www.wiley.com

Library of Congress Control Number: 2014954678

ISBN 978-1-118-85328-3 (pbk); ISBN 978-1-118-85322-1 (ebk); ISBN 978-1-118-85329-0 (ebk)

Manufactured in the United States of America

SKY10032851_012722

Contents at a Glance

Table of Contents

Introduction

This book is intended for anyone who needs to brush up on basic accounting concepts. You may use this book as a supplement to material you're learning in an undergraduate accounting course. If you're working as an accountant, this book may help you with concepts that you need to review. The book provides a basic level of accounting knowledge. After you understand these concepts, you can move on to more complex accounting issues.

What You'll Find

The 1,001 accounting questions are grouped into 14 chapters that cover everything from absorption costing to warranty expense. The last chapter of the book contains the answers, with detailed answer explanations. If you miss a question, take a close look at the answer explanation. Understanding where you went wrong will help you learn the concepts.

Beyond the Book

This product comes with a free online Cheat Sheet that helps you increase your accounting knowledge. Check it out at `www.dummies.com/cheatsheet/1001accounting`.

Where to Go for Additional Help

This book covers a great deal of accounting material. Because there are so many topics, you may struggle in some areas. If you get stuck, consider getting some additional help.

In addition to getting help from your friends, teachers, or coworkers, you can find a variety of great materials online. If you have Internet access, a simple search often turns up a treasure trove of information. You can also head to `www.dummies.com` to see the many articles and books that can help you in your studies.

1,001 Accounting Practice Problems For Dummies gives you just that — 1,001 practice questions and answers that increase your understanding and give you an opportunity to apply accounting concepts. If you need more in-depth study and direction for your accounting courses, you may want to try out the following *For Dummies* products (or their companion workbooks), all published by Wiley. There are *For Dummies* books that cover each of the major areas of study in accounting:

- ***Accounting For Dummies,* by John A. Tracy:** This book provides an introduction to the most important accounting concepts. You'll learn about cash versus accrual accounting and how accounting transactions are processed.

- ***Cost Accounting For Dummies,* by Ken Boyd:** This book explains how costs are identified and assigned to products and services. The text also explains how companies price their products and how firms calculate profit.
- ***Financial Accounting For Dummies,* by Maire Loughran:** Use this book to understand how accountants generate financial statements. This book explains how accounting information is presented to investors, lenders, and regulators.
- ***Managerial Accounting For Dummies,* by Mark P. Holtzman:** Try this book if you need to understand how management uses accounting to make decisions. For example, managers need accounting data to decide whether they should manufacture a component part themselves or buy the part from an outside firm. This book explains how accounting is used inside an organization.

Part I
The Questions

1,001 Questions

web extras

Visit www.dummies.com for free access to great *For Dummies* content online.

In this part . . .

The only way to become proficient in accounting is through a lot of practice. Fortunately, you now have 1,001 practice opportunities right in front of you. These questions cover a variety of accounting concepts and range in difficulty from easy to hard. Master these problems and you'll be well on your way to a solid foundation in accounting concepts.

Here are the types of problems that you can expect to see:

- Elements of accounting (Chapter 1)
- Financial effect of transactions (Chapter 2)
- Bookkeeping cycle and adjusting and closing entries (Chapters 3 and 4)
- Understanding and reporting profit (Chapter 5)
- Reporting financial conditions on the balance sheet (Chapter 6)
- Coupling the income statement and balance sheet (Chapter 7)
- Reporting cash flows (Chapter 8)
- Reporting changes in stockholders' equity (Chapter 9)
- Choosing accounting methods (Chapter 10)
- Profit behavior analysis (Chapter 11)
- Manufacturing cost accounting (Chapter 12)
- Investment analysis and financial statement analysis (Chapters 13 and 14)

Chapter 1

Elements of Accounting

Accounting is a subject that requires you to learn concepts in a specific order. That's because concept B builds upon what you learned about concept A. In fact, an accounting student can get very frustrated trying to learn a concept by jumping ahead and not understanding earlier concepts. This chapter provides some of the critical elements of accounting. You need these concepts before moving on to any other accounting topics.

The Problems You'll Work On

In this chapter, you see a variety of algebra problems:

- Working with transactions that change the accounting equation
- Defining assets, liabilities, equity, revenue, and expenses
- Understanding the differences between cash-basis and accrual-basis accounting
- Compiling the income statement using revenue and expense transactions
- Using the balance sheet and the income statement

What to Watch Out For

Don't let common mistakes trip you up. Some of the following suggestions may be helpful:

- Be careful when using the accounting equation. There are two versions of the formula. One is assets – liabilities = equity. The other is assets = liabilities + equity. Keep in mind which version you're using.
- The profit calculation using accrual accounting is unrelated to a firm's cash position. A firm can have a very profitable month and have a very low cash position.
- To understand the statement of cash flows, identify the investment and financing transactions first. After you identify those transactions, all the other cash flows are related to operations.
- Accounts receivable and accounts payable transactions are only posted when you use accrual accounting. If a company is using the cash basis, you don't use receivables or payables.

Types of Business Entities

1–5

1. Business entities can legally be organized in a variety of ways. What is a common characteristic among all business entity types?

2. What business type is a single-owner business?

3. Entering into a business with another person is an example of what type of business entity?

4. Why is a sole partnership not one of the ways of legally organizing a business?

5. Which business type is most difficult to create initially but, once created, makes it easier to raise funds and provides liability protection for the owners?

The Accounting Equation and Why It Balances

6–30

6. What is the proper format of the basic accounting equation?

7. What are *assets?*

8. What makes a vehicle purchased with a loan an example of an asset?

9. What are *liabilities?*

10. Why is money owed to a bank on a loan considered a liability?

11. What does it mean when a company purchases something *on account?*

12. Why is a loan from a bank not an asset?

13. Why is office equipment an example of an asset?

14. What is the name for resources owned by a company?

15. A business has assets of $135,000 and liabilities of $45,000. Calculate the amount of owners' equity.

16. A business has liabilities of $345,700 and owners' equity of $154,300. Calculate the amount of assets the company has.

17. At the end of an accounting period, a company's total assets equaled $1,450,000, and owners' equity was $654,000. How much were the company's liabilities?

18. At the end of an accounting period, a company's total assets equaled $576,000, and liabilities equaled $245,000. How much was the company's owners' equity?

19. At the end of an accounting period, a company's owners' equity equaled $2,376,000, and its liabilities equaled $142,000. How much were the company's assets?

20. What does it mean when a business has *negative retained earnings?*

21. What is the effect on the accounting equation if a company buys a truck with a cash down payment of $5,000 and borrows the remaining $25,000?

22. What is the effect on the accounting equation when a company pays cash for purchases of inventory?

23. What is the effect on the accounting equation when a company obtains a loan to purchase a delivery truck?

24. A company owes a supplier $37,000 for inventory purchased a week ago. What is the effect on the accounting equation if the company makes a $20,000 payment?

25. What is the effect on the accounting equation when owners contribute a delivery truck to a company?

26. What is the effect on the accounting equation when a company earns revenue by selling a product and collects the amount of the sale in cash?

27. What is the impact on the accounting equation when a company uses its cash to pay for office expenses such as rent and utilities?

28. What does it mean when a business is *highly leveraged?*

29. The owners of a start-up invest $1,000,000 into the business. After one year of operations, the business has assets of $850,000 and losses of $300,000. What are the total liabilities at the end of the first year?

30. The owners of a start-up invest $50,000 into the business. After one year of operations, the business has assets of $350,000 and liabilities of $200,000. How much profit or loss did the business generate during the first year?

Cash-basis Accounting versus Accrual-basis Accounting

31–52

31. What is the main characteristic of cash-basis accounting?

32. What is the main characteristic of accrual-basis accounting?

33. What is the primary difference between cash-basis and accrual-basis accounting?

34. Cash-basis accounting is most frequently used by which group?

35. Accrual-basis accounting is most frequently used by which group?

36. Why is cash-basis accounting *not* used by large businesses?

37. When are transactions recorded under accrual-basis accounting?

38. Al LaMode Ice Cream Company produces high-quality ice cream that is distributed to shops in resort areas. On July 1, the company purchased the raw materials to make the ice cream. On July 15, the process was complete, and the product was stored in the freezer ready to ship to customers. On July 31, Ken and Mary's Ice Cream Shop ordered 200 pounds of ice cream. On August 1, Al LaMode delivered the ice cream to Ken and Mary's Ice Cream Shop. Ken and Mary paid Al LaMode on August 10. Ken and Mary sold all the ice cream between August 5 and August 12. If it uses accrual-basis accounting, when will Al LaMode record the revenue from the sale to Ken and Mary?

39. Al LaMode Ice Cream Company produces high quality ice cream that is distributed to shops in resort areas. On July 1, the company purchased the raw materials to make the ice cream. On July 15, the process was complete, and the product was stored in the freezer ready to ship to customers. On July 31, Ken and Mary's Ice Cream Shop ordered 200 pounds of ice cream. On August 1, Al LaMode delivered the ice cream to Ken and Mary's Ice Cream Shop. Ken and Mary paid Al LaMode on August 10. Ken and Mary sold all the ice cream between August 5 and August 12. If it uses cash-basis accounting, when will Al LaMode record the revenue from the sale to Ken and Mary?

40. Little Falls Bandages sells medical supplies to college football teams. The teams pay a flat fee of $10,000 on August 1 for as many bandages as they need during the football season, September through November. If they use cash-basis accounting, how much revenue does Little Falls record in September?

41. Furd Buggy Company uses electricity in its retail shop during the month of May. On June 15, the company receives the bill for the May electricity usage for $759. Furd pays the bill on July 1. If Furd Buggy Company uses accrual-basis accounting, on which month's income statement will the expense appear, and how much will it be?

42. Credit Cab Corporation buys fuel from a fuel bank, paying $1,000,000 on January 1 for 250,000 gallons of fuel. The company uses the last of the 250,000 gallons on July 1. The January income statement shows a fuel expense of $1,000,000. What basis of accounting does Credit Cab use?

43–49 Use the following information to answer the questions. The following is selected information regarding Ace, Inc. for the fiscal year 2015:

- **Cash receipts from sales made in 2015: $750,000**
- **Cash payments for purchases of inventory in 2015: $325,000**
- **The company did not have a beginning inventory balance in 2015.**
- **Cash payments for other expenses: $375,000**
- **Year-end receivables balance from customers for sales made during the year 2015: $155,000**
- **Cost of products in ending inventory that have not been sold: $120,000**
- **Liability for unpaid expenses that were incurred in 2015: $450,000**

43. Calculate the amount of cash-basis revenues for Ace, Inc. for 2015.

44. Calculate the amount of cash-basis expenses for Ace, Inc. for 2015.

45. Calculate the amount of cash-basis profit or loss for Ace, Inc. for 2015.

46. Calculate the amount of accrual-basis revenues for Ace, Inc. for 2015.

47. Calculate the accrual-basis cost of goods sold for Ace, Inc. for 2015.

48. Calculate, using the accrual basis, other expenses for Ace, Inc. for 2015.

49. Calculate the accrual-basis profit or loss for Ace, Inc. for 2015.

50–52 Use the following information to answer the questions. XYZ, Inc. had the following transactions during 2015:

- **Sales on account: $5,000**
- **Cash sales: $6,000**
- **Amount collected as customer deposits in 2016: $3,000**
- **Amount paid for utilities expenses incurred in 2015: $2,000**
- **Amount paid in advance for services to be used in 2016: $1,000**

50. Calculate the amount of cash-basis revenues for XYZ, Inc. for 2015.

51. Calculate the amount of cash-basis expenses for XYZ, Inc. for 2015.

52. Calculate the amount of difference between accrual-basis revenues and cash-basis revenues for XYZ, Inc. for 2015.

Profit Activities and the Income Statement

53–72

53. What is the name of the financial statement that summarizes a company's revenues, other income, expenses, and losses?

54. What is another name for an income statement?

55. What is the financial statement that shows the business profit or loss during a period?

56. The financial statement you are looking at lists revenues and gains, along with some other items. What financial statement are you viewing?

57. Other than revenues and expenses, what other items may be found on an income statement?

58. A banker asks a borrower for information on the company's revenue growth over the last few years. What financial statement will the borrower provide the banker?

59. What information is presented on an income statement?

60. Which of the following items appear on an income statement?

A. deferred revenue

B. current liabilities

C. loss on the sale of equipment

D. cash received from customers

E. dividends paid to stockholders

61. Identify the expenses that must be listed separately on the income statement to comply with accounting rules.

62–64 *Use the following information to answer the questions. Hummus Records has the following current-year information in its accounting records:*

- Sales revenue: $47,000
- Interest revenue: $1,200
- Selling expenses: $14,000
- General expenses: $3,000
- Cost of goods sold: $20,000
- Tax expense: $2,200

62. Calculate the gross profit for Hummus Records.

63. Calculate the operating income for Hummus Records.

64. Calculate the income before taxes for Hummus Records.

65–68 *Use the following information to answer the questions. The following data is available for Koala Kuddles for 2015:*

- Sales revenue: $15,000,000
- Cost of goods sold: $12,400,000
- Interest expense: $125,000
- Selling, general, and administrative expense: $1,450,000
- Loss on the sale of equipment: $275,000
- Income tax expense: $200,000
- Cost of new equipment: $800,000

65. What is the amount of gross profit on Koala Kuddles' 2015 income statement?

66. What is the amount of operating earnings on Koala Kuddles' 2015 income statement?

67. What is the amount of earnings or loss before income taxes on Koala Kuddles' 2015 income statement?

68. What is the amount of net income or loss on Koala Kuddles' 2015 income statement?

69–72 Use the following information to answer the questions. The following data is available for Petal Bikes for 2015:

- Sales revenue: $8,000,000
- Gross margin: $2,000,000
- Operating earnings: $650,000
- Earnings before income tax: $420,000
- Net income: $180,000
- Petal Bikes had no gains or losses and no interest revenue in 2015.

69. What is the amount of income tax expense on Petal Bikes' 2015 income statement?

70. What is the amount of the cost of goods sold on Petal Bikes' 2015 income statement?

71. What is the amount of selling, general, and administrative expenses on Petal Bikes' income statement?

72. What is the amount of interest expense on Petal Bikes' 2015 income statement?

Financial Condition and the Balance Sheet

73–78

73. What are the three primary financial statements?

74. What is the balance sheet sometimes called?

75. GameTime Caterers has presented its banker with a financial statement that displays the cash balance on hand, the amount owed to its suppliers, common stock, and retained earnings as of December 31, 2015. What statement did the company give to the banker?

76–78 Use the following information to answer the questions. The following data is available for Car Bop, Inc. for 2015:

- Amounts owed by customers: $75,000
- Cost of unsold product: $90,000
- Cash balance: $110,000
- Amounts owed for unpaid purchases and expenses: $72,000
- Notes payable to bank: $73,000
- Unearned revenues: $10,000
- Cash sales for 2015: $227,000
- Credit sales for 2015: $133,000
- Cost of goods sold for 2015: $175,000

76. What are the total assets on Car Bop's balance sheet?

77. What are the total liabilities on Car Bop's balance sheet?

78. What is the total equity on Car Bop's balance sheet?

Cash Flows and the Statement of Cash Flows

79–90

79. A banker is considering a loan to finance a vehicle for a small company but wants to make sure that the company will have enough cash to make the payments over the next three years. What statement should she look at?

80. The statement of cash flows includes a section called which of the following?

A. cash outflows

B. cash inflows

C. summary of cash

D. operating activities

E. spending activities

81. During the year, Organic Bricks Co. paid cash for a new delivery truck. Where on the statement of cash flows would that event appear?

82. During the year, Organic Bricks made the last payment on the mortgage on its building. How should the company classify this on the statement of cash flows?

83. Organic Bricks sold an old truck that originally cost $76,000. The book value of the truck was $26,000, and the company received $30,000 in cash from the buyer as full payment. How should the company reflect this transaction in the cash flows from investing activities?

84. Determine the amount of change in cash during the year based on the following:

- Cash flow from operating activities: ($50,000)
- Cash flow from investing activities: $20,000
- Cash flow from financing activities: $50,000
- Significant non-cash transactions include purchase of a building with a $250,000 note.

85. Determine the cash flow from investing activities during the year based on the following:

- Cash flow from operating activities: $50,000
- Cash flow from financing activities: $25,000
- Net increase/(decrease) in cash during the year: ($40,000)

86. Determine the cash flow from financing activities during the year based on the following:

- Cash flow from operating activities: $6,000
- Cash flow from investing activities: ($5,000)
- Net increase/(decrease) in cash during the year: $13,000

87. Determine the cash flow from operating activities during the year based on the following:

- Cash flow from investing activities: $45,000
- Cash flow from financing activities: ($55,000)
- Cash at the beginning of the year: $270,000
- Cash at the end of the year: $370,000

88–90 Use the following information to answer the questions. The following data is available for Lawn Paint Yard Service:

- Proceeds received from issuance of stock: $20,000
- New equipment purchases: $130,000
- Amount of a new note payable: $65,000
- Proceeds from sale of old equipment with a book value of $40,000: $45,000
- Dividends paid: $40,000
- Dividends declared but unpaid: $10,000
- Cash flow from operating activities: $45,000

88. Calculate the cash flow from investing activities for Lawn Paint Yard Service.

89. Calculate the cash flow from financing activities for Lawn Paint Yard Service.

90. If Lawn Paint Yard Service started the year with a cash balance of $6,300, what was the balance of cash on hand at the end of the year?

Chapter 2

Financial Effects of Transactions

This chapter explains the three basic financial statements. You'll go over the information found in each type of statement. The chapter also points out the financial impact of many accounting transactions. As an accountant, you need to understand how accounting activity affects each financial statement.

The Problems You'll Work On

In this chapter, you see questions on these topics:

- Going over the three basic financial statements
- Finding out about prepaid assets and unearned revenue
- Understanding cash versus credit sales and customer deposits
- Reviewing how inventory costs are moved to cost of sales
- Working with depreciation expense

What to Watch Out For

Don't let common mistakes trip you up. Some of the following suggestions may be helpful:

- Be careful when posting customer payments. Some customer payments are deposits. A customer deposit means that you haven't delivered a product or service yet. You post customer deposits to a liability account.
- Some expenses are paid in advance. Insurance premiums, for example, are paid before the period of insurance coverage. You post these premium payments to prepaid assets. The payments are considered an asset because you don't have to pay cash later to cover the expense.
- Inventory is an asset account. When you sell inventory, you move those costs from an asset account to cost of sales expense.
- Depreciation expense is a non-cash item. Rather than crediting cash, you credit accumulated depreciation.

Classifying Business Transactions

91–99

91. What are the primary financial statements?

92. What is the name of the financial statement that summarizes a business's assets, liabilities, and owners' equity at the end of an accounting period?

93. What is the name of the financial statement that summarizes the profit-making transactions during a period of time?

94. What is the name of the financial statement that summarizes a business's cash transactions during a period of time?

95. The primary activity of a business is focused on which of the following?

A. generating assets

B. generating a profit

C. creating jobs

D. communities

E. executive compensation

96. Which of the following transactions relates to generating cost of goods sold?

A. obtaining a loan from a bank

B. selling services to customers

C. purchasing a new machine for the factory

D. hiring a new employee

E. purchasing inventory

97. Which of the following is an example of a profit-making transaction?

A. obtaining a loan from a bank

B. selling services to customers

C. purchasing a new machine for the factory

D. hiring a new employee

E. purchasing inventory

98. Which of the following is an example of an investing activity?

A. obtaining a loan from a bank

B. selling services to customers

C. purchasing a new machine for the factory

D. hiring a new employee

E. purchasing inventory

99. Which of the following is an example of a financing activity?

A. obtaining a loan from a bank

B. selling services to customers

C. purchasing a new machine for the factory

D. hiring a new employee

E. purchasing inventory

Looking at Both Sides of Business Transactions

100–109

100. Which of the following is a responsibility of an accountant?

A. executing all business transactions

B. determining the business justification of every transaction

C. auditing the financial statements for accuracy

D. the operations of the business

E. recording of the transactions in the accounting records

101. The most important assets that are found on the balance sheets of most businesses that sell products are which of the following?

A. cash, accounts receivable, goodwill, and inventory

B. accounts receivable, other assets, inventory, and fixed assets

C. cash, accounts receivable, inventory, and fixed assets

D. cash, sales, inventory, and fixed assets

E. cash, accounts receivable, inventory, sales, and fixed assets

102. What types of liabilities do not usually require the payment of interest?

103–109 Use the following information to answer the questions. The following is a condensed balance sheet for Green Power, Inc. for the fiscal year 2015:

- Cash: $125,000
- Accounts receivable: $150,000
- Inventory: $200,000
- Property, plant, and equipment: $330,000
- Total assets: $805,000
- Operating liabilities: $150,000
- Interest-bearing liabilities: $160,000
- Owners' invested capital: $120,000
- Owners' retained earnings: $375,000

103. Green Power, Inc. received $50,000 cash as a capital contribution from one of its owners. What impact did this transaction have on the balance sheet?

104. Green Power, Inc. took out a bank loan for $100,000 on January 1. The terms of the loan require Green Power to repay the loan in full in three years, plus make annual interest payments of $8,000 on December 31. What impact did this transaction have on the balance sheet on the day the company took out the loan?

105. Green Power, Inc. received a $25,000 payment from a customer as payment on the customer's account. What impact did this transaction have on the balance sheet?

106. Green Power, Inc. made a principal payment of $80,000 on its bank loan. What impact did this transaction have on the balance sheet?

107. Green Power, Inc. made a $10,000 distribution of profit to its owners. What impact did this transaction have on the balance sheet?

108. Green Power, Inc. purchased equipment that cost $20,000 by making a down payment of $5,000 and financing the remainder with a new loan. What impact did this transaction have on the balance sheet?

109. Green Power, Inc. returned $15,000 of inventory previously purchased on account. The balance has not been paid yet. What impact did this transaction have on the balance sheet?

Concentrating on Sales

110–119

110. How does a company increase profits?

111. Subtracting expenses from revenues gives what?

112. Which of the following types of sales increase assets and revenue at the time cash is received?

A. cash sales and advanced payment sales

B. advance payment sales

C. cash sales

D. credit sales and advance payment sales

E. cash sales and credit sales

113. What type of sale transaction creates a liability and no increase in profit for the company?

A. subsequent cash sale

B. cash sale

C. credit sale

D. advance credit sale

E. customer deposit

114. What type of sale transaction increases cash and profit?

A. advance cash sale

B. cash sale

C. credit sale

D. advance credit sale

E. customer deposit

115. What type of sale transaction does not increase cash but does increase profit?

A. advance cash sale

B. cash sale

C. credit sale

D. advance credit sale

E. customer deposit

116. What type of sale transaction increases cash but does not increase profit?

A. subsequent cash sale

B. cash sale

C. credit sale

D. advance credit sale

E. customer deposit

117. Cash purchase of an airline ticket for a flight next month is an example of what kind of transaction to the airline?

118. Bebebanana Co. sells its product either as a cash sale or as a customer deposit. During the year the company received $17,100,000 in cash from customers. The company fulfilled 90% of the orders. What is the effect of these exchanges on the business's financial condition?

119. A company receives $120 on January 1 as payment for a 12-month magazine subscription. Starting in January, the company will deliver the magazines at the end of each month for the next 12 months. How much is the unearned revenue balance on the company's balance sheet as of June 30?

Concentrating on Expenses

120–129

120. Which financial statement includes expenses?

121. Gold Leaves Corporation purchased $47,000 worth of its product during the year. The company had $3,000 of product on hand at the beginning of the year and sold products that it paid $43,000 for during the year. How much expense related to the products sold will Gold Leaves record for the year?

122. A company buys a building for $2,000,000 — $1,000,000 cash immediately and another $1,000,000 in two weeks. When does the company record the expense of that building?

123. Kelly's Cleaning Crew recorded expenses of $287,000 for the year. The expenses included increases to operating liabilities of $2,000 and depreciation on the van and cleaning equipment of $7,500. How did the expenses change the financial condition of the business?

124. A company pays $24,000 cash for a one-year insurance policy on October 1. As of December 31, the company has benefited from three months of insurance coverage. Calculate the amount of insurance expenses recorded as of December 31.

125. At the end of the year, the accountant for Bonnie Cameron Cosmetics notices a balance in the prepaid insurance account of $3,600 that was recorded when the three-year premium was paid on July 1. No other entries have been posted to the prepaid insurance account. How much expense should the accountant record at the end of the year?

126. Dragon Zombie Costumes had $95,000 in expenses on the income statement for the year. Of that amount, depreciation expense was $5,000. The company had no change in inventory or operating liabilities. How much cash was paid for expenses?

127. Dragon Zombie Costumes had $141,000 in expenses for the year. These expenses included depreciation expense of $8,500 and an increase in accounts payable of $2,400. How much cash did the company pay for expenses?

128. Kelly's Clean Crew recorded expenses of $500,000 for the year. The expenses included an increase to wages payable of $3,500 and depreciation on the van and cleaning equipment of $7,500. How much cash did the company pay for expenses?

129. Gray House had $139,000 in expenses for the year. Inventory increased by $2,000, prepaid rent increased by $900, depreciation expense was $9,000, wages payable increased by $12,000, and sales tax payable increased by $4,600. What was the amount of cash used to pay expenses?

Before and after Transactions of Sales and Expenses

130–134 *Use the following information to answer the questions. Assume that during the year a business had the following transactions related to sales:*

- Credit sales: $1,200,000
- Cash sales: $200,000
- Customer deposits: $500,000
- Amount of credit sales collected: $480,000
- Percentage of customer deposits delivered later in the year as completed sales to clients: 50% (of the $500,000)

130. How much did cash increase as a result of those transactions?

131. What is the total impact on receivables as a result of those transactions?

132. What is the total impact on operating liabilities as a result of those transactions?

133. Calculate the total impact on retained earnings as a result of those transactions.

134. Calculate the total impact on total assets as a result of those transactions.

135–139 Use the following information to answer the questions. Assume that during the year a business had the following transactions related to expenses:

- Total expenses: $300,000
- As a result of those expenses, inventory increased by $45,000; property, plant, and equipment increased by $5,000 as a result of purchases; operating liabilities increased by $25,000; and depreciation expenses of $15,000 were recorded during the year.

135. How did those expenses change the net balance of property, plant, and equipment?

136. How did those transactions change the balance of retained earnings?

137. Using the balance sheet equation, how did those transactions change the balance of total assets?

138. How did those transactions change the balance of total liabilities and owners' equity?

139. How did those expenses change the balance of cash?

Determining the Financial Effects of Profit or Loss

140–148

140. How do you calculate profit?

141. Which balance sheet accounts are not affected by sales and expense transactions?

142. Badabing only makes cash sales to its customers and pays all expenses in cash as incurred. During the year, sales were $53,000, and expenses were $42,000. What is the total impact on the financial position for the company as a result of operations during the past year?

143. Profit accumulated by a business since its inception is called what?

144. Badabing only makes credit sales to its customers and pays all expenses in cash as incurred. During the year, sales were $35,000, and expenses were $23,000. Collections from customers were $33,000. What is the total impact on the financial position for the company as a result of operations during the past year?

145–148 *Use the following information to answer the questions. The following information is available from the accounting records of Gold Leaves Corporation:*

- Total sales revenue for the year: $3,200,000
- As a result of the sales, the receivable balance increased by $1,200,000, and unearned revenues increased by $2,000,000. In addition, the business recorded $4,000,000 in total expenses for the year. As a result of those expenses, inventory balance increased by $2,500,000, depreciation expense was $100,000, and accounts payable increased by $500,000.

145. What is the composite change in the year-end operating liabilities balance of the business caused by its profit-making activities during the year?

146. What is the composite change in total assets caused by the business's profit-making activities during the year?

147. What is the net income or loss for the year?

148. What is the composite change in the year-end cash balance of the business caused by its profit-making activities during the year?

Chapter 3

The Bookkeeping Cycle

Bookkeeping is the nuts and bolts of accounting. It includes the most basic accounting activities. This chapter covers the chart of accounts and how accounts are created. You'll see questions on debits and credits and review nominal versus permanent accounts. The chapter provides questions on posting journal entries for a variety of transactions.

The Problems You'll Work On

In this chapter, you see problems on these accounting topics:

- Creating a chart of accounts
- Separating nominal and permanent accounts
- Understanding how each type of account is debited or credited for changes in the account balance
- Finding out about credit card fees and interest income transactions
- Working with sales returns and allowances

What to Watch Out For

Don't let common mistakes trip you up. Some of the following suggestions may be helpful:

- You adjust income statements accounts to a zero balance at the end of each accounting period. They are *nominal* (temporary) accounts.
- Debiting increases some accounts, while others are increased with a credit entry.
- An increase in credit card sales also increases credit card fee expenses.
- Gross sales less sales returns and allowances equals net sales.

Constructing Accounts

149–158

149. What is the purpose of accounts used in accounting?

150. What is the purpose of contra accounts?

151. A provided list of accounts includes depreciation expense, accounts receivable, accumulated depreciation, accounts payable, and sales revenue. Which of these accounts is an example of a commonly used contra asset?

152. What is the primary consideration when first setting up a chart of accounts?

153. What is a chart of accounts?

154. What type of account usually begins a chart of accounts?

155. What are the components of a chart of accounts?

156. What account does a business need in its chart of accounts to record expenses for renting its warehouse space?

157. What accounts does a business need in its chart of accounts to record sales to customers on account?

158. What accounts does a business need in its chart of accounts to record the receipt of cash for products to be delivered in the future?

Identifying Nominal versus Real Accounts

159–168

159. Which of the following accounts are *real* accounts (also known as *permanent* accounts)?

A. asset accounts, liability accounts, and expense accounts

B. asset accounts, liability accounts, and revenue accounts

C. revenue and expense accounts

D. asset accounts, liability accounts, and equity accounts

E. asset accounts and revenue accounts

160. Which of the following accounts are *nominal* accounts (also known as *temporary* accounts)?

A. asset accounts, liability accounts, and expense accounts

B. asset accounts, liability accounts, and revenue accounts

C. revenue and expense accounts

D. asset accounts, liability accounts, and equity accounts

E. asset accounts and revenue accounts

161. Which of the following accounts are *real* accounts?

A. balance sheet accounts

B. temporary accounts

C. profit or loss accounts

D. income statement accounts

E. revenue accounts

162. Which of the following describes nominal accounts?

A. They show balances at a point in time.

B. They're reported on the income statement.

C. They're used to determine the total assets of a business.

D. They're reported on the balance sheet.

E. They're permanent accounts.

163. Why are certain accounts closed at the end of the year?

164. Which of the following accounts is a nominal account?

A. accounts receivable

B. inventory

C. allowance for bad debt

D. prepaid insurance

E. rent expense

165. Which of the following is an example of a nominal account?

A. interest income

B. interest payable

C. accumulated depreciation

D. warranty accrual

E. unearned revenue

166. Which of the following is an example of a real account?

A. service revenue

B. inventory

C. cost of goods sold

D. interest expense

E. advertising expense

167. Which of the following is an example of a real account?

A. utilities expense

B. sales revenue

C. bad debt expense

D. unearned revenue

E. rent expense

168. Which of the following is an example of a real account?

A. interest income

B. salaries expense

C. dividend income

D. marketing expense

E. owners' capital

Knowing Your Debits from Your Credits

169–183

169. The left side of an account is

A. the name of the account

B. the running balance of the account

C. the debit side

D. the credit side

E. the type of account

170. The right side of an account is

A. the name of the account

B. the running balance of the account

C. the debit side

D. the credit side

E. the type of account

171. A *T account* is

A. the accounting record maintained by a business

B. another name for a chart of accounts

C. another name for the accounts listed in the chart of accounts

D. a special account

E. a visual way of showing the basic form of an account

172. What type of accounts increase on the debit side?

173. What type of accounts increase on the credit side?

174. How are decreases to liabilities recorded in journal entries?

175. How are increases to revenues recorded in journal entries?

176. What is the normal balance of an account?

177. What three types of accounts normally have debit balances?

178. What three types of accounts normally have credit balances?

179. What is the journal entry to record a collection of $2,000 of outstanding accounts receivables?

180. What main type of accounts has a normal debit balance?

181. *Credit to an account* means

A. an increase to an account balance

B. a decrease to an account balance

C. recording an amount on the right side of an account

D. recording an amount on the left side of an account

E. the balance of an account

182. A company recorded a debit to an asset account for $1,000 and a credit to a liability account for $200. What else should be recorded to complete the journal entry?

183. An account will have a debit balance if

A. the total debits exceed the total credits

B. the credits exceed the debits

C. the account has a normal debit balance

D. the majority of the transactions recorded in the account are debits

E. it has a normal debit balance

Making Original Journal Entries

184–198

184. *Posting* refers to

A. preparing journal entries

B. preparing financial statements

C. analyzing transactions

D. recording journal entries

E. reviewing financial statements

185. What are the components of a journal entry?

186. Which of the following isn't an example of a specialized journal?

A. sales journal

B. payroll journal

C. cash receipts journal

D. expense journal

E. disbursement journal

187. The general journal is most commonly used to record

A. recurring transactions

B. accounts receivable transactions

C. non-routine accounting entries

D. payables transactions

E. fixed asset details

188. A company records the following journal entry: cash: $5,000; sales revenue: $5,000. Provide a narrative description for the transaction.

189. A company records the following journal entry: cost of goods sold: $5,000; inventory: $5,000. Provide a narrative description for the transaction.

190. What is the proper journal entry to record a payment received from a customer on an outstanding balance?

191. What is the proper journal entry to record a $12,000 purchase of inventory on account?

192. What is the proper journal entry to record a payment on an outstanding balance owed to a supplier?

193. What is the proper entry to record a new three-year, 5% annual interest, $100,000 bank loan?

194. What is the proper entry to record a $25,000 investment in a business made by the owner?

195. What is the proper entry to record $8,000 of salaries paid to employees?

196. What is the proper entry to record a payment on a loan (principal portion only)?

197. What is the proper entry to record $1,500 of rent paid on June 30 to a landlord for the next six months' rent?

198. What is the proper entry to record a purchase of a truck for $20,000 with a 50% cash down payment and the balance financed with a loan?

Recording Revenue and Income

199–218

199. If a company has $5,000 of credit card sales but has to pay $100 of credit card fees, how much should be recorded as cash?

200. When customers pay with credit cards, the seller

A. is responsible for any amounts unpaid

B. is involved in the collection process

C. receives cash equal to the amount of sale

D. receives cash equal to the amount of sale less any credit card fees

E. is responsible for paying the credit card fees after the customer pays his or her credit card company

201. One of the primary reasons sellers are willing to pay the credit card fee is to

A. increase sales, because customers enjoy the convenience of credit cards

B. have the security of credit card transactions

C. receive cash faster

D. encourage customers to pay the fee

E. encourage customers to use credit cards

202. A retailer is charged a credit card fee of 2.5% of credit card sales. If credit card sales total $25,000, what is the total credit card fee?

203. A company has cash sales of $40,000 and no other sales. What is the correct journal entry to record this sale?

204. A company has credit card sales of $3,000, and the bank charges a credit card fee of 2%. How much cash will the seller receive after the credit card fee is paid?

205. A company has credit card sales of $50,000, and the bank charges a 2% credit card fee. What is the correct journal entry to record this sale?

206. A company has credit sales of $20,000 and no other sales. What is the correct journal entry to record this sale?

207. A company processes $120,000 of credit card sales during a day. The bank fee for the credit cards is 3.5%. The entry to record the sales will include a credit to sales revenues of $120,000 and debits to

A. accounts receivable $120,000

B. cash $115,800 and interest expense $4,200

C. accounts receivable $115,800 and credit card fees $4,200

D. accounts receivable $115,800 and interest expense $4,200

E. cash $115,800 and credit card fees $4,200

208. If a company has $10,000 of credit card sales but has to pay $250 in credit card fees, how much should be recorded as sales revenues?

209. Which of the following is *not* a source of income for a company?

A. sales revenue

B. service revenue

C. liability income

D. interest income

E. investment income

210. How is investment income reported?

211. What makes the sales returns and allowances account a contra account?

212. A company receives returns from customers totaling $3,000 and refunds the cash to the customers. What is the proper journal entry for this transaction?

213. When customers pay with credit cards, the seller records

A. revenue in the amount of sale less the credit card fees

B. a receivable

C. cash equal to the amount of sale

D. the credit card fee as a credit

E. revenue for the full sales amount before the credit card fee amount

214. The cost of a company's returned inventory is $1,000. What is the proper entry to record the returned inventory, assuming it can be sold again?

215. A company invests its cash in an interest-bearing money market account. During the month of January, it earns and receives $500 of interest. What is the proper entry to record the interest received?

216. A company has the following transactions during a day: cash sales: $13,500; credit sales: $32,500; credit card sales: $18,500. The company pays a credit card fee of 2% of credit card sales. What is the correct entry to record the day's sales?

217–218 Use the following information to answer the questions. A company has the following sales during the day:

- Sales on account: $20,000
- Cash sales: $10,000
- Credit card sales: $15,000
- The credit card fee paid to the bank is 2% of sales.

217. What is the total amount of revenue (before fees) recorded for the day?

218. What is the total amount of cash recorded for the day?

Recording Expenses and Losses

219–238

219. How many different expense accounts should a business have in its chart of accounts?

220. Expenses can be recorded by

A. decreasing assets

B. increasing assets

C. decreasing liabilities

D. increasing losses

E. increasing revenues

221. Expenses can be recorded by

A. decreasing liabilities

B. increasing assets

C. increasing liabilities

D. increasing losses

E. increasing revenues

222. What accounts are usually credited when expenses are recorded?

223. Which of the following type of expense causes a credit to inventory?

A. bad debt expense

B. depreciation expense

C. income tax expense

D. cost of goods sold

E. inventory sales expense

224. What account is credited when bad debt expense is recorded if the company doesn't record any expense until it actually writes off the account?

225. What is the financial impact of paying expenses with cash?

226. What impact in terms of increase and decrease do expenses have on the balance sheet?

227. A company receives a bill for $550 for its electric service for the month of November. No prior entries were recorded related to this bill. What is the proper journal entry to record the payment of this bill?

228. In March, a company makes a payment of $2,500 for rent of its facilities for March. No prior entries were made relating to this. What is the proper journal entry to record the payment?

229. Employees earn a total of $25,000 during a pay period. What is the proper entry to record the payment of these wages?

230. What type of account is accumulated depreciation?

231. What is the correct entry to record depreciation expense?

232. A company properly records its sales of $20,000 during the month. However, it does not record the cost of goods sold for those sales that totaled $12,000. What is the proper entry to record the cost of goods sold?

233. A company has a $100,000 outstanding balance from a customer who recently filed bankruptcy. The company won't be able to collect this balance and needs to write it off. The business doesn't record any expense caused by the uncollectible account until it actually writes off the account. What is the proper entry to record the write-off of this balance?

234. What makes accumulated depreciation a contra account?

235. A company determines that it needs to record depreciation for the period of $6,500. What is the proper entry to record this depreciation?

236. What account is debited when an employee takes paid vacation time?

237. A company receives an invoice for $5,000 for consulting services performed during the month. The payment terms are net 60 and the company intends to pay the invoice by the due date. What is the proper entry to record this invoice?

238. What are the two primary accounts that are impacted by retirement pension accounting?

Recording Preparatory and Carry-through Transactions

239–257

239. What is the main characteristic of set-up and follow-up transactions?

240. Which of the following transactions is a set-up and follow-up transaction?

A. purchasing equipment

B. obtaining a bank loan

C. selling product

D. paying for office supplies in advance

E. making a payment on a loan

241. Which of the following transactions is *not* an example of a set-up and follow-up transaction?

A. buying inventory

B. collecting receivables

C. paying liabilities for inventory

D. paying insurance expenses in advance

E. processing sales returns

242. Which of the following transactions is an example of a set-up and follow-up transaction?

A. purchasing equipment

B. collecting receivables

C. selling product

D. obtaining a loan

E. making a payment on a loan

243. What type of account is prepaid?

244. Select an asset account from the following list.

A. retained earnings

B. prepaid rent

C. salary expense

D. accounts payable

E. dividends

245. On July 1, a business paid $22,000 for six months of general liability insurance effective July 1. What is the proper entry to record the transaction?

246. What are *prepaids,* and when are they paid?

247. A company buys a large quantity of shipping supplies to obtain a big discount. The supplies will last for about two years but only cost $2,000 in cash. How should the company record the transaction?

248. A company purchases insurance coverage for the next three years. The firm pays cash of $120,000. What is the proper journal entry to record this transaction?

249. What type of inventory transaction results in an increase to inventory and a decrease to assets?

250. A company purchases $20,000 of products for sale on account and properly records the journal entry. Subsequently, the company makes a payment of 50% of the total. What is the proper entry to record this payment?

251. Identify the financial statement that is affected by the purchase of inventory.

252–257 Use the following information to answer the questions. A textbook publisher purchases $90,000 of paper on account to be used for printing of textbooks over the next three months. The company will use one-third of the paper purchased every month for the next three months to print textbooks. The supplier offers a 2% discount if the invoice is paid within ten days of sale. The textbook publisher pays the invoice within five days of the sale. At the end of the month, $10,000 of the product is determined to be defective and is returned to the supplier.

252. What is the proper entry to record the purchase?

253. What is the proper entry to record the usage of paper at the end of the first month?

254. What is the proper entry for the supplier to record when the payment is received?

255. What is the proper journal entry recorded by the textbook publisher for the return of defective paper?

256. At the end of two months, what is the balance in the prepaid expenses account?

257. How much paper expense will the company show on its income statement for the third month?

Recording Transactions with Debt Sources of Capital

258–276

258. What type of debt financing is included on the balance sheet under current liabilities?

259. Debt financing may include restrictions known as

A. interest

B. collateral

C. covenants

D. capital

E. maturity

260. Which of the following transactions is an investing transaction?

A. raising capital

B. acquisition of patents

C. distribution of dividends to shareholders

D. repayment of loans

E. acquisition of debt

261. Purchases of long-term operating assets are also called what?

262. What are fixed assets called on a balance sheet?

263. Fixed assets can be disposed of by

A. exchanging them for a new asset

B. selling them

C. scrapping them

D. either selling them, exchanging them for a new asset, or scrapping them

E. either selling them or exchanging them for a new asset

264. Which of the following types of transactions is a return of invested capital to owners?

A. investing

B. set-up

C. operating

D. follow-up

E. financing

265. A company purchases two pieces of equipment, each costing $1,000,000. For one, it makes a cash payment of $1,000,000. For the other, it takes out a loan for $1,000,000. What is the proper journal entry to record this purchase?

266. A company purchases equipment for $200,000 and takes out a five-year 5% loan to finance the purchase. What is the proper journal entry to record this purchase?

267. What are the two sources of capital?

268. On January 1, Cliche Beret Co. borrows $2,000,000 to pay for a new manufacturing facility. The loan requires annual payments of $200,000 plus 10% interest on the unpaid balance. How is this transaction represented on the financial statements on January 1?

269. Go Go Golf Corporation has had a very good year and decides to distribute some profits to the owners of the corporation. What journal entry will the company make when it distributes $250,000 to the stockholders?

270. Which of the following transactions is a capital expenditure?

A. buying a piece of land to be used in constructing a new factory

B. buying inventory for resale

C. renting a truck for a month

D. declaring $250,000 in dividends

E. selling 4,000 shares of common stock

271. Companies sometimes finance operating cash needs via

A. fixed assets

B. investing

C. retained earnings

D. debt

E. expenses

272–276 *Use the following information to answer the questions. A company makes the following purchases during the month:*

- Computers: $2,000 paid with cash immediately
- Inventory: $30,000 on credit
- Building: $350,000, 20% cash down payment and a five-year, 5% loan for the balance
- Office furniture: $5,000 on credit
- Machinery: $50,000, 30% cash down payment and a three-year, 5% loan for the balance

272. Which of these purchases is *not* a capital expenditure?

273. What is the total amount recorded as a credit to cash as a result of these transactions?

274. What is the impact to accounts receivable or accounts payable of these transactions?

275. What is the credit side of the entry to record the total loans payable?

276. Calculate total fixed assets.

Recording Transactions with Equity Sources of Capital

277–296

277. Compared to other types of transactions, how frequently do financing and investing transactions occur?

A. Financing and investing transactions are the most frequently occurring transactions.

B. Financing and investing transactions occur very rarely.

C. Financing and investing transactions occur on a daily basis.

D. Financing and investing transactions are just as frequent as other types of transactions.

E. Financing and investing transactions are not as frequent as other types of business transactions.

278. Financing and investing activities are usually reported on which financial statement?

279. Which of the following would not usually provide equity capital?

A. institutions

B. individuals

C. employees

D. banks

E. venture capitalists

280. How is equity capital reported?

281. A company receives $1,000,000 as an investment from owners. What is the proper journal entry to record this transaction?

***282–284** Use the following information to answer the questions. A company makes a cash dividend distribution to its owners totaling $500,000.*

282. What is the proper entry to record this transaction (using the single-entry approach)?

283. What is the first entry to properly record this dividend if retained earnings are not immediately changed?

284. What is the second entry to properly record this dividend once dividends have been debited?

285. What are the two types of stock issued by companies?

286. How is an issuance of stock recorded?

287. Paying day-to-day liabilities is an example of what type of activity on the statement of cash flows?

288. What is *equity?*

289. How is total equity calculated?

290. If a business has $5,000,000 of assets and $3,000,000 of liabilities, what can you assume about its equity?

291. What is another term for total owners' equity?

292. Which of the following is an example of equity source of capital?

A. issuing debt

B. paying dividends

C. issuing shares of stock

D. obtaining a loan

E. issuing bonds

293. What type of stock is most frequently issued by corporations to raise equity capital?

294. What is a key advantage of common stock over preferred stock?

295. What is the primary benefit of preferred stock over other classes of stock?

296. TaDaa Theater Corporation is raising funds to buy a new theater. A venture capital firm provides $5,000,000 in cash. TaDaa Theater signs a $3,000,000 interest-bearing note due in three years and issues $2,000,000 in common stock to the venture capital firm. By how much does revenue increase as a result of this transaction?

Chapter 4

The Bookkeeping Cycle: Adjusting and Closing Entries

Bookkeeping includes the most basic accounting activities. To generate financial statements, a company must perform more accounting work. One task is to post adjusting entries. Adjustments help the company post revenue and expenses to the proper accounting period. This chapter also covers closing entries. After the accounting records are closed, the firm's accountants can generate financial statements. Those are the topics covered here.

The Problems You'll Work On

In this chapter, you see problems on these accounting topics:

- **Understanding the purpose of adjusting entries**
- **Posting depreciation and amortization expenses**
- **Using accrual entries for revenue and expenses**
- **Finding out about deferrals**
- **Working with closing entries**

What to Watch Out For

Don't let common mistakes trip you up. Some of the following suggestions may be helpful:

- **Keep in mind that adjusting entries nearly always involve one balance sheet account and one income statement account.**
- **The most you can depreciate from any asset is that asset's depreciable base. That remains true regardless of the depreciation method chosen.**
- **A business can't create an intangible asset and then add that asset to the balance sheet. Intangible assets are posted when they're purchased.**
- **When the books are closed at the end of an accounting period, you adjust all income statement accounts to zero.**

Achieving Accuracy with Adjusting Entries

297–306

297. Who prepares the year-end financial statements of a business?

298. What is the purpose of adjusting entries?

299. Why are adjusting entries necessary?

300. At the end of the year, an accountant finds paperwork for a sale of product already shipped to the customer that was not fully recorded. The amount of the sale was $50,000, and the cost of the inventory was $20,000. The proper entry for the sale was recorded correctly. What is the proper adjusting entry to record the cost of the transaction?

301. An accountant realizes that the bill for electricity for December was not received, and therefore, the associated expense was not recorded. After speaking with the utility company, he estimates the December bill will total approximately $500. What is the proper entry to record the required entry adjustment related to this invoice?

302. A company purchases inventory for $12,450 and records a debit to equipment and a credit to accounts payable for $12,540. Are any adjusting entries necessary at year-end?

303. At the end of the year, an accountant finds paperwork for a sale of product on account already shipped to the customer that was not fully recorded. The amount of the sale was $40,000. The proper entry for the cost of the transaction was recorded correctly. What is the proper adjusting entry to record the sale?

304. A company forgets to record an entry for salaries earned and paid during the last week of the year for a total of $2,000. What is the proper adjusting entry to correct this error?

305. At the end of the year, an accountant notices an error where a credit sale for $55,000 was accidentally recorded as $60,000. The cost of the sale was recorded at the correct amount. What is the proper adjusting entry to correct this mistake?

306. During the year a company receives an invoice for consulting services for $1,240. The invoice has not been paid as of the end of the year. While preparing to pay the invoice, an accountant notices that the bill was mistakenly recorded as $2,140. What adjustment entry is necessary to correct this error?

Classifying End-of-period Adjusting Entries

307–309

307. What is the title used to designate the chief accountant of a company?

308. What is a controller's responsibility in relation to year-end adjusting entries?

309. How does the term *bookkeeping* compare to accounting?

Recording Depreciation Expense

310–319

310. What is the purpose of depreciation?

311. How are estimated lives of fixed assets determined?

312. How does the straight-line deprecation method allocate costs?

313. A company purchases a machine for its manufacturing facility for $90,000 in January and as of December has recorded only 11 months of depreciation. The machinery is estimated to have a useful life of 5 years. What is the proper entry to record the year-end adjustment for depreciation, assuming the straight-line method is used?

314. A company purchased a truck for $25,000 on January 1 and as of December has not recorded any depreciation. The truck is estimated to have a useful life of 5 years, and straight-line depreciation is used. What is the proper entry to record the year-end adjustment for depreciation?

315. A company purchases computer equipment totaling $24,000 on October 1. As of December, the company has not recorded any depreciation. The computer equipment is estimated to have a useful life of 3 years. What is the proper entry to record the year-end adjustment for depreciation, assuming the straight-line method is used?

316. A company has disposed a fixed asset originally purchased for $10,000 and fully depreciated. What is the proper entry to record the disposal?

317. A company purchases a building for $450,000 on January 1 and estimates that the building will have a useful life of 40 years and a salvage value at the end of its life of $50,000. What is the correct amount of annual depreciation that should be recorded, assuming straight-line depreciation?

318. Classy Clickers buys manufacturing equipment at the beginning of the year for $450,000. The equipment will be used for 10 years and will be sold for about $50,000 at the end of 10 years. Classy Clickers forgets to record the depreciation expense in the first year. What is the amount of misstatement of income before tax as a result of this error?

319. Classy Clickers records depreciation expense for the year. What is the effect on total assets?

Recording Amortization Expense

320–329

320. A common characteristic of all intangible assets is that

A. they're depreciated over their useful life

B. they're revalued annually

C. they have no physical substance

D. they're purchased

E. they're internally developed

321. A company lists the following assets as intangible assets: capitalized equipment, patent, franchise, customer list, and trademark. Which of those assets should not be classified as an intangible?

322. What is the name of the accounting process that allocates the cost of intangible assets over their useful lives?

323. What accounts are debited and credited when amortization expenses are recorded?

324. Trademarks are reported on the balance sheet as

A. investments

B. current assets

C. long-term investments

D. fixed assets

E. intangible assets

325. A company purchases customer lists for $240,000 on January 1. The estimated life of the customer lists is 5 years. What is the proper amount of amortization that should be recorded for the year?

326. At the beginning of a year, a company invests in a franchise and, as part of the franchise contract, pays a franchise fee of $40,000 to use the franchise logo for 8 years. The amount paid is recorded as a debit to franchise. What is the proper adjusting entry that should be recorded at the end of the year to account for the use of the franchise logo?

327. Beta Company acquires a patent to produce glowing fish. The cost of the patent is $500,000. The patent expires in 10 years. Beta plans to use the patented process in the production of glowing fish for the next 5 years, after which the demand for glowing fish will no longer exist and the patent will be worthless. How much amortization should Beta record each year?

328–329 *Use the following information to answer the questions. On July 1, a company pays $1,000,000 cash for the right to use a patent for 5 years.*

328. What is the effect of the purchase of the patent on total assets?

329. The company neglects to make the adjusting entry for the year's amortization. What is the effect on income and assets?

Accrual of Unpaid Expenses

330–339

330. What is the purpose of an aging analysis?

331. What method of accounting for bad debt records the bad debt expense in the same period that the revenue is earned?

332. A company has total receivables of $1,000,000 and estimates that $50,000 of those receivable balances are not collectible. What is the proper journal entry to record the year-end adjustment for bad debt?

333. A company has total receivables of $500,000 and, after discussions with customers, determines that $10,000 of those receivable balances are not collectible. What is the proper journal entry to record the uncollectible accounts?

334. A company earns $500 in interest on savings bonds during the year, but as of the end of the year, the company has not received the interest. What is the proper year-end adjusting entry to record this interest?

335. An expense that has been incurred but not paid is called a what?

336. In October 2015, a company receives an invoice from the county for property taxes of $3,000 for 2015. The bill is not due until February 2016. What entry or entries should be recorded in 2015?

337. A company usually incurs approximately $1,000 of legal expenses every month. As of December, the company has not received the invoice for legal services performed during the last quarter of the year. What adjusting entry (if any) should be recorded at year-end?

338. What is the proper adjusting entry to record accrued interest expense on a loan payable?

339. Which of the following is *not* a typical year-end adjusting entry?

A. recording a liability for warranty costs

B. recording bad debt expenses

C. recording investment income earned but not received

D. recording inventory purchases

E. recording asset impairments

Deferral of Prepaid Expenses

340–344

340. What do prepaids represent?

341. Which one of the following accounts should be classified as a prepaid on the balance sheet?

A. inventory

B. insurance

C. unearned revenue

D. cost of goods sold

E. utilities

342. A company pays $12,000 on March 1 for a 12-month insurance policy effective on the day of payment. It properly records the purchase as a prepaid. What adjusting entry should be recorded at year-end if no other entries have been recorded during the year?

343. Foggy Glass Company purchases insurance coverage for three years on March 1. The cost of the coverage is $6,000. What is the effect on total assets on the date of purchase?

344. Foggy Glass Company purchases insurance coverage for two years on March 1, 2015. The cost of the coverage is $6,000. Identify the transaction that will decrease total assets by $3,000.

A. recording the payment of the invoice

B. recording the adjusting entry for 2015

C. recording the payment for the insurance coverage

D. recording the adjusting entry for insurance expense for 2016

E. recording the adjusting entry for insurance expense for 2017

Closing the Books on the Year

345–363

345. What accounts are closed in the process of closing the books?

346. What is the purpose of recording closing entries?

347. What important function do closing entries perform?

348. When closing the books, what accounts are closed?

349. What type of journal entries are recorded at the end of the year to prepare the income statement accounts for the next year?

350. After all the closing entries are posted, to what account is the net income or loss for the period transferred to?

351. What type of account would usually be debited with a closing entry?

352. Which of the following accounts should be closed at the end of the year?

A. accumulated depreciation

B. service revenue

C. inventory

D. short-term investments

E. accounts payable

353. Which of the following accounts should not be closed at the end of the year?

A. sales revenues

B. cost of goods sold

C. insurance expense

D. prepaid insurance

E. interest income

354. Which of the following accounts will have a zero balance after closing entries are posted?

A. property, plant, and equipment

B. accumulated depreciation

C. depreciation expense

D. patents

E. trademarks

355. What entry is recorded when closing the sales revenue account?

356. What type of balances do temporary accounts have on the first day of a new accounting period?

357. Which of the following would you find in a closing entry?

A. debit expense accounts

B. credit expense accounts

C. credit to revenue accounts

D. debit to asset accounts

E. debit owners' equity

358. Which of the following accounts should be closed at the end of the accounting period?

A. litigation liability

B. retained earnings

C. cost of goods sold

D. inventory

E. unearned revenue

359. When a company experiences a loss for the year, how is the closing entry recorded?

360–363 *Use the following information to answer the questions. At the end of the first year of operations, a company had the following amounts in its accounting records:*

- Cash: $5,000
- Accounts receivable: $7,000
- Cost of goods sold: $20,000
- Salary expense: $1,950
- Inventory: $8,000
- Owners' invested capital: $10,000
- Sales revenues: $30,000
- Accounts payable: $4,000
- Gross profit: $10,000
- Office expenses: $2,000
- Income tax expense: $50

360. When the company records the year-end closing entry, what should the debit be?

361. What is the net income or loss for the year?

362. What is the total credit amount recorded to expense accounts when the closing entry is recorded?

363. What is recorded to transfer net income to retained earnings?

Testing You on Internal Controls

364–380

364. What kind of errors should be expected in an accounting system?

365. Who is primarily involved in internal controls of an organization?

366. Why are internal controls necessary?

367. Who designs a company's internal controls?

368. What is the primary reason management commits financial fraud?

369. What is increased when one person authorizes all cash disbursement, regardless of the amount?

370. Which of the following assets is most vulnerable to fraud?

A. cash

B. inventory

C. accounts receivable

D. fixed assets

E. prepaids

371. How often should companies prepare bank statement reconciliations?

372. Who usually commits financial statement (accounting) fraud?

373. What action by fraudsters can cause controls to be ineffective?

374. Which of the following is *not* an internal control?

A. using prenumbered documents

B. requiring a second signature on checks over a certain amount

C. requiring all adjusting entries to be recorded before the books are closed

D. taking surprise inventory counts

E. requiring employees to take mandatory vacation time

375. What is a good system of internal controls designed to safeguard?

376. What can well-designed internal controls protect a company from?

377. Which of the following is *not* an example of a strong internal control procedure?

A. performing a monthly bank reconciliation

B. accepting only cash payments

C. allowing only certain people to approve payments

D. making sure that the person approving the payment is different from the person preparing it

E. only ordering from preapproved suppliers

378. What types of transactions are most likely to be identified as not recorded in the accounting records when bank reconciliation is completed?

A. bank charges

B. outstanding checks

C. deposits in transit

D. cost of goods sold

E. sales revenue

379. What is the name of the main principle of internal controls that requires multiple people to be involved in a process?

380. What is a common control regarding payments?

A. requiring a company's controller to take vacation every year

B. requiring monthly bank reconciliations by someone other than the person recording cash

C. requiring the person who prepares payments to open mail

D. requiring a second signature on checks over a certain amount

E. requiring the person who inspects shipments delivered to a business to be different from the person who approves vendors' invoices for payment

Chapter 5

Understanding and Reporting Profit

The primary goal of a business is to generate a profit. Understanding exactly how the profit is generated, however, can be complicated. This chapter covers those details. Here you go over the single-step and multi-step income statement formats. The chapter also addresses operating versus non-operating income and expenses. You'll also see questions that relate the income statement to the balance sheet.

The Problems You'll Work On

In this chapter, you see problems on these accounting topics:

- Understanding gross margin
- Separating operating income from non-operating income
- Going over the concept of materiality
- Finding out about net worth
- Connecting the income statement to the balance sheet

What to Watch Out For

Don't let common mistakes trip you up. Some of the following suggestions may be helpful:

- Keep in mind that *gross margin* is not a term used in a single-step income statement.
- If income or expenses relate to a company's day-to-day business, that activity is considered to be operating income or expense.
- *Gross margin* is defined as sales less cost of sales. Selling, general, and administration (SG and A) expenses are not part of the gross margin calculation.
- Sometimes, gross margin is called *gross profit,* but the calculation is the same: sales less cost of sales.
- The Securities and Exchange Commission (SEC) regulates publicly traded companies. Those companies have issued stock to the general public.

Nature of Profit and Loss

381–385

381. How is profit calculated?

382. What does GAAP stand for?

383. What primary business activity influences profit the most?

384. What is the impact of an increase in sales revenues on the balance sheet?

385. A company reported net income of $550,000 for the year. If liabilities decreased by $250,000, what was the impact (if any) on the balance of assets?

Formats for the Income Statement

386–400

386. The income statement provides what three main pieces of information?

387. What does the single-step income statement focus on?

388. What line item is found only on the multi-step income statement?

389. What is the most common expense of a merchandiser (non-service-oriented business) related to the product?

390. Which of the following is *not* reported on an income statement?

A. assets

B. revenues

C. gross profit

D. expenses

E. net income

391. What are the two formats of an income statement?

392. How is gross margin calculated?

393. What is the primary tool used by decision makers to evaluate a company's performance and estimate its future performance?

394. What line item is found only on the multi-step income statement?

395. What income statement format(s) are earnings before income tax reported on?

396. Which of the following expenses is considered an operating expense?

A. interest expense

B. rent expense

C. loss on sale of marketable securities

D. other income

E. income tax expense

397. Which of the following items is presented below operating income on a typical multi-step income statement?

A. cost of goods sold

B. gross margin

C. revenues

D. selling expenses

E. income tax expense

398. A company has the following balances at the end of the year:

- Income tax expense: $10,000
- Sales revenue: $50,000
- Selling and general expenses: $12,000
- Interest expense: $2,000
- Cost of goods sold: $28,000
- Income tax: $1,000

How much will this company report on its single-step income statement as gross profit?

399. What line item is found on both the single-step and the multi-step income statement formats?

400. Which income statement format doesn't separate operating expenses from non-operating expenses?

Disclosure in Income Statements

401–405

401. What entity regulates financial statement disclosures?

402. SEC regulations require publicly traded companies to disclose various kinds of information in their financial statements. However, companies sometimes try to disclose as little as possible. What is the main reason why companies try to minimize their disclosures?

403. What concept relates to reporting only significant information?

404. Sometimes putting too much information in an income statement can be considered counterproductive. What is the term that describes this concept?

405. What are the four main considerations when deciding on income statement disclosures?

Examining How Sales and Expenses Change Assets and Liabilities

406–410

406. What is the first relationship between the income statement and the balance sheet?

407. What line item on the balance sheet is also reported on the statement of cash flows?

408. What other financial statements are impacted by the activity on the income statement?

409. How do sales recorded on the income statement impact the balance sheet?

410. How do sales recorded on the income statement impact the statement of cash flows?

Summing Up the Diverse Financial Effects from Making Profit

411–425

411. How is net worth determined?

412. When accounts receivable increase, what else changes in the financial statements?

413. When sales revenues increase, what else should be debited or credited in the financial statements?

414. When cost of goods sold increases, what else should be debited or credited in the financial statements?

415–425 *Use the following information to answer the questions.*

- A company has depreciation expense of $1,200 and inventory purchases of $10,000. Its cost of goods sold is $7,000.
- The company added $400 to its prepaid expenses during the year.
- Accounts payable for inventory purchases increased $2,000.
- The interest expense is $600, and selling and general expenses are $5,000.
- Unpaid expenses at the end of the year included $1,500 of accrued expenses payable and $2,000 of accounts payable (unrelated to inventory).
- The company paid $200 for interest during the year.

415. How is the difference between interest expense and interest paid recorded?

416. What is the balance sheet impact to accounts payable as a result of the inventory purchases?

417. In what category of expenses on the income statement is the change in accumulated depreciation included?

418. What is the balance sheet impact to cash as a result of the increase in prepaids?

419. The decrease in inventory is recorded as part of what journal entry?

420. What is the amount of debit or credit to cash as a result of the cost of goods sold summary journal entry?

421. What is the cash impact of the interest expense summary journal entry?

422. What is the balance sheet impact to inventory as a result of the increase in cost of goods sold?

423. The selling and general expenses summary journal entry includes what credit related to accrued expenses?

424. How is cash impacted in the selling and general expenses summary journal entry?

425. What is the balance sheet impact to cash as a result of the increase in cost of goods sold?

Chapter 6

Reporting Financial Conditions on the Balance Sheet

The balance sheet reports a company's assets, liabilities, and equity as of a specific date. This chapter goes over each type of account you'll use on a balance sheet. The chapter covers the concept of current versus noncurrent assets and liabilities. You'll also work with several types of financial ratios in this chapter.

The Problems You'll Work On

In this chapter, you see problems on these accounting topics:

- Understanding the purpose of an audit opinion
- Separating current from noncurrent assets and liabilities
- Going over the concept of retained earnings
- Finding out about solvency and liquidity
- Using financial ratios to assess a company's performance

What to Watch Out For

Don't let common mistakes trip you up. Some of the following suggestions may be helpful:

- Keep in mind that the return of an investor's investment reduces a company's total equity balance.
- The balance sheet is reported as of a certain date. An income statement, on the other hand, covers a period of time.
- *Liquidity* assesses a company's ability to generate current assets and pay current liabilities. *Solvency* measures a firm's ability to survive over the long term.
- An *audit opinion* states whether the financial statements are materially correct.

Getting Started on the Balance Sheet

426–439

426. What is the purpose of a confidentiality agreement?

427. What are the four essential elements of an annual financial report?

428. What is the purpose of an audit opinion?

429. What is the most common presentation format used for balance sheets?

430. Why do businesses like the portrait format of a balance sheet?

431. What does a balance sheet summarize?

432. What should a prospective buyer consider when purchasing an existing business?

433. The balance sheet is also frequently referred to as what?

434. What do liabilities represent?

435. What is *owners' equity?*

436. What are the two sources of equity?

437. How are profits earned and retained by a business reported in the financial statements?

438. For what time period is the balance sheet usually presented?

439. What can't a prospective buyer determine about a business by looking at the balance sheet?

Building a Balance Sheet

440–448

440. What are the three types of transactions that are the building blocks of a balance sheet?

441. Which of the following would be classified as financing activity?

A. the purchase of long-lived assets used in the operations of a business

B. investment of capital in a company by its owners

C. the profit-making activities of a company

D. the purchase of intangible assets

E. transactions related to expenses

442. Which of the following would be classified as operating activity?

A. the purchase of long-lived assets used in the operations of a business

B. transactions related to expenses

C. investment of capital in a company by its owners

D. the purchase of intangible assets

E. all of the above

443. Which of the following would be classified as investing activity?

A. the purchase of intangible assets

B. the return of capital to its owners

C. the profit-making activities of a company

D. the investment of capital in a company by its owners

E. transactions related to expenses

444. Which of the following would be classified as financing activity?

A. the purchase of intangible assets

B. the profit-making activities of a company

C. transactions related to expenses

D. the return of capital to its owners

E. the purchase of long-lived assets used in the operations of a business

445. Which of the following would be classified as investing activity?

A. the return of capital to its owners

B. the profit-making activities of a company

C. the purchase of long-lived assets used in the operations of a business

D. investment of capital in a company by its owners

E. transactions related to revenues

446. Which of the following would be classified as operating activity?

A. the purchase of long-lived assets used in the operations of a business

B. investment of capital in a company by its owners

C. the return of capital to its owners

D. the purchase of intangible assets

E. the profit-making activities of a company

447. A new business has incurred only financing and investing transactions. What account would you not expect to find on a balance sheet?

A. cash

B. accounts receivable

C. long-term debt

D. capital stock

E. total assets

448. When a business manufactures its first batch of products, what is recorded in the balance sheet as a result of the manufacturing activity?

Fleshing Out the Balance Sheet

449–463

449. If a company does not borrow any money, which account would not be presented on its balance sheet?

A. accounts payable

B. accrued liabilities

C. short-term notes

D. accumulated depreciation

E. prepaid expenses

450. If a company only provides services and does not sell any product, which account would not be presented on its balance sheet?

A. accounts receivable

B. inventory

C. prepaid expenses

D. accounts payable

E. accrued expenses

451. Which of the following could be determined based on a review of a company's balance sheet?

A. the replacement cost of the company's fixed assets

B. the fixed asset depreciation method

C. the amount of money borrowed

D. total revenues

E. total expenses

452–463 Use the following information to answer the questions. A company reports the following on its balance sheet:

- Cash: $10,000
- Accounts receivable: $20,000
- Inventory: $14,000
- Prepaid expenses: $3,000
- Property, plant, and equipment: $35,000
- Accumulated depreciation: $2,000
- Accounts payable: $5,000
- Accrued expenses: $6,000
- Short-term notes: $7,000
- Long-term notes: $10,000
- Capital stock: $40,000
- Retained earnings: $12,000

452. What are the company's total liabilities?

453. What is the company's total equity?

454. What are the company's total assets?

455. What are the company's total current assets?

456. What does the $12,000 in retained earnings mean?

457. What are the company's current liabilities?

458. If the company did not accept credit payments and only made cash sales, what account would *not* be included on its balance sheet?

459. Is this company a service provider or a merchandiser (sells merchandise)?

460. How does the company get paid by its customers?

461. When does the company pay for its expenses?

462. What is the net value of fixed assets reported on the balance sheet?

463. What do the accrued expenses on the balance sheet mean about the company's expenses?

Classifying Assets and Liabilities (Which Are Not Listed Haphazardly)

464–476

464. Accounts receivable would be classified as which of the following?

A. current liability

B. current asset

C. long-term asset

D. long-term liability

E. equity

465. A company has current assets of $500,000 and current liabilities of $200,000. Calculate the current ratio.

466. How is the quick ratio calculated?

467. Which of the following is a current asset?

A. inventory

B. accounts payable

C. note receivable

D. retained earnings

E. long-term investment

468. Which of the following is *not* a current asset?

A. property, plant, and equipment

B. inventory

C. accounts receivable

D. cash

E. cash equivalents

469. How is land classified on a balance sheet?

470. What is the formula for calculating the current ratio?

471. Which of the following is *not* considered a current liability?

A. payroll payable

B. tax payable

C. accounts payable

D. customer deposits

E. bonds payable

472. A financially healthy company's current ratio should be at least

A. 1 or less

B. 1 or more

C. less than 2

D. more than 2

E. less than 3

473. Which of the following would be considered a current asset?

A. land held for use

B. trade payables

C. patent

D. inventory

E. accrued expenses

474. What is *solvency*?

475. What does the asset turnover ratio measure?

476. Which of the following statements is correct about capital-intensive businesses?

A. Capital-intensive companies have very high asset turnover ratios.

B. A capital-intensive business requires a significant amount of assets to attract investors.

C. An example of a capital-intensive business is a retail store.

D. An example of a capital-intensive business is a company developing websites.

E. A capital-intensive business requires a significant amount of assets to generate sales.

Role of the Balance Sheet in Business Valuation

477–490

477. What items on the balance sheet are recorded at historical cost?

478. What is the focus of a business valuation?

479. What is the main estimate used for business valuations?

480. What is the most common basis for the values reported on the balance sheet?

481–484 *Use the following information to answer the questions. A company has the following balances:*

- Cash: $100,000
- Cash equivalents: $200,000
- Total current assets: $600,000
- Total assets: $1,000,000
- Total current liabilities: $300,000
- Revenues: $2,400,000

481. What is the company's current ratio?

482. What is the company's quick ratio?

483. What is the company's asset turnover ratio?

484. What is the impact on the current ratio of making a large payment on accounts payable?

485. If a company has a current ratio greater than 1, which of the following will *not* impact the current ratio?

A. using long-term debt to pay off current liabilities

B. collection of accounts receivable

C. paying off accounts payable

D. selling fixed assets for cash

E. purchasing fixed assets for cash

486. Which of the following is a characteristic of business valuation?

A. It's performed by accountants.

B. It's determined solely based on the financial statements.

C. It reflects how much one might pay for a business.

D. It's part of the financial statements.

E. It's a simple calculation based on historical performance of a company.

487. How do past and future earnings impact business valuation?

488. Which of the following is correct regarding the earnings multiple valuation method?

A. It does not consider the values in the balance sheet.

B. It's the most accurate business valuation method.

C. It considers only the values in the balance sheet.

D. It's a very complex calculation.

E. It looks at future estimated earnings.

489. Which of the following is correct regarding recording the investment when a buyer purchases a business for a price greater than the balance in the owners' equity accounts?

A. An adjustment to owners' equity must be recorded.

B. An adjustment to assets must be recorded.

C. No adjustment is necessary.

D. The previously recorded owners' equity was incorrect and must be corrected.

E. The buyer should record the investment at the value of owners' equity accounts, not the price paid.

490. What section of a balance sheet is *not* affected by the type of depreciation method a company uses?

Chapter 7

Coupling the Income Statement and the Balance Sheet

The balance sheet and the income statement are closely related. In fact, many accounting transactions affect both a balance sheet account and an income statement account. This chapter covers those relationships. You'll review how sales are tied to cash collections and accounts receivable and how inventory, purchases, and cost of sales are connected.

The Problems You'll Work On

In this chapter, you see problems on these accounting topics:

- Understanding how balance sheet account balances carry over to the next accounting period
- Separating cash sales from accounts receivable
- Going over inventory, purchases, and cost of sales
- Finding out about revenue recognition
- Distinguishing between fixed assets and intangible assets

What to Watch Out For

Don't let common mistakes trip you up. Some of the following suggestions may be helpful:

- Keep in mind that balance sheet account balances carry over to the next accounting period, while income statement accounts are adjusted to zero at the end of each period.
- Revenue should be recognized when the sales process is complete. For many firms, a product or service must be delivered to the client before revenue is recognized.
- Fixed assets are kept separate from intangible assets. Intangible assets can be intellectual property, such as a patent or a copyright.
- Net income increases retained earnings, while dividends reduce retained earnings.

Rejoining the Income Statement and the Balance Sheet

491–495

491. How are the balance sheet and income statement usually presented in relation to each other?

492–495 *Use the following information to answer the questions. The following information is available about a company for 2014:*

- Annual sales: $13,000,000
- Annual cost of goods sold: $7,150,000
- Historically, accounts receivable at the end of the year equal about 3 weeks of annual sales.
- Average amount of debt during the year was $3,600,000.
- Historically, inventory balance at the end of the year equals about 8 weeks of annual cost of goods sold.
- Historically, accounts payable for inventory purchases is about 4 weeks of annual cost of goods sold.
- Average annual interest rate on debt was 5.25%.

492. What is the expected balance of accounts receivable at the end of the year?

493. What is the expected inventory balance at the end of the year?

494. What is the accounts payable from inventory purchases balance at the end of the year?

495. What is the interest expense at the end of the year?

Making the Vital Connections

496–498

496. What are normative operating ratios?

497. What income statement account can affect liabilities on the balance sheet?

498. What item connects the income statement and the balance sheet?

Sales Revenue → Accounts Receivable

499–508

499. When customers buy products on credit or on account, in what asset account is the transaction recorded?

500. What entry is recorded when a previously recorded account receivable is collected?

501. When should outstanding receivables be collected?

502. What is the journal entry to record a sale in which the buyer agrees to pay later?

503. What is the journal entry to record the cost of a sale?

504. When does GAAP (Generally Accepted Accounting Principles) require revenue to be recorded?

505. What does a decrease in the balance of accounts receivable during the year mean to a company's cash flow?

506. What does the balance in accounts receivable represent?

507. A company makes a $25,000 sale on account. The company expects that $10,000 will be collected within a week and the balance within a month. What is the proper entry to record the transaction at the time of sale?

508. A company makes a $30,000 sale on account but with a 10% cash down payment. What is the proper entry to record this transaction?

Cost of Goods Sold Expense → Inventory

509–518

509. Identify an expense specific to companies that sell a physical product.

510. What does cost of goods sold reflect?

511. When a company purchases product for sale, in what account is the cost recorded?

512. What happens with the cost of the sold inventory when a company sells products from the inventory account?

513. What does the inventory balance on the balance sheet represent?

514. On what financial statement and where on that statement is cost of goods sold recorded?

515. Which of the following is correct about gross margin?

A. It applies only to service industries.

B. It's the difference between revenues and cost of goods sold.

C. It's rarely reported in the financial statements.

D. It's reported on the balance sheet.

E. It's reported on the statement of cash flows.

516. Which of the following is incorrectly classified as inventory?

A. items on shelves at a grocery store

B. cars at a car dealership

C. cars at a car rental facility

D. computers for sale at an electronics store

E. large farm equipment held by an implement dealer for sale to farmers in the fall

517. Which of the following triggers the recording of cost of goods sold?

A. the receipt of a purchase order

B. the time that a customer pays for a product

C. when a product sold is ready for shipment

D. the time that a sale is collected

E. the time that a product is shipped to a buyer

518. A company makes a mistake and records a cost of goods sold transaction for $10,000 instead of $100,000. How would this error affect the financial statements?

Fixed Assets → Depreciation Expense

519–528

519. What is the main characteristic of a fixed asset?

520. Which of the following assets should not be classified as a fixed asset?

A. factory building

B. inventory held for sale

C. office equipment

D. delivery vehicle

E. factory equipment

521. What is *depreciation?*

522. What is the formula to calculate the annual amount of straight-line depreciation?

523. How is the annual amount of depreciation recorded on the balance sheet?

524. How does depreciation impact the financial statements?

525. Which of the following assets is incorrectly classified as fixed assets?

A. furniture in the sales office

B. car used in the ordinary sales operations of a business

C. equipment held for resale by an equipment dealer

D. factory building

E. fence around a factory building owned by a company

526. Why do companies record depreciation expense?

527. Instead of recording building expense for the cost, what does a company do to record the cost of a building?

528. Company A buys a delivery truck for $40,000 and depreciates it using the straight-line method over 5 years, assuming it will be worth $5,000 when the company disposes of it. If the company forgets to record the depreciation expense in the second year, what amounts will be wrong on the financial statements?

Intangible Assets → Amortization Expense

529–538

529. What is the primary characteristic of an intangible asset?

530. What is the name of the rational process of allocating the cost of an intangible asset?

531. Which of the following assets is incorrectly classified as intangibles?

A. goodwill

B. delivery vehicle

C. patents

D. purchased trademarks

E. customer lists

532. What type of asset is a patent?

533. What is *amortization*?

534. What is the impact of amortization of intangibles on the income statement?

535. Which of the following items should be classified as an intangible asset?

A. unsold inventory

B. vendor payables

C. customers' receivables

D. customer lists

E. approved vendor list

536. How are internally developed and purchased intangible assets recorded?

537. How are purchases of intangibles recorded?

538. What is the impact of amortization of intangibles on the balance sheet?

Operating Assets → Their Assets and Liabilities

539–548

539. Which of the following is *not* a prepaid expense?

A. insurance premium paid ahead of time

B. supplies purchased in bulk

C. rent paid in advance

D. magazine subscription received

E. expenses paid ahead of time

540. Where on the balance sheet are prepaid expenses usually presented?

541. When are prepaid expenses recorded?

542. How do prepaids impact expenses?

543. When are operating expenses usually paid?

544. How are unpaid expenses reported on the balance sheet?

545. Where on the balance sheet are accounts payable presented?

546. Why are prepaid expenses recorded as assets on the balance sheet?

547. How should a company record estimates of unpaid costs for which invoices have not been received?

548. Badabing Company has not received the electricity bill for December when it closes the books for the year. The company does not record the cost of the electricity used in December in the accounting records. What error(s) will be in the annual financial statements?

Debt → Interest Expense

549–558

549. Which of the following is not a characteristic of debt?

A. money borrowed

B. credit instrument

C. liability

D. interest-bearing

E. informal agreement

550. What is a characteristic that classifies debt as short term?

551. Why do companies obtain debt?

552. What is the primary disadvantage of debt financing?

553. Where is interest expense reported on the income statement?

554. When is interest expense recorded?

555. What parts of the balance sheet are impacted by obtaining debt?

556. Which of the following is *not* a negative consequence of defaulting on debt agreements?

A. additional infusion of equity

B. forced sale of assets

C. bankruptcy

D. liquidation

E. All of the above are negative consequences of defaulting on debt.

557. How is interest payable usually presented on the balance sheet if the amount is not large?

558. If a company reports debt of $3,050,000 and interest expense for the year of $175,000, calculate the approximate annual interest rate on the debt.

Income Tax → Income Tax Payable

559–563

559. What is the account used to record amounts due to the IRS called?

560. How is the unpaid portion of income tax reported?

561. What is *taxable income?*

562. How does the income tax payable compare to the income tax expense at the end of the year?

563. What causes a company to have a liability for income tax payable on its balance sheet?

Net Income → Retained Earnings

564–568

564. How does net income impact retained earnings and owners' equity?

565. What is the usual payment schedule for dividends?

566. How is net income impacted by dividends and income tax expense?

567. What are the typical expenses that are excluded from operating income?

568. How do distributions to owners impact net income and retained earnings?

Chapter 8

Reporting Cash Flows

For most companies, managing cash is a critical accounting task. That's because all companies need cash to operate. Without proper cash planning, a company can't produce its product or service. This chapter covers the statement of cash flows. This financial statement is the tool accountants use to track their sources and uses of cash.

The Problems You'll Work On

In this chapter, you see problems on these accounting topics:

- Understanding how to calculate profit using comparative balance sheets
- Posting net income as equity on the balance sheet
- Going over the three types of cash flows
- Finding out how to post cash transactions to the statement of cash flows
- Distinguishing between the direct and indirect cash flow method for cash flow from operations

What to Watch Out For

Don't let common mistakes trip you up. Some of the following suggestions may be helpful:

- Keep in mind that *equity* and *net worth* mean the same thing. Both terms refer to a company's total assets less liabilities.
- The indirect method of cash flows is only used for cash flow from operations. The two other types of cash flows are not affected.
- Depreciation expense does not impact cash.
- You post net income from the income statement as an increase to equity in the balance sheet.

Figuring Profit from Comparative Balance Sheets

569–578

569. What financial statements are affected when sales transactions are recorded?

570. Net income is found on the income statement, but it also links the income statement and the balance sheet. Where on the balance sheet is this link?

571. A company has total assets of $1,200,000, total current liabilities of $500,000, and total long-term liabilities of $350,000. Calculate the total net worth.

572. What can cause net worth to be negative?

573. At the end of its first year, a company estimates its end-of-year balances to be:

- Total assets: $2,500,000
- Total current liabilities: $800,000
- Total long-term liabilities: $200,000

If there are no other equity transactions, what is the net income for the year?

574. How do cash dividends and owners' capital contributions affect net worth?

575. At the end of its first year of operations, a company has total assets of $1,200,000, total current liabilities of $500,000, total long-term liabilities of $350,000, and paid cash dividends of $45,000. Calculate the total net income.

576. At the end of its first year of operations, a company has total assets of $1,200,000, total current liabilities of $500,000, and total long-term liabilities of $350,000, and it issued $30,000 of stock during the year. Calculate the total net income.

577. At the end of its first year of operations, a company has total assets of $800,000, total current liabilities of $200,000, and total long-term liabilities of $100,000. It issued $80,000 of stock during the year and paid cash dividends of $20,000. Calculate the total net income.

578. At the end of its first year, a company estimates its end-of-year balances to be:

- Total assets: $2,500,000
- Total current liabilities: $800,000
- Total long-term liabilities: $200,000

If the company also paid a $200,000 cash dividend, what is the net income for the year?

Putting on Your Trifocals: Separating the Three Types of Cash Flows

579–583

579. What financial statement provides data about sources and uses of cash?

580. What type of cash flows are always listed first on the statement of cash flows?

581. A company buys new equipment for $450,000 cash, sells some old delivery trucks for $5,700 cash, and receives $1,300,000 cash from the sale of stock. Which of those events involve investing activities?

582. On a company's year-end balance sheet, you notice that the fixed assets account increased by $570,000. The company did not dispose of any fixed assets during the year and did not take on any additional debt. What will you expect to find on the statement of cash flows to explain this change?

583. Shoot Some Hoops Rec Center, Inc., had the following transactions: Sale of investments for $38,000 cash, sale of common stock for $300,000 cash, payment of $30,000 in cash dividends, and receipt of $10,000 in dividends from ownership of Spalding common stock. Which of these transactions will be reflected in the financing section of the statement of cash flows prepared by Shoot Some Hoops at the end of the year?

Reporting Cash Flow from Operating Activities by the Direct Method

584–588

584. What is the primary characteristic of the direct method of preparing the statement of cash flows?

585. What line item is included in the indirect method statement of cash flows but not in the direct method statement of cash flows?

586. What line item description is specific to the cash flow from operations?

587. Which of the following is true about the preparation of a statement of cash flows?

A. The direct method is preferred and required.

B. The indirect method is preferred and required.

C. The indirect method is preferred but not required.

D. Neither method is preferred nor required.

E. Neither method is preferred, but the direct method is required.

588. What varies between the direct and indirect methods in the statement of cash flows?

Reporting Cash Flow from Operating Activities by the Indirect Method

589–593

589. How often is the indirect statement of cash flows method used?

590. What is the name of the cash flow statement method that adjusts net income for transactions that did not impact cash?

591. What is the most common adjustment to net income under the indirect method?

592. Shoot Some Hoops Rec Center, Inc., prepares its statement of cash flows using the indirect method. How will the result for cash flows from operating activities compare if the company uses the direct method?

593. How does the indirect method determine cash provided by operating activities?

Adjusting for Changes in Operating Assets

594–598

594. Which of the following accounts is *not* an operating asset account?

A. accounts receivable

B. accrued liabilities

C. inventory

D. prepaid insurance

E. prepaid rent

595. The following information is taken from the accounting records of Badabing Sound Effects, Inc.:

	2015	2016
Inventory	7,000	5,000

How would this change be reflected in the statement of cash flows prepared using the indirect method?

596. How is a decrease in the balance of accounts receivable treated on the statement of cash flows under the indirect method?

597. How is an increase in the balance of prepaid expenses treated on the statement of cash flows under the indirect method?

598. What is the impact of an increase in accounts receivable on the statement of cash flows?

Adjusting for Changes in Operating Liabilities

599–603

599. Which of the following accounts should *not* be classified as operating liabilities?

A. accounts payable

B. long-term loans

C. accrued expenses

D. income tax payable

E. salaries payable

600. How does an increase in income taxes payable impact the statement of cash flows?

601. During a year, a company reports a net income of $20,000 and an accounts payable increase of $5,000. No other operating assets or liabilities changed. How much was cash provided by operating activities?

602. During a year, a company reports a net income of $50,000, an accounts receivable increase of $5,000, and an accounts payable decrease of $2,000. How much was cash provided by operating activities?

603. During a year, a company reports a net income of $100,000, an accounts receivable increase of $8,000, and an accrued liabilities increase of $12,000. How much was cash provided by operating activities?

Adjusting for Depreciation and Other Non-cash Items

604–608

604. How does recording the depreciation impact cash?

605. How is the depreciation expense treated on the statement of cash flows using the indirect method?

606. How is the depreciation expense treated on the statement of cash flows using the direct method?

607. During a year, a company reports a net income of $155,000, a depreciation expense of $35,000, an accounts receivable increase of $25,000, and an accounts payable increase of $10,000. How much was cash provided by operating activities?

608. During a year, a company reports a net income of $80,000, a depreciation expense of $5,000, an amortization expense of $2,000, and an accounts receivable decrease of $3,000. In addition, the company sold bonds for $400,000 cash. How much was cash provided by operating activities?

Chapter 9

Reporting Changes in Owners' Equity

The equity section of the balance sheet represents the true value of a business. *Equity,* also called *net worth,* is defined as assets less liabilities. If you sell all your assets and use the cash to pay off all liabilities, the amount remaining in cash is your equity. This chapter explains equity increases and decreases.

The Problems You'll Work On

In this chapter, you see problems on these accounting topics:

- Understanding that equity represents claims on assets by shareholders
- Posting net income and net losses to the equity account
- Going over dividends and the impact of dividends on equity
- Finding out how to calculate return on equity
- Using the debt-to-equity ratio to manage a business

What to Watch Out For

Don't let common mistakes trip you up. Some of the following suggestions may be helpful:

- Keep in mind that equity represents an owner's interest in the company. If a firm raises money by issuing bonds, those cash proceeds are considered debt, the lender's interest in the company.
- Net income increases equity, while generating net losses decreases equity.
- Cash proceeds from the issuance of stock increases equity.
- An owner's personal expenses are excluded from that owner's business transactions, even if the owner is a sole proprietor.

The Fourth Financial Statement

609–613

609. Which of the following is not included on the statement of changes in stockholders' equity?

A. capital invested by the owners

B. capital returned to the owners

C. dividends

D. total assets

E. annual profit

610. Who are the primary users of the statement of changes in stockholders' equity?

611. Which of the following is *not* one of the primary four financial statements?

A. balance sheet

B. income statement

C. income tax statement

D. statement of cash flows

E. statement of changes in equity

612. List the four main company financial statements.

613. Which of the following would not be found on the statement of changes in stockholders' equity?

A. net loss

B. sale of common stock

C. payment of cash dividends

D. proceeds from the sale of bonds

E. distribution of stock dividends

The Statement of Changes in Owners' (Shareholders') Equity

614–618

614. How does net income impact the balance sheet?

615. What type of companies would not need to prepare the statement of changes in owners' equity?

A. privately held companies

B. small publicly traded companies

C. companies that only report owners' capital transactions in their equity accounts

D. companies that only report dividends in their equity accounts

E. companies that only report profit in their equity accounts

616. What is the purpose of the statement of changes in owners' equity?

617. What is the presentation format of the statement of changes in owners' equity?

618. Which of the following would *not* be included in a simple statement of changes in owners' equity for a business?

A. equity balance at the end of the period

B. owners' contributions of capital

C. owners' personal expenses

D. net income

E. equity balance at the beginning of the period

Information Reported in This Financial Statement

619–623

619. What type of transaction is the most common transaction presented as a decrease to retained earnings on the statement of changes in owners' equity?

620. What special transactions are recorded in accumulated other comprehensive income?

621. Where in the financial statements can accumulated other comprehensive income be presented?

622. Which of the following would *not* be one of the line items on the statement of changes in owners' equity?

A. accumulated other comprehensive income

B. net earnings

C. dividends to stockholders

D. stock issued

E. debt issued

623. Which of the following should *not* be reported in accumulated other comprehensive income?

A. foreign currency translation gains

B. foreign currency translation losses

C. unrealized gains and losses from certain types of securities

D. realized gains and losses from certain types of securities

E. changes in liabilities for unfunded pension fund obligations

Analyzing the Information in This Financial Statement

624–628

624. Under what circumstances can a company omit presenting a statement of changes in owners' equity?

A. Because it's an optional statement, any company can choose not to present it.

B. when the company has generated losses

C. when the company also shows accumulated other comprehensive income

D. when earnings are the only equity transaction

E. when the company is not publicly traded

625. How is return on equity calculated?

626. A company has a net income of $5,000,000 and owners' equity of $18,000,000. Calculate the return on equity.

627. How do you calculate the debt-to-equity ratio?

628. Which of the following statements is incorrect?

A. A high debt-to-equity ratio means the company has a lot of debt in relation to equity.

B. The higher the debt-to-equity ratio, the more debt the company has on its balance sheet.

C. The higher the debt-to-equity ratio, the more challenging it might be for the business to obtain debt financing.

D. The debt-to-equity ratio analyzes the relationship between total liabilities and total equity.

E. The higher the debt-to-equity ratio, the more profit the company has recorded.

Chapter 10

Choosing Accounting Methods

This chapter covers three important types of accounting methods. One is the choice of an inventory valuation method. The chapter addresses four choices that an accountant might consider and goes over several depreciation methods. Finally, this chapter reviews methods for recognizing bad debt expense. Each accounting method has an impact on a company's financial statements.

The Problems You'll Work On

In this chapter, you see problems on these accounting topics:

- Understanding LIFO, FIFO, and weighted average inventory valuation methods
- Posting inventory purchases and sales in the accounting records
- Going over the lower of cost or market method for asset valuations
- Finding out about accelerated methods of depreciation
- Using the allowance method to recognize bad debt expense

What to Watch Out For

Don't let common mistakes trip you up. Some of the following suggestions may be helpful:

- Regardless of which inventory method you choose, the total cost of inventory eventually posted to cost of sales will be the same over the life of the organization.
- The lower of cost of market method may require you to evaluate four different values. To keep the numbers straight, make sure to label each value as *fair market value, original cost,* and so on.
- When using the allowance method for bad debt expense, understand the difference between an adjusting entry and the ending balance you need. These may be two different amounts.
- Different accounting methods for inventory valuation and depreciation will generate different levels of net income and expense. A company can change an accounting method to manipulate company earnings.

Determining Whether Products Are Unique or Fungible

629–638

629. Which of the following is a fungible good?

A. corn

B. original oil paintings

C. designer jewelry pieces

D. new cars

E. Native American hand-woven tapestries

630. Which of the following is not fungible?

A. gallons of oil

B. 4-foot by 8-foot pieces of plywood

C. bottles of aspirin

D. bags of kitty litter

E. hand-painted portraits of kings and queens of England

631. What is the first thing a business must consider when deciding how to account for cost of goods sold expense?

632. What type of goods does a business sell that uses specific identification to record the cost of goods sold expense?

633. Gail's Art House has the following items in inventory (total inventory cost is $24,000):

- Small painting of trees by artist A, unframed, cost was $2,000
- Large painting of trees by artist A, framed, cost was $10,000
- Large painting of lake by artist A, framed, cost was $12,000.

If Gail sells the small painting of trees, what is the cost of goods sold using the method most appropriate for her inventory?

634. If a jeweler sells designer pieces, what information is necessary to record the cost of goods sold expense?

635. What are two characteristics of non-fungible goods?

636. Why is it necessary to determine whether goods are fungible or non-fungible?

637. Name three fungible goods.

A. 400 gallons of water to be sold to different customers, 400 gallons of special mix paint to be sold to one customer, 400 gallons of sweet crude oil

B. 2,000 bushels of corn, 2,000 bushels of tomatoes, 2,000 bushels of soybeans

C. a painting by Norman Rockwell, a painting by Grandma Moses, a painting by Claude Monet

D. a new convertible, a new truck, a new minivan

E. a diamond ring, an emerald ring, a sapphire ring

638. If a car dealership sells vehicles to individuals, what method is used to record the cost of the vehicles sold?

Contrasting Cost of Goods Sold Expense Methods

639–650

639. Placebo Clip-On Tie Company had one tie in inventory at the beginning of the year, and it cost $5. On February 10, the company bought another tie for inventory, and it cost $8. On March 10, the company bought another tie for $10; on April 3, it purchased another for $12; and on May 12, it bought another for $15. In June, Placebo sold three ties. If the company uses the LIFO method of recording cost of goods sold expense, how much is cost of goods sold?

640. Placebo Clip-On Tie Company had one tie in inventory at the beginning of the year, and it cost $5. On February 10, the company bought another tie for inventory, and it cost $8. On March 10, the company bought another tie for $10; on April 3, it purchased another for $12; and on May 12, it bought another for $15. In June, Placebo sold three ties. What is the value of the ending inventory if Placebo uses the LIFO method of recording ending inventory?

641. Placebo Clip-On Tie Company had one tie in inventory at the beginning of the year, and it cost $5. On February 10, the company bought another tie for inventory, and it cost $8. On March 10, the company bought another tie for $10; on April 3, it purchased another for $12; and on May 12, it bought another for $15. In June, Placebo sold three ties. If the company uses the average cost method of recording cost of goods sold expense, how much is cost of goods sold?

642. Placebo Clip-On Tie Company had one tie in inventory at the beginning of the year, and it cost $5. On February 10, the company bought another tie for inventory, and it cost $8. On March 10, the company bought another tie for $10; on April 3, it purchased another for $12; and on May 12, it bought another for $15. In June, Placebo sold three ties. If the company uses the FIFO method of recording cost of goods sold expense, how much is cost of goods sold?

643. Placebo Clip-On Tie Company had one tie in inventory at the beginning of the year, and it cost $5. On February 10, the company bought another tie for inventory, and it cost $8. On March 10, the company bought another tie for $10; on April 3, it purchased another for $12; and on May 12, it bought another for $15. In June, Placebo sold three ties. What is the value of the ending inventory if Placebo uses the average cost method of recording ending inventory?

644. Placebo Clip-On Tie Company had one tie in inventory at the beginning of the year, and it cost $5. On February 10, the company bought another tie for inventory, and it cost $8. On March 10, the company bought another tie for $10; on April 3, it purchased another for $12; and on May 12, it bought another for $15. In June, Placebo sold three ties. What is the value of the ending inventory if Placebo uses the FIFO method of recording ending inventory?

645. Which method of recording cost of goods sold expense moves the cost of the most recent inventory purchases to cost of goods sold?

646. Which method of recording cost of goods sold expense uses the cost of the oldest inventory purchases to determine cost of goods sold?

647. Which method of recording cost of goods sold expense and ending inventory uses a weighted average cost per unit based on the cost of all goods available for sale to calculate cost of goods sold expense?

648. Which method of recording cost of goods sold expense and ending inventory uses a weighted average cost per unit based on the cost of all goods available for sale to calculate the value of ending inventory?

649. Which method of recording cost of goods sold expense and ending inventory uses the cost of the oldest inventory purchases to determine the ending inventory value?

650. Which method of recording cost of goods sold expense and ending inventory uses the cost of the most recently acquired inventory purchases to determine the ending inventory value?

Moving Forward: The First-in, First-out (FIFO) Method

651–660

651. Exercise Boots starts the month of May with 4,251 pairs of boots in inventory. Each pair, or unit, has a cost of $3 associated with it. On May 5, the company purchases 5,000 more pairs and pays $5 per unit. Then, on May 24, it adds 7,300 more units to inventory, and each unit costs $6. At the end of the month, Exercise Boots has 5,010 units left in inventory. If the company uses the FIFO method to record the cost of goods sold expense, what is the value of ending inventory at the end of the month?

652. Stone Stuff sells big, heavy things for $500 each. The company begins November with 13 units in inventory, and each unit has an assigned cost of $204. During the month, it makes three purchases. On the 10th, it buys 20 more units for $210 each. On the 20th, it buys another 18 units at a cost of $220 per unit. And on the 29th, it purchases 12 units and pays $227 per unit. If Stone Stuff uses FIFO to record the cost of goods sold expense, what is the value of ending inventory for November if 14 units are left unsold?

653. Rich Red Company sells its product for $15. It begins 2015 with 10 units in inventory at a cost of $6 each. On February 2, Rich purchases an additional 12 units at a cost of $8 each. Another purchase, on June 9, consists of 15 units at a cost of $11 each. Then, on October 31, it buys another 15 units at a cost of $11 each. At year-end, 12 units are left in inventory. What is the cost of goods sold expense using the FIFO method?

654. Rich Red Company sells its product for $15. It begins 2015 with 10 units in inventory at a cost of $6 each. On February 2, Rich purchases an additional 12 units at a cost of $8 each. Another purchase, on June 9, consists of 15 units at a cost of $11 each. Then, on October 31, it buys another 15 units at a cost of $11 each. At year-end, 12 units are left in inventory. What is the value of ending inventory using the FIFO method?

655. Gray Paints has 40,000 units of Product A in inventory at a cost of $10 at the beginning of the year. On February 2, it purchases another 100,000 units at $12. On April 1, it purchases 50,000 units at $15 each. On June 1, it purchases 75,000 units and pays $16 per unit. On August 2, it purchases 50,000 units at a cost of $18 each, and the final purchase of the year occurs on October 1, when Gray buys 80,000 units for $19 each. During the year, Gray Paints sells 353,000 units at $35 each. If Gray Paints uses the FIFO method, what is cost of goods sold expense for the year?

656. Gray Paints has 40,000 units of Product A in inventory at a cost of $10 at the beginning of the year. On February 2, it purchases another 100,000 units at $12. On April 1, it purchases 50,000 units at $15 each. On June 1, it purchases 75,000 units and pays $16 per unit. On August 2, it purchases 50,000 units at a cost of $18 each, and the final purchase of the year occurs on October 1, when Gray buys 80,000 units for $19 each. During the year, Gray Paints sells 353,000 units at $35 each. If Gray Paints uses the FIFO method of recording cost of goods sold expense, what is the value of ending inventory at the end of the year?

657. Exercise Boots starts the month of May with 4,251 pairs of boots in inventory. Each pair, or unit, has a cost of $3 associated with it. On May 5, the company purchases 5,000 more units and pays $5 per unit. Then, on May 24, it adds 7,300 more units to inventory, and each unit costs $6. At the end of the month, Exercise Boots has 5,010 units left in inventory. Calculate the cost of goods sold for the month if the company uses FIFO.

658. Stone Stuff sells big, heavy things for $500 each. The company begins November with 13 units in inventory, and each unit has an assigned cost of $204. During the month, it makes three purchases. On the 10th, it buys 20 more units for $210 each. On the 20th, it buys another 18 units at a cost of $220 per unit. And on the 29th, it purchases 12 units and pays $227 per unit. If Stone Stuff uses FIFO to record the cost of goods sold expense, what is cost of goods sold for November if 14 units are left unsold?

659. Core Corporation is the leading supplier of apple corers. It begins the period with 43,172 units in beginning inventory. Each of those units has a $2 cost attached to it. During the period, Core makes the following purchases:

- Feb. 3: 67,000 at $4
- May 5: 132,000 at $5
- Aug. 25: 125,000 at $5
- Nov. 11: 83,000 at $7

At the end of the period, Core has 45,669 units left in inventory. Calculate cost of goods sold expense if Core uses the FIFO method.

660. Core Corporation is the leading supplier of apple corers. It begins the period with 43,172 units in beginning inventory. Each of those units has a $2 cost attached to it. During the period, Core makes the following purchases:

- Feb. 3: 67,000 at $4
- May 5: 132,000 at $5
- Aug. 25: 125,000 at $5
- Nov. 11: 83,000 at $7

At the end of the period, Core has 45,669 units left in inventory. What is the value of ending inventory if Core uses the FIFO method of recording cost of goods sold expense?

Moving in Reverse: The Last-in, First-out (LIFO) Method

661–670

661. Exercise Boots starts the month of May with 4,251 pairs of boots in inventory. Each pair, or unit, has a cost of $3 associated with it. On May 5, the company purchases 5,000 more pairs and pays $5 per unit. Then, on May 24, it adds 7,300 more units to inventory, and each unit costs $6. At the end of the month, Exercise Boots has 5,010 units left in inventory. If the company uses the LIFO method to record the cost of goods sold expense, what is the value of ending inventory at the end of the month?

662. Stone Stuff sells big, heavy things for $500 each. The company begins November with 13 units in inventory, and each unit has an assigned cost of $204. During the month, it makes three purchases. On the 10th, it buys 20 more units for $210 each. On the 20th, it buys another 18 units at a cost of $220 per unit. And on the 29th, it purchases 12 units and pays $227 per unit. If Stone Stuff uses LIFO to record the cost of goods sold expense, what is the value of ending inventory for November if 14 units are left unsold?

663. Core Corporation is the leading supplier of apple corers. It begins the period with 43,172 units in beginning inventory. Each of those units has a $2 cost attached to it. During the period, Core makes the following purchases:

- Feb. 3: 67,000 at $4
- May 5: 132,000 at $5
- Aug. 25: 125,000 at $5
- Nov. 11: 83,000 at $7

At the end of the period, Core has 45,669 units left in inventory. What is the value of ending inventory if Core uses the LIFO method of recording cost of goods sold expense?

664. Boomerang Grenade Company sells its product for $15. It begins 2015 with 10 units in inventory at a cost of $6 each. On February 2, the company purchases an additional 12 units at a cost of $8 each. Another purchase, on June 9, consists of 15 units at a cost of $11 each. Then, on October 31, the company purchases another 15 units at a cost of $11 each. At year-end, 12 units are left in inventory. What is the cost of goods sold expense using the LIFO method?

665. Boomerang Grenade Company sells its product for $15. It begins 2015 with 10 units in inventory at a cost of $6 each. On February 2, the company purchases an additional 12 units at a cost of $8 each. Another purchase, on June 9, consists of 15 units at a cost of $11 each. Then, on October 31, the company buys another 15 units at a cost of $11 each. At year-end, 12 units are left in inventory. What is the value of ending inventory using the LIFO method?

666. Gray Paints has 40,000 units of Product A in inventory at a cost of $10 at the beginning of the year. On February 2, it purchases another 100,000 units at $12. On April 1, it purchases 50,000 units at $15 each. On June 1, it purchases 75,000 units and pays $16 per unit. On August 2, it purchases 50,000 units at a cost of $18 each, and the final purchase of the year occurs on October 1, when Gray buys 80,000 units for $19 each. During the year, Gray Paints sells 353,000 units at $35 each. If Gray Paints uses the LIFO method, what is the cost of goods sold expense for the year?

667. Gray Paints has 40,000 units of Product A in inventory at a cost of $10 at the beginning of the year. On February 2, it purchases another 100,000 units at $12. On April 1, it purchases 50,000 units at $15 each. On June 1, it purchases 75,000 units and pays $16 per unit. On August 2, it purchases 50,000 units at a cost of $18 each, and the final purchase of the year occurs on October 1, when Gray buys 80,000 units for $19 each. During the year, Gray Paints sells 353,000 units at $35 each. If Gray Paints uses the LIFO method, what is the cost of ending inventory at year-end?

668. Exercise Boots starts the month of May with 4,251 pairs of boots in inventory. Each pair, or unit, has a cost of $3 associated with it. On May 5, the company purchases 5,000 more units and pays $5 per unit. Then, on May 24, it adds 7,300 more units to inventory, and each unit cost $6. At the end of the month, Exercise Boots has 5,010 units left in inventory. Calculate the cost of goods sold for the month if the company uses LIFO.

669. Stone Stuff sells big, heavy things for $500 each. The company begins November with 13 units in inventory, and each unit has an assigned cost of $204. During the month, it makes three purchases. On the 10th, it buys 20 more units for $210 each. On the 20th, it buys another 18 units at a cost of $220 per unit. And on the 29th, it purchases 12 units and pays $227 per unit. At the end of November, 14 units are left unsold. Calculate the cost of goods sold expense if Stone Stuff uses the LIFO method.

670. Core Corporation is the leading supplier of apple corers. It begins the period with 43,172 units in beginning inventory. Each of those units has a $2 cost attached to it. During the period, Core makes the following purchases:

- Feb. 3: 67,000 at $4
- May 5: 132,000 at $5
- Aug. 25: 125,000 at $5
- Nov. 11: 83,000 at $7

At the end of the period, Core has 45,669 units left in inventory. Calculate the cost of goods sold expense if Core uses the LIFO method.

Compromising: The Average Cost Method

671–682

671. Stone Stuff sells big, heavy things for $500 each. The company begins November with 13 units in inventory, and each unit has an assigned cost of $204. During the month, it makes three purchases. On the 10th, it buys 20 more units for $210 each. On the 20th, it buys another 18 units at a cost of $220 per unit. And on the 29th, it purchases 12 units and pays $227 per unit. At the end of November, 14 units are left unsold. Calculate the value of ending inventory if Stone Stuff uses the average cost method to record cost of goods sold expense.

672. Stone Stuff sells big, heavy things for $500 each. The company begins November with 13 units in inventory, and each unit has an assigned cost of $204. During the month, it makes three purchases. On the 10th, it buys 20 more units for $210 each. On the 20th, it buys another 18 units at a cost of $220 per unit. And on the 29th, it purchases 12 units and pays $227 per unit. At the end of November, 14 units are left unsold. If the company uses the average cost method to record cost of goods sold expense, what is the average cost per unit?

673. Gray Paints has 40,000 units of Product A in inventory at a cost of $10 at the beginning of the year. On February 2, it purchases another 100,000 units at $12. On April 1, it purchases 50,000 units at $15 each. On June 1, it purchases 75,000 units and pays $16 per unit. On August 2, it purchases 50,000 units at a cost of $18 each, and the final purchase of the year occurs on October 1, when Gray buys 80,000 units for $19 each. During the year, Gray Paints sells 353,000 units at $35 each. If Gray Paints uses the average cost method for recording cost of goods sold expense, what is the average cost per unit that it will use?

674. Gray Paints uses the average cost method to record cost of goods sold expense. Gray Paints has 40,000 units of Product A in inventory at a cost of $10 at the beginning of the year. On February 2, it purchases another 100,000 units at $12. On April 1, it purchases 50,000 units at $15 each. On June 1, it purchases 75,000 units and pays $16 per unit. On August 2, it purchases 50,000 units at a cost of $18 each, and the final purchase of the year occurs on October 1, when Gray buys 80,000 units for $19 each. During the year, Gray Paints sells 353,000 units at $35 each and has 42,000 units left in inventory. Calculate the cost of goods sold expense if the company has determined the weighted average cost per unit is $15.11 and the simple average cost per unit is $15.

675. Gray Paints uses the average cost method to record cost of goods sold expense. Gray Paints has 40,000 units of Product A in inventory at a cost of $10 at the beginning of the year. On February 2, it purchases another 100,000 units at $12. On April 1, it purchases 50,000 units at $15 each. On June 1, it purchases 75,000 units and pays $16 per unit. On August 2, it purchases 50,000 units at a cost of $18 each, and the final purchase of the year occurs on October 1, when Gray buys 80,000 units for $19 each. During the year, Gray Paints sells 353,000 units at $35 each and has 42,000 units left in inventory. Calculate the cost of goods sold expense if the company has determined the weighted average cost per unit is $15.11 and the simple average cost per unit is $15.

676. Core Corporation is the leading supplier of apple corers. It begins the period with 43,172 units in beginning inventory. Each of those units has a $2 cost attached to it. During the period, Core makes the following purchases:

- Feb. 3: 67,000 at $4
- May 5: 132,000 at $5
- Aug. 25: 125,000 at $5
- Nov. 11: 83,000 at $7

At the end of the period, Core has 45,669 units left in inventory. Calculate the average cost per unit that Core would use to record cost of goods sold if the company uses the average cost method.

677. Core Corporation is the leading supplier of apple corers. It begins the period with 43,172 units in beginning inventory. Each of those units has a $2 cost attached to it. During the period, Core makes the following purchases:

- Feb. 3: 67,000 at $4
- May 5: 132,000 at $5
- Aug. 25: 125,000 at $5
- Nov. 11: 83,000 at $7

At the end of the period, Core has 45,669 units left in inventory. Calculate the value of ending inventory if Core uses the average cost method.

678. Rich Red Company sells its product for $15. It begins 2015 with 10 units in inventory at a cost of $6 each. On February 2, Rich purchases an additional 12 units at a cost of $8 each. Another purchase, on June 9, consists of 15 units at a cost of $11 each. Then, on October 31, it buys another 15 units at a cost of $11 each. At year-end, 12 units are left in inventory. Calculate the cost per unit Rich Red would use to record cost of goods sold expense if the company uses the average cost method.

679. Rich Red Company sells its product for $15. It begins 2015 with 10 units in inventory at a cost of $6 each. On February 2, Rich purchases an additional 12 units at a cost of $8 each. Another purchase, on June 9, consists of 15 units at a cost of $11 each. Then, on October 31, it buys another 15 units at a cost of $11 each. At year-end, 12 units are left in inventory. Calculate the cost of goods sold expense if Rich Red uses the average cost method of inventory cost flow.

680. Rich Red Company sells its product for $15. It begins 2015 with 10 units in inventory at a cost of $6 each. On February 2, Rich purchases an additional 12 units at a cost of $8 each. Another purchase, on June 9, consists of 15 units at a cost of $11 each. Then, on October 31, it buys another 15 units at a cost of $11 each. At year-end, 12 units are left in inventory. If the company uses the average cost method, calculate the cost of ending inventory.

681. Stone Stuff sells big, heavy things for $500 each. The company begins November with 13 units in inventory, and each unit has an assigned cost of $204. During the month, it makes three purchases. On the 10th, it buys 20 more units for $210 each. On the 20th, it buys another 18 units at a cost of $220 per unit. And on the 29th, it purchases 12 units and pays $227 per unit. At the end of November, 14 units are left unsold. Calculate the cost of goods sold expense if Stone Stuff uses the average cost method for its inventory cost flow.

682. Core Corporation is the leading supplier of apple corers. It begins the period with 43,172 units in beginning inventory. Each of those units has a $2 cost attached to it. During the period, Core makes the following purchases:

- Feb. 3: 67,000 at $4
- May 5: 132,000 at $5
- Aug. 25: 125,000 at $5
- Nov. 11: 83,000 at $7

At the end of the period, Core has 45,669 units left in inventory. Calculate the cost of goods sold expense if Core uses the average cost method.

Remembering to Apply the Lower of Cost or Market Rule

683–692

683. When valuing inventories using the lower of cost or market rule, what is considered the market value?

684. Snow Company sells big shovels for $20 each. The company has 3,000 big shovels on hand at the end of the year. After using LIFO, the inventory is valued at $4,000. The current replacement cost of those big shovels is $4,100. What is the amount of inventory listed on the year-end balance sheet?

685. Henrietta's Helmets sells high quality bike helmets for $100 each. The cost of the 394 helmets in inventory at year-end is $14,552. The current cost to replace the helmets in ending inventory is $15,039. What is the value of ending inventory on the balance sheet?

686. Spring Works, Inc. uses average cost to record cost of goods sold expense. At year-end, Spring Works determines the value of the 580 units in ending inventory to be $375,800. However, when it compares that value to the market value using the current replacement cost, the value of the inventory is $400,500. What is the amount of the adjustment that Spring Works must make to apply the lower of cost or market rule?

687. Henrietta's Helmets sells high quality bike helmets for $100 each. The cost of the 394 helmets in inventory at year-end is $14,552. The current cost to replace the helmets in ending inventory is $15,039. What is the amount of the adjustment to inventory and income that Henrietta must make to comply with the lower of cost or market rule?

688. Snow Company sells big shovels for $20 each. The company has 3,000 big shovels on hand at the end of the year. After using LIFO, the inventory is valued at $4,100. The current replacement cost of those big shovels is $4,000. How much will income decrease because of the difference between the inventory values?

689. Great Games sells three different products: card games, electronic games, and board games. The cost of the card games in ending inventory is $12,000, and the market value is $11,000. The cost of the electronic games in ending inventory is $300,000, and the market value is $310,000. The cost of the board games in ending inventory is $57,000, and the market value is $48,000. What is the total value of ending inventory on the year-end balance sheet?

690. Vase Land has inventory at the end of the year of 3,100 vases. Vase Land uses average cost to record cost of goods sold expense. The average cost per unit for the year is $12. The beginning inventory for the year consisted of 3,000 vases with an average cost of $11. The current replacement cost for the 3,100 vases is $9 per vase. What is the amount of the adjustment necessary to apply the lower of cost or market rule to the ending inventory?

691. Snow Company sells big shovels for $20 each. The company has 3,000 big shovels on hand at the end of the year. After using LIFO, the inventory is valued at $4,000. The current replacement cost of those big shovels is $4,100. How much will income change because of the difference between the inventory values?

692. Henrietta's Helmets sells high quality bike helmets for $100 each. The cost of the 394 helmets in inventory at year-end is $15,039. The current cost to replace the helmets in ending inventory is $14,552. What is the amount of the adjustment that Henrietta must make to comply with the lower of cost or market rule?

Choosing Depreciation Methods

693–706

693. What is the purpose of recording depreciation expense?

694. Describe the main characteristic of accelerated depreciation methods.

695. On January 1, Tropics Company purchases a food truck to drive around the island and sell lunch items to beachgoers and surfers. The cost of the truck is $75,000. Tropics plans to use the truck for 5 years and then assess whether to expand or give it up. Either way, the company figures it should be able to sell the truck for about $10,000. Assuming Tropics decides to use the straight line depreciation method, calculate the depreciation expense on the income statement and the book value of the truck on the balance sheet at the end of the first year.

696. On January 1, Country Weddings buys a beautiful mansion situated on an old farm. It plans to rent out the property for weddings. It buys the land and building for $800,000 and allocates half the purchase price to the land and half to the house. The house has a useful life of 25 years and a salvage value of $100,000. If Country Weddings uses straight line depreciation, what is the total depreciation expense for a full year of use?

697. Green Careers is a staffing agency specializing in jobs in environmentally friendly companies. The company rents an office and phone equipment but bought desks, computers, printers, and file cabinets. Which of the items listed must Green Careers depreciate?

698. Minnesota Cookie Company buys new mixing equipment for the factory. The order for the equipment is placed on June 15, 2015. The equipment is delivered on June 20 but isn't installed and ready for use until July 1, 2015. The cost of the equipment is $19,250. The company believes that it will last for 10 years. At the end of 10 years, the company expects to sell it for $500. If the company uses straight line depreciation, how much depreciation expense should the company record for 2015?

699. Minnesota Cookie Company buys new mixing equipment for the factory. The order for the equipment is placed on June 1, 2015. The equipment is delivered on June 20 but isn't installed and ready for use until July 1, 2015. The cost of the equipment is $19,250. The company believes that it will last for 10 years. At the end of 10 years, the company expects to sell it for $500. If the company uses straight line depreciation, how much depreciation expense should the company record for 2016?

700. On January 1, Tropics Company purchases a food truck to drive around the island and sell lunch items to beachgoers and surfers. The cost of the truck is $75,000. Tropics plans to use the truck for 5 years and then assess whether to expand or give it up. Either way, the company figures it should be able to sell the truck for about $10,000 at the end of 5 years. Assuming Tropics decides to use the straight line depreciation method, calculate the depreciation expense on the income statement and the book value of the truck on the balance sheet at the end of the fifth year.

701. Minnesota Cookie Company buys new mixing equipment for the factory. The order for the equipment is placed on June 1, 2015. The equipment is delivered on June 20 but isn't installed and ready for use until July 1, 2015. The cost of the equipment is $19,250. The company believes that it will last for 10 years. At the end of 10 years, the company expects to sell it for $500. The company properly records depreciation expense using the straight line method for 2015 and 2016. What is the book value of the asset at the end of 2016?

702. On January 1, Country Weddings buys a beautiful mansion situated on an old farm. It plans to rent out the property for weddings. It buys the land and building for $800,000 and allocates half the purchase price to the land and half to the house. The house has a useful life of 25 years and a salvage value of $100,000. If Country Weddings uses double-declining depreciation, what is the total depreciation expense for the first year of use?

703. On January 1, Country Weddings buys a beautiful mansion situated on an old farm. It plans to rent out the property for weddings. It buys the land and building for $800,000 and allocates half the purchase price to the land and half to the house. The house has a useful life of 25 years and a salvage value of $100,000. If Country Weddings uses double-declining balance depreciation, what is the total depreciation expense for the third year of use?

704. On January 1, Country Weddings buys a beautiful mansion situated on an old farm. It plans to rent out the property for weddings. It buys the land and building for $800,000 and allocates half the purchase price to the land and half to the house. The house has a useful life of 25 years and a salvage value of $100,000. Over the life of the asset, how much more depreciation expense will Country Weddings record using double-declining balance versus straight line depreciation?

705. On January 1, Tropics Company purchases a food truck to drive around the island and sell lunch items to beachgoers and surfers. The cost of the truck is $75,000. Tropics plans to use the truck for 5 years and then assess whether to expand or give it up. Either way, the company figures it should be able to sell the truck for about $10,000 at the end of 5 years. The company uses straight line depreciation. Seven years later, Tropics is still using the truck. How much is the depreciation expense in the seventh year of use?

706. Minnesota Cookie Company buys new mixing equipment for the factory. The order for the equipment is placed on June 1, 2015. The equipment is delivered on June 20 but isn't installed and ready for use until July 1, 2015. The cost of the equipment is $19,250. The company believes that it will last for 10 years. At the end of 10 years, the company expects to sell it for $500. If the company uses the equipment for 10 years, what is the total depreciation expense recorded for all years?

Other Areas of Alternative Accounting Methods

707–716

707. Beach Sports has the following information in its accounting records before adjusting for estimated bad debts:

- Accounts receivable: $865,000 (debit balance)
- Allowance for bad debts: $2,100 (credit balance)
- Sales, net: $756,000 (credit balance)

Calculate the bad debt expense if the company uses the allowance method and estimates bad debts of .8% of net sales.

708. Beach Sports has the following information in its accounting records before adjusting for estimated bad debts:

- Accounts receivable: $865,000 (debit balance)
- Allowance for bad debts: $2,100 (credit balance)
- Sales, net: $756,000 (credit balance)

Calculate the balance in the allowance for bad debts after the adjustment is made if the allowance method assumes bad debts of .8% of net sales.

709. Geyser Goods has the following information in its accounting records before adjusting for estimated bad debts:

- Accounts receivable: $865,000 (debit balance)
- Allowance for uncollectibles: $2,100 (debit balance)
- Sales: $756,000 (credit balance)
- Sales returns: $6,000 (debit balance)

Calculate the bad debt expense if the company uses the allowance method and assumes bad debts of .5% of net sales.

710. Beach Sports has the following information in its accounting records before adjusting for estimated bad debts:

- Accounts receivable: $865,000 (debit balance)
- Allowance for bad debts: $2,100 (credit balance)
- Sales, net: $756,000 (credit balance)

Calculate the amount of accounts receivable, net on the balance sheet after the adjustment is made if the allowance method assumes bad debts of .8% of net sales.

711. Beach Sports has the following information in its accounting records before adjusting for estimated bad debts using the allowance method:

- Accounts receivable: $865,000 (debit balance)
- Allowance for bad debts: $2,100 (credit balance)
- Sales, net: $756,000 (credit balance)

Calculate the bad debt expense if the method assumes 1% of gross accounts receivable are possibly uncollectible.

712. Beach Sports has the following information in its accounting records before adjusting for estimated bad debts:

- Accounts receivable: $865,000 (debit balance)
- Allowance for bad debts: $2,100 (credit balance)
- Sales, net: $756,000 (credit balance)

Calculate the balance in the allowance for bad debt if the method assumes 1% of gross accounts receivable are possibly uncollectible.

713. Beach Sports has the following information in its accounting records before adjusting for estimated bad debts using the allowance method:

- Accounts receivable: $865,000 (debit balance)
- Allowance for bad debts: $2,100 (credit balance)
- Sales, net: $756,000 (credit balance)

Calculate accounts receivable, net if the method assumes 1% of gross accounts receivable are possibly uncollectible.

714. Geyser Goods has the following information in its accounting records before adjusting for estimated bad debts:

- Accounts receivable: $865,000 (debit balance)
- Allowance for uncollectibles: $2,100 (debit balance)
- Sales: $756,000 (credit balance)
- Sales returns: $6,000 (debit balance)

Calculate the balance in the allowance for uncollectibles after the adjustment is made if the company uses the allowance method and assumes bad debts of .5% of net sales.

715. Geyser Goods has the following information in its accounting records before adjusting for estimated bad debts:

- Accounts receivable: $865,000 (debit balance)
- Allowance for uncollectibles: $2,100 (debit balance)
- Sales: $756,000 (credit balance)
- Sales returns: $6,000 (debit balance)

Calculate the bad debt expense if the company uses the allowance method and assumes .8% of gross accounts receivable are possibly uncollectible.

716. Geyser Goods has the following information in its accounting records before adjusting for estimated bad debts:

- Accounts receivable: $865,000 (debit balance)
- Allowance for uncollectibles: $2,100 (debit balance)
- Sales: $756,000 (credit balance)
- Sales returns: $6,000 (debit balance)

Calculate accounts receivable, net if the method assumes .8% of gross accounts receivable are possibly uncollectible.

Massaging the Numbers and Manipulating Reported Profit

717–728

717. Permanent Lipstick Co. is worried about meeting its earnings forecast. The company bought a new, very expensive piece of manufacturing equipment during the year and is trying to decide which method of depreciation to use to minimize the expense. What method do you recommend?

718. Which method of depreciation produces the highest amount of depreciation expense in the first year of an asset's life?

719. Purple Beauty Pots is concerned about achieving its forecast for $4,000,000 in earnings. Preliminary numbers make it look like the company will be about $500,000 short. It currently estimate bad debts as 2% of net sales. This year, sales were $50,000,000. What estimate of bad debts would help the company meet the forecast?

720. Identify two conservative accounting methods.

A. straight line depreciation for new equipment and FIFO when prices are falling

B. double-declining balance depreciation for new equipment and LIFO when prices are rising

C. double-declining balance depreciation for old equipment and LIFO when prices are rising

D. straight line depreciation for new equipment and LIFO when prices are rising

E. double-declining balance depreciation for new equipment and FIFO when prices are falling

721. Gourmet Convenience Corp. is trying to minimize taxes and is considering the following alternative accounting methods:

- Depreciation on new machinery: double-declining balance, 150% declining balance, or straight line
- Inventory cost flow (costs are increasing): LIFO or FIFO

What combination do you recommend to minimize taxes?

722. High Water Wading Pants is choosing accounting methods to maximize income and is considering the following choices:

- Inventory: LIFO, FIFO, or weighted average (prices are rising)
- Depreciation: double-declining balance or straight line (equipment is new)
- Bad debt expense: 50-year average of bad debts, 1%; 2-year average of bad debts during an economic downturn, 4% (sales of $3,000,000)

What combination of methods will produce the highest income?

723. Which method of recording depreciation will produce the highest depreciation expense on new equipment?

A. double-declining balance

B. straight line

C. 150% declining balance

D. LIFO

E. residual value allocation

724. Companies often use different accounting methods for tax purposes than they use for financial reporting. The goal for tax purposes is to reduce taxable income as much as possible to avoid paying taxes. The goal for financial reporting is to make income as high as possible to make the company look more valuable. Identify which method of depreciation a company with new assets should use for tax purposes and which it should use for financial reporting to achieve the goals.

A. Use straight line for tax purposes and double-declining for financial reporting.

B. Use straight line for both tax and financial reporting.

C. Use double-declining balance for tax purposes and straight line for financial reporting.

D. Use double-declining for both tax and financial reporting.

E. It doesn't matter because both methods produce the same expense.

725. The following information is taken from the books of Annoying Telemarketers Co.: Equipment, useful life of 5 years, $10,000 salvage, purchased this year for $81,000 cash. By how much will income increase if the company uses the straight line method, rather than the double-declining balance method for depreciation?

726. Brain Cell Bar sells treatments to improve intelligence. The company is preparing the financial statements for the venture capital team that will consider investing in the company. The investors require statements that are prepared using generally accepted accounting principles, GAAP. The company is trying to maximize income to impress the investors. It is considering the following different accounting methods:

- Depreciation on new equipment: straight line or double-declining balance
- Inventory cost flows (prices are increasing): LIFO or FIFO
- Bad debt expense: direct write off or percent of sales

What combination will maximize income while still following GAAP?

727. The following information is taken from the books of Annoying Telemarketers Co.:

- Sales: $57,000
- Estimate of bad debts expense from the Association of Telemarketers: 1% of net sales
- Estimate of bad debts expense based on nonpayment during January and February: 3%

By how much will income change if the company uses a conservative accounting method for bad debt?

728. White Ear Plugs is considering which method of recording inventory cost flows will produce the lowest cost of goods sold expense during a period when the price of materials is falling. Suggest the method the company should use.

Chapter 11

Profit Behavior Analysis

This chapter reviews how you calculate a company's break-even point in sales. It moves on to cover contribution margin and gross margin. These two formulas help explain why a company is profitable. You also go over rate of return formulas, such as return on equity (ROE) and return on assets (ROA). These calculations reveal how well a firm is using the balance sheet accounts to generate a profit.

The Problems You'll Work On

In this chapter, you see problems on these accounting topics:

- Understanding how to calculate the break-even point in dollars and units sold
- Going over contribution margin and gross margin
- Using operating leverage to analyze the use of debt and equity
- Finding out about operating profit
- Using return on equity and return on assets to assess profitability

What to Watch Out For

Don't let common mistakes trip you up. Some of the following suggestions may be helpful:

- You calculate contribution margin as sales less variable costs. You don't use fixed costs in the calculation.
- You can calculate the break-even point in sale dollars or in units sold.
- Operating profit represents profit generated from normal, day-to-day business operations. Non-operating income is profit from unusual transactions.
- You calculate gross margin as sales less cost of sales. Gross margin is not a company's total profit.

Mapping Profit for Managers

729–738

729. Pine Hill Products has the following information:

- Sales: $10,000
- Cost of goods sold: $3,000
- Variable costs: $2,000
- Fixed costs: $3,000

Calculate the contribution margin.

730. Pine Hill Products has the following information:

- Sales: $10,000
- Cost of goods sold: $3,000
- Variable costs: $2,000
- Fixed costs: $4,000

Calculate the gross profit, also called gross margin.

731. Golden State Products has sales of $7,632,614. Cost of goods sold expense is $2,531,636. Variable costs associated with sales equal $3,631,011, and fixed costs are $800,000. Calculate gross profit, also called gross margin.

732. Golden State Products has sales of $7,632,614. Cost of goods sold expense is $2,531,636. Variable costs associated with sales equal $3,631,011, and fixed costs are $800,000. Calculate contribution margin.

733. Golden State Products has sales of $7,632,614. Cost of goods sold expense is $2,531,636. Variable costs associated with sales equal $3,631,011, and fixed costs are $800,000. Calculate operating profit.

734. Green Glass Corporation has sales of $800,000, gross profit of $300,000, and a contribution margin of $200,000. It also has fixed costs of $50,000. Calculate cost of goods sold.

735. Green Glass Corporation has sales of $800,000, gross profit of $300,000, and a contribution margin of $200,000. It also has fixed costs of $50,000. Calculate variable costs other than cost of goods sold.

736. Green Glass Corporation has sales of $800,000, gross profit of $300,000, and a contribution margin of $200,000. The operating profit is $150,000. Calculate fixed costs.

737. Exotic Case has the following information available in its internal reporting system:

- Sales volume, in units: 47,350
- Selling price per unit: $300
- Cost of goods sold per unit: $140
- Variable costs associated with each unit (sales commission): $30
- Fixed costs: $3,500,000

Calculate gross profit, also called gross margin.

738. Exotic Case has the following information available in its internal reporting system:

- Sales volume, in units: 47,350
- Selling price per unit: $300
- Cost of goods sold per unit: $140
- Variable costs associated with each unit (sales commission): $30
- Fixed costs: $3,500,000

Calculate the contribution margin.

Analyzing Operating Profit

739–748

739. Lake City Products sells its product for $45 per unit. The costs associated with the product consist of $30 per unit of variable cost and $150,000 of fixed costs. What is the contribution margin per unit?

740. Rick's Wheelbarrows manufactures and sells wheelbarrows. The selling price is $80. The total cost to produce 1,000 units is $27,000, and the total cost to produce 1,500 units is $35,000. Estimate the variable cost per unit.

741. Rick's Wheelbarrows manufactures and sells wheelbarrows. The selling price is $80. The total cost to produce 1,000 units is $27,000, and the total cost to produce 1,500 units is $35,000. Estimate total fixed costs.

742. Rick's Wheelbarrows manufactures and sells wheelbarrows. The selling price is $80. The total cost to produce 1,000 units is $27,000, and the total cost to produce 1,500 units is $35,000. Estimate the contribution margin per unit.

743. Short Elliott Corporation sells 15,000 units of its product and has sales revenue of $87,000,000. Total variable costs are $54,000,000, and fixed costs are $20,000,000. Calculate variable cost per unit.

744. Lake City Products sells its product for $45 per unit. The costs associated with the product consist of $30 per unit of variable cost and $150,000 of fixed costs. How many units must the company sell to earn $1,000,000?

745. Lake City Products sells its product for $45 per unit. The costs associated with the product consist of $30 per unit of variable cost and $150,000 of fixed costs. How many units must the company sell to reach its break-even point?

746. Short Elliott Corporation sells 15,000 units of its product and has sales revenue of $87,000,000. Total variable costs are $54,000,000, and fixed costs are $20,000,000. Calculate the contribution margin per unit.

747. Short Elliott Corporation sells 15,000 units of its product and has sales revenue of $87,000,000. Total variable costs are $54,000,000, and fixed costs are $20,000,000. Calculate the number of units Short Elliott must sell to double the operating profit to $26,000,000.

748. Short Elliott Corporation sells 15,000 units of its product and has sales revenue of $87,000,000. Total variable costs are $54,000,000, and fixed costs are $20,000,000. Calculate the number of units Short Elliott must sell to triple the operating profit to $39,000,000.

Contribution Margin over Fixed Costs

749–758

749. Kalia's Company produces a product that sells for $10, has variable cost per unit of $4, and has fixed costs of $535,000. Calculate Kalia's operating profit if it sells 150,000 units during the year.

750. Zoomski's Company produces a product that sells for $135, has variable cost per unit of $125, and has fixed costs of $553,000. Calculate Zoomski's operating profit if it sells 87,000 units during the year.

751. Harris Hair Goo sells tubes of goo for $20. The contribution margin is $15 per tube, and fixed costs for the period are $12,000,000. Calculate the operating profit for the period if the company sells 2,000,000 tubes of goo.

752. Pasquale's produces a product that has a selling price of $10 and a contribution margin of $4. Fixed costs are $1,400,000. Calculate the operating profit if the company sells 450,000 units.

753. Shea's Honey Company sells honey in gallon jars for $40 per jar. The contribution margin per jar is $15, and fixed costs are $238,000 per year. Calculate Shea's operating profit if the company has sales revenue of $680,000.

754. VLM Necklace Corporation sells necklaces to elementary school girls. Each necklace sells for $5, and the company sells 1,000,000 necklaces during the year. The fixed costs for the year are $3,700,000, and operating profit is $850,000. Calculate contribution margin per unit.

755. VLM Necklace Corporation sells necklaces to elementary school girls. Each necklace sells for $5, and the company sells 1,000,000 necklaces during the year. The fixed costs for the year are $3,700,000, and variable cost per unit is $1. Calculate the operating profit for the year.

756. VLM Necklace Corporation sells necklaces to elementary school girls. Each necklace sells for $5, and the company sells 1,000,000 necklaces during the year. The fixed costs for the year are $3,700,000, and variable cost per unit is $1. Calculate the contribution margin in dollars.

757. Vi's Quilts produces beautiful, warm quilts that sell for $560. The variable cost per quilt is $130. Fixed costs for the year total $11,350,000. Calculate the operating profit if the company sells 37,500 quilts during the year.

758. Harvey Racing Skis sells 9,310 sets of skis and has a profit of $373,000. Calculate the contribution margin per unit if fixed costs are $92,500.

Excess over Break-even

759–768

759. Quasi Motors sells 1,200 vehicles during the year. The company's break-even point is the sale of 800 vehicles. If the contribution margin per unit is $430, what operating profit did Quasi Motors earn?

760. Zombie Bikes sells 8,000 apocalypse bikes during the year. If the company sells 6,000 of these special bikes, the fixed costs are covered, and the company breaks even. The selling price is $450, and the contribution margin is $103. What operating profit did Zombie Bikes earn selling 8,000 apocalypse bikes?

761. Then He Goes Like, Inc. translates documents for a flat fee of $50 per document. In July the company translates 4,000 documents. Its break-even sales level is 3,800 documents, and the contribution margin per document is $5. What is the operating profit for July?

762. Happy Day Breakfast Food sells 120,000 boxes of its product for $6.75 per box. The variable cost per box is $4. If Happy Day sells 107,000 boxes of breakfast food, it covers its fixed costs. What is the operating profit for the year?

763. Wild Wind Fans has fixed costs that require the sale of 3,710 fans to break even. Each fan sells for $400, and the variable cost per fan is $175. What operating profit will Wild Wind Fans earn if it sells 3,975 fans?

764. Bebebanana sells one-piece workout suits for $80 each. The variable cost per suit is $73. Break-even occurs at a sales level of 190,000 suits. The suits are featured on a new reality show, and sales soar to 238,000 suits. Calculate the company's operating profit at that level of sales.

765. Splendid Treats sells fruit drinks from a shack at the beach for $15 per drink. If it sells 1,240 drinks per month, it covers the fixed costs and breaks even. How much operating profit will Splendid Treats earn if the variable cost per unit is $12 and it sells 1,500 units during the month?

766. Ghost Bedding sells 7,000 sheets resulting in $560,000 in sales revenue. Variable costs per sheet are $35. Break-even occurs at 5,300 units. Calculate the operating profit for Ghost Bedding.

767. Golf Gear has a break-even sales level of 12,500 units. The company sells 20,000 units resulting in sales revenue of $300,000 and total variable costs of $170,000. Calculate the operating profit.

768. TextType sells applications for cellphones. It sells 970,000 apps resulting in $960,300 in sales revenue. Variable costs per app are 5¢. Break-even occurs at 850,000 units. Calculate the operating profit for TextType.

Minimizing Fixed Cost per Unit

769–778

769. The Yard Guys, Inc. sells lawn care equipment to homeowners. The contribution margin per piece of equipment is $400. Average fixed cost per unit is $220 at a sales volume of 4,500 units. Calculate the operating profit if Yard Guys, Inc. makes 4,500 sales.

770. Organic Bricks sells hypoallergenic bricks to hospitals. The contribution margin per brick is $2.75. The average fixed cost per unit is $1.50 at a sales volume of 4,000,000 units. Calculate the operating profit if the company sells 4,000,000 bricks.

771. Foxy Paint Cosmetics sells an all-purpose face cream for $495 per quart jar. The variable costs per jar are $35. The contribution margin per jar is $460. Total fixed costs are $3,500,000. What is the average fixed cost per unit if Foxy Paint sells 1,000,000 jars of face cream?

772. Foxy Paint Cosmetics sells an all-purpose face cream for $500 per quart jar. The variable costs per jar are $35. Total fixed costs are $3,500,000. What is the profit per unit if Foxy Paint sells 1,000,000 jars of face cream?

773. Edible Fungus Mushroom Farms sells boxes of exotic mushrooms. The contribution margin per box is $47. The fixed costs are $35,000 for production of up to 1,000 boxes. Calculate the operating profit if Edible Fungus Mushroom Farms sells 950 boxes.

774. Middle Age Tune-up Clinics provides a package of medical tests that sells for $350 per package and has variable costs per package of $120. Fixed costs per package are $85. Calculate the operating profit if the company sells 4,600 packages.

775. Perfect Bag, Inc. sells the perfect briefcase for both men and women. The contribution margin for the product is $90 per bag. Average fixed cost per bag is $40 when the company sells 10,000 bags. By how much does profit decline if the company sells 8,000 bags?

776. Middle Age Tune-up Clinic provides a package of medical tests that sells for $350 per package and has variable costs per package of $120. Total fixed costs are $208,000. The company is only open weekdays and does 8 test packages per day for 2,080 per year. The company has the capacity to do 10 test packages every day with no change in fixed costs. What would be the average profit per package if the company does 10 packages per day for a total of 2,600 per year?

777. Middle Age Tune-up Clinic provides a package of medical tests. The contribution margin per product is $230. Variable costs per product are $120. Total fixed costs are $330,000. How much more in profit will the company earn if it sells 4,400 packages instead of the usual 4,000 per year?

778. Perfect Bag, Inc. sells the perfect briefcase for both men and women. The contribution margin for the product is $90 per bag. Profit per bag is $50 when the company sells 10,000 bags. The company can increase sales by 500 bags with no increase in fixed costs. What would be the total profit if Perfect Bag sells 10,500 bags?

Analyzing Return on Capital

779–788

779. Trendy Touring Company, which has $3,500,000 in assets, earns $120,000 in operating profit using $1,000,000 in capital. Calculate the return on capital for Trendy Touring Company.

780. Trendy Touring Company, which has $3,500,000 in assets, earns $120,000 in operating profit using $1,000,000 in capital. Of the capital, $750,000 is owners' equity. Interest expense is $15,000. Calculate the return on equity for Trendy Touring Company.

781. A company earns $27,000 in operating profit using $140,000 in assets. Current liabilities are $40,000, long-term debt is $60,000, and owners' equity is $40,000. Calculate the return on capital for the year.

782. A company earns $27,000 in operating profit using $140,000 in assets. Current liabilities are $40,000, long-term debt is $60,000, and owners' equity is $40,000. The interest expense for the year is $3,000. Calculate the return on equity for the year.

783. At the end of the year, Bruce's Bees has the following balance sheet accounts:

- Total assets: $400,000
- Current liabilities: $80,000
- Long-term debt: $200,000
- Owners' equity: $120,000

Operating profit for the year is $41,600, and interest expense is $14,000. Calculate the return on capital for the year.

784. At the end of the year, Bruce's Bees has the following balance sheet accounts:

- Total assets: $400,000
- Current liabilities: $80,000
- Long-term debt: $200,000
- Owners' equity: $120,000

Operating profit for the year is $41,600, and interest expense is $14,000. Calculate the return on equity for the year.

785. The following information is from the financial statements of Fiber Palace:

- Total assets: $585,000
- Current liabilities: $200,000
- Long-term debt: $85,000
- Owners' equity: $300,000
- Operating profit: $37,000
- Interest expense: $6,800

Calculate the return on capital for the year.

786. The following information is from the financial statements of Fiber Palace:

- Total assets: $585,000
- Current liabilities: $200,000
- Long-term debt: $85,000
- Owners' equity: $300,000
- Operating profit: $37,000
- Interest expense: $6,800

Calculate the return on equity for the year.

787. Dorm Lofts Engineering has the following year-end balance sheet and income statement for the year.

- Balance Sheet
  - Current assets: $64,000
  - Equipment: $536,000
  - Total assets: $600,000
  - Current liabilities: $30,000
  - Long-term debt: $250,000
  - Total liabilities: $280,000
  - Owners' equity: $320,000
  - Total liabilities and owners' equity: $600,000
- Income Statement
  - Revenue: $110,000
  - Cost of goods sold: ($70,000)
  - Gross profit: $40,000
  - Operating expenses: ($8,000)
  - Operating profit: $32,000
  - Interest expense: ($11,250)
  - Income before taxes: $20,750
  - Tax expense: ($5,810)
  - Net income: $14,940

Calculate the return on capital for the year.

788. Dorm Lofts Engineering has the following year-end balance sheet and income statement for the year.

- Balance Sheet
  - Current assets: $64,000
  - Equipment: $536,000
  - Total assets: $600,000
  - Current liabilities: $30,000
  - Long-term debt: $250,000
  - Total liabilities: $280,000
  - Owners' equity: $320,000
  - Total liabilities and owners' equity: $600,000
- Income Statement
  - Revenue: $110,000
  - Cost of goods sold: ($70,000)
  - Gross profit: $40,000
  - Operating expenses: ($8,000)
  - Operating profit: $32,000
  - Interest expense: ($11,250)
  - Income before taxes: $20,750
  - Tax expense: ($5,810)
  - Net income: $14,940

Calculate the return on equity for the year.

Improving Profit Performance

789–798

789. ASV Manufacturing has fixed costs of $10,000 that allow the company to produce between 100 and 180 units. Each unit sells for $185 and has variable costs per unit of $5. Last year the company sold 100 units. What happens to operating profit if the company sells 10% more units?

790. What is the term for the situation in which an increase in sales volume produces a larger increase in operating profit?

791. Brain Cell Bar sells treatments to improve intelligence. Each treatment sells for $4,000. The contribution margin per treatment is $2,000. Total fixed costs are $250,000, which allow the company to provide between 200 and 300 treatments per year. The company sold 200 treatments last year. If the company increases sales by 10%, how much will operating profit increase?

792. ASV Manufacturing has fixed costs of $10,000 that allow the company to produce between 100 and 180 units. Each unit sells for $185 and has variable costs per unit of $5. Last year the company sold 100 units. What is the percent increase in operating profit if the company manages to increase sales by 50%?

793. ASV Manufacturing has fixed costs of $7,000 that allow the company to produce between 100 and 180 units. Each unit sells for $185 and has variable costs per unit of $5. Last year the company sold 100 units. What is the percent decrease in operating profit if the company has a bad year and sells 10% fewer units?

794. Green Grass Lawn Painters sells yard maintenance packages for $300. The variable cost associated with each package is $200. Fixed costs of $13,000 allow the company to service 300 to 400 packages. When a competitor goes out of business, Green Grass Lawn Painters is able to increase sales by 20%, from 300 packages to 360 packages. What happens to operating profit if sales increase by 20%?

795. High Water Wading Pants sells short, waterproof pants for $80 each. The variable cost associated with each pair of pants is $15. Fixed costs of $1,200,000 allow the company to produce and sell 30,000 to 40,000 pairs of pants. Severe rains have resulted in expanding markets in many areas of the country. High Water Wading Pants plans to increase sales by 15%, from 30,000 pairs to 34,500 pairs. What happens to operating profit if sales increase by 15%?

796. Green Grass Lawn Painters sells yard maintenance packages for $300. The variable cost associated with each package is $200. Fixed costs of $13,000 allow the company to service 300 to 400 packages. Green Grass Lawn Painters faces increased competition and anticipates a decrease in sales of 20%, from 375 packages to 300 packages. What happens to operating profit if sales decrease by 20%?

797. High Water Wading Pants sells short, waterproof pants for $80 each. The variable cost associated with each pair of pants is $15. Fixed costs of $1,200,000 allow the company to produce and sell 30,000 to 40,000 pairs of pants. Drought conditions have affected sales, and the company anticipates a 15% decrease in sales, from 36,000 pairs of pants to 30,600. What happens to operating profit if sales decrease by 15%?

798. Brain Cell Bar sells treatments to improve intelligence. Each treatment sells for $4,000. The variable costs associated with each treatment are $2,000. Total fixed costs are $250,000, which allow the company to provide between 200 and 300 treatments per year. Last year it sold 200 treatments. If the company is able to increase sales by 10%, by what percent will profit increase?

Selling More Units

799–808

799. Red Thumb Corporation is planning to increase sales by a small amount because it has excess capacity. What is the relationship between the increase in sales and the increase in operating profit?

800. What is a company's *capacity?*

801. Dragon Zombie Costumes Co. can produce and sell up to 10,000 costumes. It currently sells 8,000. The selling price for the costumes is $89, and the variable cost for each costume is $40. What is the increase in operating profit if the company increases sales to 9,000?

802. Document Destruction Specialists manage the shredding of secret documents for an annual fee of $10,000. The current level of sales is 150,000 annual contracts. The company could handle another 50,000 contracts without any increase in fixed costs. The contribution margin per contract is $2,000. If the company increases sales by 15,000 contracts, what is the dollar amount of the increase in operating profit?

803. Travel Fridge, Inc. produces and sells a mini refrigerator that fits inside a backpack and runs on batteries. Each unit sells for $120. The contribution margin for each unit is $40. Last year the company sold 25,000 units. Favorable reviews on social media sites make the company think it can increase sales by 2,000 without decreasing the price or incurring any additional fixed costs. Calculate the increase in operating profit assuming the increase in sales.

804. Fiber Palace sells packages of fibers for $39. The variable cost per package is $25. The company believes it can increase sales by 5% from last year's sales of 100,000 packages without any increase in fixed costs. Calculate the amount of the increase in operating profit that Fiber Palace is anticipating.

805. Document Destruction Specialists manage the shredding of secret documents for an annual fee of $10,000. The current level of sales is 150,000 annual contracts. The company could handle another 50,000 contracts without any increase in fixed costs. The variable cost per unit is $9,000. If the company increases sales by 10% without changing the selling price, what is the dollar amount of increase in operating profit?

806. Cold Pack Athletic Gear produces and sells workout shirts with built-in cold packs. The user stores the clothing in the freezer and then wears the cold shirt during workouts. Each shirt sells for $150 and has a contribution margin of $60. Last year the company sold 100,000 shirts and had $3,000,000 in operating profit. With the aging baby boomers, the company anticipates an increase of 14% in the next year with no reduction in the selling price or increase in fixed costs. What is the expected operating profit with the 14% increase in sales next year?

807. Gourmet Convenience sells all-inclusive takeout gourmet dinners for $57 each. Each dinner has a variable cost of $25. The current level of sales is $1,140,000. An improving economy indicates that the company could increase sales by 15% without any change in selling price or fixed costs. Calculate the increase in operating profit if the company achieves an increase in sales of 15%.

808. Amazing Key Chains sells truly amazing key chains that combine a cellphone and a garage door opener for $650. The variable cost of each key chain is $200. Last year the company had sales revenue of $21,450,000. Reliability issues with a competitor's device give the company a chance to increase sales by 10% without any change in selling price or fixed costs. Calculate the increase in operating profit if the company achieves an increase in sales of 10% over last year.

Improving Margins

809–818

809. Identify two actions that increase the contribution margin per unit.

A. increase sales volume and selling price

B. increase sales volume and decrease variable cost per unit

C. increase selling price and decrease variable cost per unit

D. increase sales volume and decrease fixed costs

E. decrease fixed costs and increase variable cost per unit

810. Frosty Inc. would like a 2% increase in operating profit from its current level of $1,200,000. The company doesn't believe it can increase either selling price or sales volume from the 40,000 units sold last year, so it wants to decrease variable costs. By how much will variable cost per unit need to decrease to achieve the desired increased operating profit?

811. Perfect Bag, Inc. sells the perfect briefcase for both men and women. Last year the contribution margin per bag was $87. Total fixed costs for the year were $4,900,000 and are expected to be the same next year. However, increased competition has forced the company to reduce the selling price by $5 to maintain its current sales volume of 70,000 bags. Determine the amount of change in operating profit for next year if the company reduces the selling price and maintains the sales volume.

812. Perfect Bag, Inc. sells the perfect briefcase for both men and women. Last year the contribution margin per bag was $87. Total fixed costs for the year were $4,900,000 and are expected to be the same next year. However, increased competition has forced the company to reduce the selling price by $5 to maintain its current sales volume of 70,000 bags. Determine the change in break-even sales volume next year if the company reduces the selling price and maintains the sales volume.

813. Bright Children Publications sells summer learning packets for children in elementary school. Each packet costs $125. The cost of goods sold expense per unit is $8. Variable operating expenses per unit are $5, and total fixed costs are $4,000,000. The company has determined it can maintain sales volume only if it reduces the selling price of the packet to $110. Calculate the change in break-even sales volume next year if the company reduces the selling price.

814. Bright Children Publications sells summer learning packets for children in elementary school. Each packet costs $125. The cost of goods sold expense per unit is $8. Variable operating expenses per unit are $5, and total fixed costs are $4,000,000. The company has determined it can maintain sales volume only if it reduces the selling price of the packet to $110. Calculate the change in operating profit next year if the company reduces the selling price and maintains the current sales volume of 100,000 units.

815. Cloud Glasses Company sells glasses that protect the wearer from supposedly dangerous ultra-blue rays emitted by clouds. The following information is taken from the business's records:

- Sales volume in units: 60,000
- Selling price per unit: $300
- Cost of goods sold expense per unit: $160
- Variable operating expenses per unit: $75
- Contribution margin per unit: $65
- Fixed operating expenses: $1,950,000

Calculate the increase in operating profit if the cost of goods sold expense per unit is reduced to $155.

816. The following information relates to Purple Beauty Pots, a company that manufactures and sells ever-blooming garden pots.

- Sales volume in units: 160,000
- Selling price per unit: $129
- Cost of goods sold expense per unit: $65
- Variable operating expenses per unit: $12
- Contribution margin per unit: $52
- Fixed operating expenses: $2,100,000

The cost of raw materials used in manufacturing the pots has increased, resulting in an increase in cost of goods sold expense to $68 per unit. Calculate the change in operating profit resulting from the increase in cost of goods sold expense per unit.

817. The following information relates to Purple Beauty Pots, a company that manufactures and sells ever-blooming garden pots:

- Sales volume in units: 160,000
- Selling price per unit: $129
- Cost of goods sold expense per unit: $65
- Variable operating expenses per unit: $12
- Contribution margin per unit: $52
- Fixed operating expenses: $2,100,000

The cost of raw materials used in manufacturing the pots has increased, resulting in an increase in cost of goods sold expense to $68 per unit. Calculate the change in break-even sales volume resulting from the increase in cost of goods sold expense per unit.

818. Cloud Glasses Company sells glasses that protect the wearer from supposedly dangerous ultra-blue rays emitted by clouds. The following information is taken from the business's records:

- Sales volume in units: 60,000
- Selling price per unit: $300
- Cost of goods sold expense per unit: $160
- Variable operating expenses per unit: $75
- Contribution margin per unit: $65
- Fixed operating expenses: $1,950,000

The company has found a way to decrease the cost of goods sold expense per unit by $5 to $155. How does this affect the break-even sales volume?

Making Trade-offs

819–828

819. A company sells 80,000 units during the year and has total fixed costs of $200,000. If the company lowers the selling price of its product by 10%, from $10 to $9, reduces contribution margin from $4 to $3, and achieves a 12% increase in sales volume, will operating profit increase?

820. The following information is taken from the records of Cloud Glasses Co., a company that sells glasses that protect the wearer from supposedly dangerous ultra-blue rays emitted by clouds:

- Selling price: $100
- Variable cost per unit: $30
- Contribution margin per unit: $70

The company has fixed costs of $4,000,000 and sold 100,000 units last year. Unfortunately, because of increased materials cost, variable cost per unit is increasing by a third, to $40 per unit. The company plans to offset this with a 5% increase in price that will result in a 2% decrease in sales. What is the new break-even sales volume?

821. The following information is taken from the records of EconoCar, Inc.:

- Selling price: $23,000
- Contribution margin: $7,000
- Fixed costs are $70,000,000.

How much sales revenue is needed to produce $980,000 in operating profit?

822. The following information is taken from the records of Cloud Glasses Co.:

- Selling price: $100
- Variable cost per unit: $30
- Contribution margin per unit: $70

The company has fixed costs of $4,000,000 and sold 100,000 units last year. Unfortunately, because of increased materials cost, variable cost per unit is increasing by a third, to $40 per unit. The company plans to offset this with a 5% increase in price that will result in a 2% decrease in sales volume. What will be the new operating profit?

823. The following information is taken from the records of EconoCar, Inc.:

- Selling price: $23,000
- Variable cost per unit: $16,000
- Fixed costs: $70,000,000

How many cars must the company sell to earn $1,000,000 in operating profit?

824. Perfect Bag, Inc. sells briefcases to men and women. The bags retail for $400, and the variable costs are 40% of sales. Fixed costs are $12,000,000. The company sells 100,000 bags per year. It believes with $500,000 in additional advertising, it could increase sales by 10%. What is the increase in operating profit if the company is successful?

825. Perfect Bag, Inc. sells briefcases to men and women. The bags retail for $400, and the variable costs are 40% of sales. Fixed costs are $12,000,000. The company makes drastic cuts to executive salaries, and fixed costs are reduced by 25%, to $9,000,000. What is the change in operating profit as a result of these cuts if the company sells 100,000 bags?

826. Yummy Goat operates a food truck at summer festivals. The sandwiches sell for $10, and the contribution margin is $6. If sales increase by $25,000 without any increase in the current fixed cost of $8,000, by how much will the company's operating profit increase?

827. A company sells 80,000 units during the year and has total fixed costs of $200,000. If the company lowers the selling price of its product by 10%, from $10 to $9, and reduces contribution margin from $4 to $3, calculate the sales volume needed to earn the same operating profit as prior to the price reduction.

828. Terry Bears manufactures and distributes stuffed bears that sell for $50. The company's variable cost per unit is $18, and fixed costs total $560,000. Last year the company sold 18,000 bears. The company's sales manager suggests that a 5% reduction in selling price, combined with a $120,000 increase in advertising, will result in a 30% increase in sales volume over last year. If the company institutes the price reduction and the increase in advertising, what is the change in operating profit over last year?

Chapter 12

Manufacturing Cost Accounting

This chapter explains how costs move through the manufacturing process for a product. You'll go over how material, labor, and overhead costs are moved into production. The chapter reviews the concept of work-in-process, which are the costs incurred for a partially completed product. You assign spending as either a product cost or period cost. This chapter also connects manufacturing costs to the calculation of profit.

The Problems You'll Work On

In this chapter, you see problems on these accounting topics:

- Understanding that material, labor, and overhead costs are added to work-in-process
- Moving costs from work-in-process to finished goods
- Calculating cost of goods sold
- Finding out about product costs and period costs
- Using total manufacturing costs to compute operating profit

What to Watch Out For

Don't let common mistakes trip you up. Some of the following suggestions may be helpful:

- Keep in mind that costs flow from work-in-process to finished goods to cost of sales.
- Work-in-process and finished goods are inventory (asset) accounts. Cost of sales is an expense account.
- Product costs are included in the cost of the product. These costs become expenses when the product is sold. Period costs, on the other hand, are expensed immediately when they're incurred.
- Overhead costs can't be directly traced to a unit of product in production. Instead, these costs are allocated, based on some sort of activity level.

Classifying Manufacturing and Non-manufacturing Costs

829–838

829. A shirt manufacturer has the following costs: Life insurance on the CEO, bolts of cloth for making shirts, sales commissions paid to salespeople, costs of sending the HR manager to attend a training conference, and cost of the annual audit. Which is a manufacturing cost?

830. A company that manufactures kayaks has the following costs: salary for the HR manager, salary for the technician who maintains the computerized billing system, wages for assemblers who build the kayaks, commissions paid to salespeople, and wages for the CEO's administrative assistant. Which is a manufacturing cost?

831. Identify the four basic types of manufacturing costs.

832. Red Cow Sleeping Drinks has the following costs:

- Direct materials: $3,507,000
- Direct labor: $1,200,000
- Variable overhead: $700,000
- Fixed overhead: $250,000
- Selling expenses: $890,000
- General expenses: $400,500
- Administrative expenses: $500,000

Calculate the total manufacturing costs.

833. Herb's Herbs packages high-quality dried herbs for home use. The following costs are taken from Herb's accounting records:

- Fresh herbs: $137,000
- Depreciation on the drying machine: $8,100
- Glass jars for packaging the herbs: $5,000
- Electricity to run the drying machines: $15,000
- Gasoline for delivery trucks: $24,000
- Internet advertising: $3,000
- Depreciation on the computer used to do the accounting for the company: $1,000

Calculate the total manufacturing costs.

834. EconoCar Co. produces and sells inexpensive vehicles. The following list of costs pertains to the company:

- Direct material: $405,000
- Factory workers' wages: $827,000
- Sales commissions: $267,000
- Depreciation on the manufacturing facility: $130,000
- Insurance on the manufacturing facility: $84,000
- Utilities at the manufacturing facility: $12,500

Calculate the total manufacturing costs.

835. Fiber Palace produces beautiful fibers and sells them in bundles to artists. The following list of costs pertains to the company:

- Wool: $57,000
- Packaging for wool bundles: $10,000
- Advertising in art magazines: $7,000
- Depreciation on delivery trucks: $3,600
- Wages for workers who wash and package the spun wool: $119,000
- Salary for CEO and CFO, who never work in the factory: $400,000
- Depreciation on the factory building: $12,400

Calculate the total manufacturing costs from the list.

836. Which of the following is a manufacturing cost?

A. the material used to produce the window coverings in a president's office

B. the material used to patch body damage on a delivery truck

C. the material used to prepare advertising campaigns

D. the material used in making a product

E. the materials used by a CFO to prepare the annual report

837. The following are costs experienced by Goody Picnic Tables, a company that manufactures and sells wooden picnic tables. Which of the costs is a manufacturing cost?

A. depreciation on the machines that smooth the wood for the tables

B. depreciation on the office equipment at the company headquarters

C. depreciation on the cars supplied to salespeople

D. depreciation on the office building that houses only the administrative functions and no manufacturing

E. depreciation on cellphones supplied to salespeople

838. Which of the following is a manufacturing cost?

A. insurance on a factory

B. insurance on a warehouse

C. insurance on company cars used by a sales force

D. insurance on delivery vehicles

E. insurance on the life of a CEO

Minding Manufacturing Costs

839–853

839. Terry Bears Co. produces stuffed animals. Last year the company had the following costs to produce 50,000 animals:

- Direct materials: $60,000
- Direct labor: $80,000
- Variable overhead: $10,000
- Fixed overhead: $5,000

What is the cost per animal?

840. Purple Beauty Pots manufactured 28,000 pots and sold 25,000 pots last year. The cost per pot was $30, and each pot sold for $75. Calculate the total manufacturing costs for the year.

841. Goody Picnic Tables Inc. has the following per-unit information:

- Selling price: $450
- Raw materials used to construct the product: $95
- Labor to build the product: $75
- Overhead associated with building the product: $14
- Sales commission: $25
- Administrative costs: $12

The company produced 250 units and sold 240. Calculate the product cost per unit.

842. Lily Valley Drain Tiles produces 100,000 tiles per year. The manufacturing cost per unit is $118. The sales commission on the $225 selling price is $20 per unit. Calculate the cost of goods sold expense if the company sells 97,000 tiles.

843. Lily Valley Drain Tiles produces 100,000 tiles per year. The manufacturing cost per unit is $118. The sales commission on the $225 selling price is $20 per unit. Calculate total manufacturing costs if the company sells 97,000 tiles.

844. Lily Valley Drain Tiles produces 100,000 tiles per year. The manufacturing cost per unit is $118. The sales commission on the $225 selling price is $20 per unit. Calculate the amount of manufacturing costs that will be added to inventory if the company sells 97,000 tiles.

845. Terry Bears Co. produces stuffed animals and sold 5,000 animals last year. The company had the following costs last year to produce 6,000 animals:

- Fabric used to construct the animals: $30,000
- Stuffing for the animals: $5,000
- Depreciation on the sewing machines used to construct the animals: $2,500
- Depreciation on delivery trucks: $1,500
- Wages for the workers who sew and stuff the animals: $40,000
- Wages for salespeople: $13,000
- Utilities to heat and light the factory and power the sewing machines: $12,000
- Utilities to heat and light the corporate headquarters: $6,000

What is the cost per animal?

846. Goody Picnic Tables Inc. has the following per-unit information:

- Selling price: $450
- Raw materials used to construct the product: $95
- Labor to build the product: $75
- Overhead associated with building the product: $14
- Sales commission: $25
- Administrative costs: $12

The company produces 250 units and sells 240. Calculate cost of goods sold expense.

847. Bright Children Publications sells summer learning packets for $140 per packet. The costs for assembling the packets in a factory are as follows:

- Rent for the building: $12,000
- Rent for the work tables and stools: $10,000
- Utilities to heat, cool, and light the building: $24,000
- Instruction sheets for the packets: $300
- Worksheets for the packets: $20,000
- Envelopes for the packets: $100
- Wages for the workers assembling the packets: $192,000
- Wages for the supervisor: $48,000
- Wages for the quality control inspector: $36,000
- Advertising: $6,000

The company produces 10,000 packets and sells 8,500. Calculate the cost of goods sold expense for the year.

848. Bright Children Publications sells summer learning packets for $140 per packet. The costs for assembling the packets in a factory are as follows:

- Rent for the building: $12,000
- Rent for the work tables and stools: $10,000
- Utilities to heat, cool, and light the building: $24,000
- Instruction sheets for the packets: $300
- Worksheets for the packets: $20,000
- Envelopes for the packets: $100
- Wages for the workers assembling the packets: $192,000
- Wages for the supervisor: $48,000
- Wages for the quality control inspector: $36,000
- Advertising: $6,000

The company produces 10,000 packets and sells 8,500. What is the product cost per unit?

849. Happy Birds Wild Bird Feeders manufactures bird feeders. Last year it produced 5,000 feeders and sold 3,500. The following is taken from the company's records:

- Sales revenue: $280,000
- Materials used to produce the feeders: $150,000
- Wages paid to production workers: $50,000
- Factory utilities and other variable overhead: $15,000
- Factory depreciation and other fixed overhead: $10,000
- Sales commissions: $28,000
- General and administrative expenses: $120,000

Calculate the product cost per unit.

850. Happy Birds Wild Bird Feeders manufactures bird feeders. Last year it produced 5,000 feeders and sold 3,500. The following is taken from the company's records:

- Sales revenue: $280,000
- Materials used to produce the feeders: $150,000
- Wages paid to production workers: $50,000
- Factory utilities and other variable overhead: $15,000
- Factory depreciation and other fixed overhead: $10,000
- Sales commissions: $28,000
- General and administrative expenses: $120,000

Calculate cost of goods sold expense.

851. Happy Birds Wild Bird Feeders manufactures bird feeders. Last year it produced 5,000 feeders and sold 3,500. The following is taken from the company's records:

- Sales revenue: $280,000
- Materials used to produce the feeders: $150,000
- Wages paid to production workers: $50,000
- Factory utilities and other variable overhead: $15,000
- Factory depreciation and other fixed overhead: $10,000
- Sales commissions: $28,000
- General and administrative expenses: $120,000

Calculate the amount of manufacturing costs that will be added to inventory.

852. Bright Children Publications sells summer learning packets for $140 per packet. The costs for assembling the packets in a factory are as follows:

- Rent for the building: $12,000
- Rent for the work tables and stools: $10,000
- Utilities to heat, cool, and light the building: $24,000
- Instruction sheets for the packets: $300
- Worksheets for the packets: $20,000
- Envelopes for the packets: $100
- Wages for the workers assembling the packets: $192,000
- Wages for the supervisor: $48,000
- Wages for the quality control inspector: $36,000
- Advertising: $6,000

The company produces 10,000 packets and sells 8,500. Calculate the amount of manufacturing costs that will be added to inventory.

853. Goody Picnic Tables Inc. has the following per-unit information:

- Selling price: $450
- Raw materials used to construct the product: $95
- Labor to build the product: $75
- Overhead associated with building the product: $14
- Sales commission: $25
- Administrative costs: $12

The company produces 250 units and sells 240. Calculate the amount of manufacturing cost that will be added to inventory after all the sales are completed.

Product Costs versus Period Costs

854–868

854. Happy Birds Wild Bird Feeders records depreciation on delivery trucks and pays for the following items:

- Wood to construct the feeders
- Nails and glue used in construction of the feeders
- Skilled workers to construct the feeders
- A supervisor for the factory
- Utilities for the factory
- Sales commissions
- Insurance on the factory
- Property taxes on the factory

Which of the items recorded or paid is a period cost?

855. Cloud Glasses Company sells glasses that protect the wearer from supposedly dangerous ultra-blue rays emitted by clouds. The company has the following information:

- Indirect materials used in products: $6,400
- Depreciation on delivery equipment: $10,200
- Gas and oil for delivery trucks: $2,200
- President's salary: $92,000
- Materials used in products: $120,000
- Labor costs of assembly line workers: $110,000
- Factory supplies used: $24,000
- Advertising expense: $25,000
- Property taxes on the factory: $45,000
- Repairs on office equipment: $1,800
- Factory utilities: $39,000

Determine the total amount of product costs.

856. Cloud Glasses Company sells glasses that protect the wearer from supposedly dangerous ultra-blue rays emitted by clouds. The company has the following information:

- Indirect materials used in products: $6,400
- Depreciation on delivery equipment: $10,200
- Gas and oil for delivery trucks: $2,200
- President's salary: $92,000
- Materials used in products: $120,000
- Labor costs of assembly line workers: $110,000
- Factory supplies used: $24,000
- Advertising expense: $25,000
- Property taxes on the factory: $45,000
- Repairs on office equipment: $1,800
- Factory utilities: $39,000

Determine the total amount of period costs.

857. Terry Bears Co. paid wages to the following groups of employees:

- Factory workers
- Factory manager
- Chief executive officer
- Corporate attorney
- Salespeople
- Administrative support for executives
- Delivery drivers

Identify the employees whose wages will be included in product costs.

858. Terry Bears Co paid wages to the following groups of employees:

- Factory workers
- Factory manager
- Chief executive officer
- Corporate attorney
- Salespeople
- Administrative support for executives
- Delivery drivers

Identify the employees whose wages are period costs.

859. Dragon Zombie Costume Manufacturer is trying to determine the product costs from this list of costs to manufacture costumes:

- Wages paid to designers of the costumes
- Fabric used in the costumes
- Wages paid to sewing machine operators
- Depreciation on sewing machines
- Commissions paid to salespeople
- Charges for cellphones issued to salespeople
- Depreciation on delivery vehicles
- Gas and maintenance on delivery vehicles
- Insurance on the factory building
- Insurance on the delivery vehicles
- Amounts paid to CPAs who do the accounting and taxes

Of the listed costs, which are product costs?

860. Dragon Zombie Costume Manufacturer is trying to determine the period costs from this list of costs to manufacture costumes.

- Wages paid to designers of the costumes
- Fabric used in the costumes
- Wages paid to sewing machine operators
- Depreciation on sewing machines
- Commissions paid to salespeople
- Charges for cellphones issued to salespeople
- Depreciation on delivery vehicles
- Gas and maintenance on delivery vehicles
- Insurance on the factory building
- Insurance on the delivery vehicles
- Amounts paid to CPAs who do the accounting and taxes

Of the listed costs, which are period costs?

861. Which category of cost does the cost of the ingredients in a frozen pizza belong to?

862. Which category of cost do the wages of workers at a truck assembly plant belong to?

863. Jimmy Choo designs and sells luxury footwear. Which category of cost does the depreciation on the factory machines that produce the shoes belong to?

864. Dorm Lofts Engineering has the following costs to produce and sell its product. The lofts are constructed on-site, and the carpenter uses a truck to get the materials to the dorm.

- CEO's salary: $27,000
- Carpenter's wages: $24,000
- Salesperson's wages: $13,000
- Insurance on the truck: $1,200
- Bank charges: $600
- Wood, nails, and glue: $87,000
- Depreciation on tools: $130
- Depreciation on the truck: $250
- Gas and maintenance for the truck: $1,500
- Advertising: $80
- Accounting services: $120

Determine the total product cost.

865. How would you categorize the cost of advertising this book?

866. Dorm Lofts Engineering has the following costs to produce and sell its product. The lofts are constructed on-site, and the carpenter uses a truck to get the materials to the dorm.

- CEO's salary: $27,000
- Carpenter's wages: $24,000
- Salesperson's wages: $13,000
- Insurance on the truck: $1,200
- Bank charges: $600
- Wood, nails, and glue: $87,000
- Depreciation on tools: $130
- Depreciation on the truck: $250
- Gas and maintenance for the truck: $1,500
- Advertising: $80
- Accounting services: $120

Determine the total period costs.

867. Dorm Lofts Engineering has the following costs to produce and sell its product. The lofts are constructed on-site, and the carpenter uses a truck to get the materials to the dorm.

- CEO's salary: $27,000
- Carpenter's wages: $24,000
- Salesperson's wages: $13,000
- Insurance on the truck: $1,200
- Bank charges: $600
- Wood, nails, and glue: $87,000
- Depreciation on tools: $130
- Depreciation on the truck: $250
- Gas and maintenance for the truck: $1,500
- Advertising: $80
- Accounting services: $120

Categorize the costs as direct materials, direct labor, overhead, or period costs.

868. How would you categorize the cost of heating and cooling a factory that produces computers?

Recording Product and Period Costs

869–883

869. What journal entry will a manufacturing company make when buying the raw materials used in production, assuming it buys on credit?

870. What account is decreased and what account is increased when materials are added to the production process at Perfect Bag, Inc., a company that manufactures the perfect briefcase for men and women?

871. Identify the accounts and the debits and credits that a company records when paying cash to buy raw materials for the production process.

872. Identify the accounts and the debits and credits that a company records when depreciating the machines used in production.

873. Assuming all purchases of raw materials are made on credit, what journal entry will Nike make when adding fabric and foam padding into the production process?

874. UnderStuff Clothing Company has the following costs during the month:

- Cotton knit fabric added to production: $45,000
- Sewing machine operators' wages: $30,000
- Electricity to run the machines, cool the factory, and light the factory: $2,000
- Factory manager's salary: $3,000
- Elastic and thread used in making the garments: $1,500
- Insurance on the factory: $200
- CEO's salary: $40,000
- Wages for the accounting department: $22,000
- Advertising: $3,000
- Depreciation on the sewing machines: $2,100

By how much will the Work-in-Process Inventory account increase as a result of these costs?

875. Assuming wages are paid in cash, what journal entries will Bob's Boats make when paying the following employees?

- Factory workers: $157,500
- Salespeople: $89,000
- Factory manager: $5,000
- Delivery drivers: $12,000

876. Purple Magic Pots has no Work-in-Process Inventory at the beginning or end of the year. The following costs are from the accounting records:

- Clay used to form the pots: $157,300
- Wages for the potters: $143,000
- Salaries for the president, secretary, and billing clerk: $160,000
- Electricity to run the wheels, kilns, lights, and cooling: $48,000
- Utilities for the office: $3,600
- Depreciation on office equipment: $1,300
- Depreciation on the wheels and kilns: $3,000
- Rent for the studio: $36,000
- Rent for the business office: $12,000
- Office expenses: $500

How much is transferred from Work-in-Process Inventory to Finished Goods Inventory?

877. Identify the accounts and the debits and credits that a company records when paying the employees who work in the factory.

878. Identify the accounts and the debits and credits that a company records when the manufacturing process is complete and products are ready for sale.

879. High Water Wading Pants produces and sells short, waterproof pants. In its production process it uses various small items like buttons, thread, seam tape, and pins, which are all bought on credit, just in time to use in making the pants. The cost of these items used in producing 10,000 pairs of pants last month was $450. Identify the accounts and debits and credits the company will record to account for the cost of these things.

880. Herb's Herbs has its production facility and office in the same building. The office occupies about 20% of the building with computers and other office machines. The production area occupies the other 80% and has filling and watering machines, plus tables and benches for work surfaces. The electric bill for the month is $3,750. Identify the accounts and the debits and credits that Herb records when paying the electric bill.

881. Identify the accounts and the debits and credits that a company records when paying lawyers for defending the company in a product liability lawsuit.

882. Yummy Jams has the following payroll taxes, which consist of the matching FICA and both state and federal unemployment insurance amounts:

- Factory workers: $89,350
- Executives: $180,000
- Administrative staff: $65,000
- Sales staff: $78,400

What journal entries will the company make to record the payroll taxes?

883. Gourmet Convenience Inc. had no beginning or ending Work-in-Process Inventory. During the period, direct materials of $217,500 were put into production. Direct labor of $464,000 converted the materials into finished products. The production also required $100,000 in overhead costs. What journal entry will the company make to transfer the goods when they are ready to sell?

Basic Cycle of Manufacturing Entries

884–893

884. Cold Pack Athletic Gear produces and sells workout shirts with built-in cold packs to soothe sore muscles. The company, which had no unfinished production at the start of the year, put $156,000 in raw materials into production. The labor necessary to produce the shirts was applied and cost $298,000. Overhead items necessary to complete the shirts cost $81,000. All shirts were finished. Sales commissions of $33,250 were paid to the sales force, who sold 95% of the finished shirts. What journal entry did the company make when the materials were added to the production process?

885. Cold Pack Athletic Gear produces and sells workout shirts with built-in cold packs to soothe sore muscles. The company, which had no unfinished production at the start of the year, put $156,000 in raw materials into production. The labor necessary to produce the shirts was applied and cost $298,000. Overhead items necessary to complete the shirts cost $81,000. All shirts were finished. Sales commissions of $33,250 were paid to the sales force, who sold 95% of the finished shirts. What journal entry did the company make to record the sale of the shirts?

886. Amazing Key Chains produces and sells truly amazing devices that combine a garage door opener and a cellphone. The following costs are taken from its year-end records:

- Direct materials: $42,000
- Direct labor: $97,000
- Overhead: $61,000
- Selling expenses: $27,000
- General and administrative expenses: $41,000

The company had no unfinished products at either the beginning of the year or the end of the year. The company produced 50,000 units during the year and sold 48,000 for $25 each. What journal entry did the company make when the materials were added to the production process?

887. Cold Pack Athletic Gear produces and sells workout shirts with built-in cold packs to soothe sore muscles. The company, which had no unfinished production at the start of the year, put $156,000 in raw materials into production. The labor necessary to produce the shirts was applied and cost $298,000. The payroll included wages paid in cash of $248,000 and $50,000 in payroll taxes. Overhead items necessary to complete the shirts cost $81,000. All shirts were finished. Sales commissions of $33,250 were paid to the sales force, who sold 95% of the finished shirts. What journal entry did the company make when paying the employees who worked in the factory?

888. Cold Pack Athletic Gear produces and sells workout shirts with built-in cold packs to soothe sore muscles. The company, which had no unfinished production at the start of the year, put $156,000 in raw materials into production. The labor necessary to produce the shirts was applied and cost $298,000. Overhead items necessary to complete the shirts cost $81,000 and consisted of depreciation of $35,000, utilities paid in cash of $24,000, and maintenance of $22,000, also paid in cash. All shirts were finished. Sales commissions of $33,250 were paid to the sales force, who sold 95% of the finished shirts. What journal entry did the company make to record the overhead costs?

889. Amazing Key Chains produces and sells truly amazing devices that combine a garage door opener and a cellphone. The following costs are taken from its year-end records:

- Direct materials: $42,000
- Direct labor: $97,000, of which $80,800 was paid in cash and $16,200 is the amount of payroll taxes
- Overhead: $61,000
- Selling expenses: $27,000
- General and administrative expenses: $41,000

The company had no unfinished products at either the beginning of the year or the end of the year. The company produced 50,000 units during the year and sold 48,000 for $25 each. What journal entry did the company make when applying the labor to the production process?

890. Amazing Key Chains produces and sells truly amazing devices that combine a garage door opener and a cellphone. The following costs are taken from its year-end records:

- Direct materials: $42,000
- Direct labor: $97,000
- Overhead: $61,000
- Selling expenses: $27,000
- General and administrative expenses: $41,000

The company had no unfinished products at either the beginning of the year or the end of the year. The company produced 50,000 units during the year and sold 48,000 for $25 each. What journal entry did the company make when the production of the key chains was complete and they were ready to sell?

891. Amazing Key Chains produces and sells truly amazing devices that combine a garage door opener and a cellphone. The following costs are taken from its year-end records:

- Direct materials: $42,000
- Direct labor: $97,000
- Overhead: $61,000
- Selling expenses: $27,000
- General and administrative expenses: $41,000

The company had no unfinished products at either the beginning of the year or the end of the year. The company produced 50,000 units during the year and sold 48,000 for $25 each. What journal entry did the company make when the goods were sold?

892. Cold Pack Athletic Gear produces and sells workout shirts with built-in cold packs to soothe sore muscles. The company, which had no unfinished production at the start of the year, put $156,000 in raw materials into production. The labor necessary to produce the shirts was applied and cost $298,000. Overhead items necessary to complete the shirts cost $81,000. All shirts were finished during the year. Sales commissions of $33,250 were paid to the sales force, who sold 95% of the finished shirts. What is the balance in the Work-in-Process Inventory and the Finished Goods Inventory at the end of the year?

893. Cold Pack Athletic Gear produces and sells workout shirts with built-in cold packs to soothe sore muscles. The company, which had no unfinished production at the start of the year, put $156,000 in raw materials into production. The labor necessary to produce the shirts was applied and cost $298,000. Overhead items necessary to complete the shirts cost $81,000. All shirts were finished. Sales commissions of $33,250 were paid to the sales force, who sold 95% of the finished shirts. What journal entry did the company make when the shirts were completed?

Basic Problems in Calculating Product Costs

894–903

894. Trendy Royal Coaches manufactures and sells horse-drawn coaches for royalty. Last year the company manufactured 150 coaches. The company had the following costs associated with the production of the 150 coaches:

- Direct materials: $1,000,000
- Direct labor: $2,000,000
- Variable overhead: $500,000
- Fixed overhead: $300,000

Calculate the burden rate for last year.

895. Trendy Royal Coaches manufactures and sells horse-drawn coaches for royalty. Last year the company manufactured and sold 150 coaches. The variable cost per unit was $23,000, and fixed manufacturing costs were $300,000. Calculate total manufacturing costs for the year.

896. The following information is taken from the records of Granny's Golf Carts:

- Raw materials per unit: $800
- Direct labor per unit: $1,200
- Variable manufacturing overhead per unit: $100
- Total fixed manufacturing costs: $8,250,000

Calculate the new cost per unit if the company increases production by 20% from the 5,000 units it produced last year.

897. The following information is taken from the accounting records of Granny's Golf Carts:

Per-unit information

- Selling price: $6,500
- Cost of goods sold: $3,200
- Gross margin: $3,300
- Variable operating expenses: $1,500
- Contribution margin: $1,800
- Raw materials: $800
- Direct labor: $1,200
- Variable overhead: $100
- Fixed overhead: $1,100

The company produced and sold 7,500 units and had an operating profit of $7,250,000. Total fixed manufacturing overhead cost is $8,250,000, and total fixed operating expenses are $6,250,000. The company believes it can increase production and sales by one-third, to 10,000 units, with its current capacity. Calculate the new burden rate if the company is successful.

898. Trendy Royal Coaches manufactures and sells horse-drawn coaches for royalty. Last year the company manufactured and sold 150 coaches, and it has the capacity to produce up to 400 per year. The company's variable cost per unit last year was $23,000, and fixed manufacturing costs per unit were $2,000. If the company increases production by 20%, to 180 coaches, what is the new variable cost per unit?

899. Trendy Royal Coaches manufactures and sells horse-drawn coaches for royalty. Last year the company manufactured and sold 150 coaches, and it has the capacity to produce up to 400 per year. The company's variable cost per unit last year was $23,000, and fixed manufacturing costs per unit were $2,000. If the company increases production by 20%, to 180 units, what is the new burden rate?

900. The following information is taken from the accounting records of Granny's Golf Carts:

Per-unit information

- Selling price: $6,500
- Cost of goods sold: $3,200
- Gross margin: $3,300
- Variable operating expenses: $1,500
- Contribution margin: $1,800
- Raw materials: $800
- Direct labor: $1,200
- Variable overhead: $100
- Fixed overhead: $1,100

The company produced and sold 7,500 units. Total fixed manufacturing overhead cost is $8,250,000, and total fixed operating expenses are $6,250,000. The company believes it can increase production and sales by one-third, to 10,000 units. Calculate the new cost per unit if the company is successful.

901. The following information is taken from the accounting records of Granny's Golf Carts:

Per-unit information

- Selling price: $6,500
- Cost of goods sold: $3,200
- Gross margin: $3,300
- Variable operating expenses: $1,500
- Contribution margin: $1,800
- Raw materials: $800
- Direct labor: $1,200
- Variable overhead: $100
- Fixed overhead: $1,100

The company produced and sold 7,500 units and had an operating profit of $7,250,000. Total fixed manufacturing overhead cost is $8,250,000, and total fixed operating expenses are $6,250,000. The company believes it can increase production and sales by one-third, to 10,000 units, with its current capacity. Calculate the new operating profit if the company is successful.

902. Trendy Royal Coaches manufactures and sells horse-drawn coaches for royalty. Last year the company manufactured and sold 150 coaches, and it has the capacity to produce up to 400 per year. The company's variable cost per unit last year was $23,000, and fixed manufacturing costs per unit were $2,000. If the company increases production by 20%, to 180 units, what is the new cost per unit?

903. Trendy Royal Coaches manufactures and sells horse-drawn coaches for royalty. Last year the company manufactured and sold 150 coaches, and it has the capacity to produce up to 400 per year. The company's variable cost per unit last year was $23,000, and fixed manufacturing costs per unit were $2,000. If production increases 200 coaches next year, what will be the cost per unit?

When Production and Sales Levels Are Seriously Out of Sync

904–908

904. Very Cool Things, Inc. produces and sells things. The following information is taken from its records for the month of June:

- Total units produced: 500
- Raw materials per unit: $750
- Direct labor per unit: $1,200
- Variable manufacturing overhead per unit: $50
- Fixed manufacturing overhead per unit: $100

The cost per unit seemed high to the factory manager, and after investigating, he found that about $75,000 in materials had been wasted because of water problems in the storage area. Calculate the best estimate of cost per unit.

905. Happy Birds Bird Feeders produces and sells high-quality bird feeders. The feeders sell for $80 each. Last year the company had idle capacity and could have produced 20% more feeders for the same amount of fixed manufacturing overhead costs, which were $100,000 last year. Calculate the cost of idle capacity.

906. Very Cool Things, Inc. produces and sells things. The following information is taken from its records for the month of June:

- Total units produced: 500
- Raw materials per unit: $500
- Direct labor per unit: $1,200
- Overhead per unit: $200

The factory supervisor was looking over the numbers and noticed that direct labor per unit was about 25% higher than normal and investigated. She found that the electricity that ran the machines was unreliable and that workers were often standing around waiting for the machines to start up again. Calculate a cost per unit that is more reflective of the actual cost to produce a thing.

907. Baby Games manufactures board games with extra-large playing pieces. The company has total fixed manufacturing overhead cost of $195,000, which gives Baby Games capacity to produce between 12,000 and 18,000 units. If the company produces 15,000 units, what is the cost of the idle capacity?

908. Baby Games manufactures board games with extra-large playing pieces. The company has discovered that its most recent results misrepresent the cost per unit because raw materials were wasted. The waste is estimated at a significant amount, $14,000,000. How should Baby Games adjust its operating results to reflect the waste?

Chapter 13

Investment Analysis Fundamentals

Accountants need to know how to perform investment analysis. Understanding this type of analysis allows managers to evaluate business decisions. This chapter spends time on how you calculate interest on a variety of debt instruments. You'll cover compound interest and the rule of 72. The chapter also covers the present value and future value of a series of cash flows. Return on investment is also covered in this chapter.

The Problems You'll Work On

In this chapter, you see problems on these accounting topics:

- Understanding how compounding interest impacts the total interest expense on a debt
- Connecting return on investment to profit margin and asset turnover
- Calculating the cost of capital for a investment
- Finding out about present value and future value of cash flows
- Using the internal rate of return to judge an investment's attractiveness

What to Watch Out For

Don't let common mistakes trip you up. Some of the following suggestions may be helpful:

- The more often interest is compounded, the greater the total interest owed on a debt.
- The rule of 72 explains how long it takes for an amount of money to double, given a particular interest rate that is compounded.
- Companies can issue either debt or equity to raise capital.
- *Internal rate of return* (IRR) is the rate of interest that adjusts the present value of all cash flows to a sum of zero. IRR assumes that there are both cash inflows and outflows for a particular project.

Calculating Interest — Simple Case

909–916

909. Green Grass Paint Co. borrows $50,000 from the bank for one year and is required to pay 4% annual interest. How much cash will the company repay the bank when the loan is due?

910. Edible Fungus Mushroom Farms borrows $65,000 at 10% for one year. The company receives the cash on May 1. How much interest will the company pay in cash on the maturity date?

911. Edible Fungus Mushroom Farms signs a promissory note that specifies 9% annual interest and a repayment date in three months. The company receives $100,000. What is the principal amount of the note?

912. Green Grass Paint Co. borrows $24,000 from the bank. The terms of the loan include annual interest of 6% and repayment in one year. What is the maturity value of the loan?

913. Green Grass Paint Co. gets $24,000 cash from a bank loan and must repay $25,200 in one year. What is the interest rate on the loan?

914. Green Grass Paint Co. borrows $37,000 from the bank. The terms of the loan include annual interest of 5% and repayment in 6 months. How much interest will the company pay the bank?

915. Permanent Lipstick Corporation borrows $275,000 on March 1. The terms of the loan call for repayment in one year and interest charges of 8%. What adjusting entry does the company make on December 31, the company's year-end?

916. Edible Fungus Mushroom Farms signs a promissory note that specifies 6.5% annual interest and a repayment date in three months. The company receives $100,000. What is the maturity value of the note?

Nominal and Effective Interest Rates

917–920

917. Awesome Goods Co. borrows $12,000 from the bank and agrees to repay the principal and interest in one year. The paperwork states that the annual rate is 4.5% but that the effective interest rate is 4.5766%. What is the explanation?

918. Awesome Goods Co. borrows $12,000 from the bank and agrees to repay the principal and interest in one year. The paperwork states that the annual rate is 4.5% but that the effective interest rate is 4.5766%. How much cash will the company give the bank when the loan is repaid?

919. Travel Fridge, Inc. borrows $45,000 from the bank for one year at an annual rate of 8% compounded quarterly. How much interest will the company pay on this loan?

920. Travel Fridge, Inc. borrows $45,000 from the bank for one year at an annual rate of 8% compounded quarterly. What is the effective rate of the loan?

Discounting Loans

921–924

921. Boomerang Grenade Co. signs a note agreeing to pay $15,000 in one year and receives a check for $14,151. Assuming that the interest is compounded annually, what is the rate the bank is charging?

922. Placebo Clip-on Tie signs a note agreeing to pay $150,000 to the bank in one year. The interest rate is 20% compounded quarterly. How much cash does the company receive at the signing of the note? To compute your answer, refer to present value tables, which you can find at `www.flexstudy.com/demo/demopdf/96019_appendix.pdf`.

923. Then He Goes Translation Services signs a note agreeing to pay $30,000 to the bank in one year. The interest rate is 12% compounded semiannually. How much cash does the company receive at the signing of the note? To compute your answer, refer to present value tables, which you can find at `www.flexstudy.com/demo/demopdf/96019_appendix.pdf`.

924. Grunt-N-Groan Fitness Centers signs a note agreeing to pay the bank $250,000 in one year. The rate on the note is 24% compounded quarterly. How much interest will the company pay on this note if it repays it on time? To compute your answer, refer to present and future value tables, which you can find at `www.flexstudy.com/demo/demopdf/96019_appendix.pdf`.

Compound Interest

925–928

925. When Marcia Devlin was born, her godmother deposited $10,000 in an account that earned 5% compounded annually. How much will Marcia receive on her 18th birthday? To compute your answer, refer to future value tables, which you can find at www.flexstudy.com/demo/demopdf/96019_appendix.pdf.

926. Terry Tim received a nice bonus at the end of the year, $127,000. Terry has decided to put it in a retirement account that earns 8% compounded quarterly. Terry intends to retire in 10 years. How much will be in the retirement account at that time? To compute your answer, refer to future value tables, which you can find at www.flexstudy.com/demo/demopdf/96019_appendix.pdf.

927. Jen Zomby decides to invest her very first bonus check, $6,000, in a retirement account that pays an average of 8% annual return. Jen plans to retire in 40 years. How much will she have? To compute your answer, refer to future value tables, which you can find at www.flexstudy.com/demo/demopdf/96019_appendix.pdf.

928. Snowman wants to invest his $100,000 inheritance so that he can retire in the Arctic in 20 years. He has the choice of investing at 4% but can choose to have the rate compounded annually, semiannually, quarterly, or monthly. Which should he choose?

Borrowing and Investing in Installments

929–932

929. Organic Bricks borrows $20,000 from the bank. The loan calls for repayment over 2 years in equal annual payments at the end of each year. The interest rate is 12%. When calculating the amount of the payment, what is the number of periods, *n*, and the rate, *i*, that will result in the correct payment?

930. Car Bop Company borrows $50,000 to buy a delivery truck for the business. The loan carries a 6% interest rate and must be paid back in equal annual payments over 5 years. How much is each payment? To compute your answer, refer to present value of an ordinary annuity tables, which you can find at www.flexstudy.com/demo/demopdf/96019_appendix.pdf.

931. Snappy Suits borrows $265,000 to buy a building. The loan calls for repayment over 20 years in equal monthly payments. The interest rate is 6%. When calculating the amount of the payment, what is the number of periods, *n*, and the rate, *i*, that will result in the correct payment?

932. Harris Hair Goo takes out a loan from Sharkey Loan Company. The amount of the loan is $10,000, and Harris agrees to pay it back in equal payments over 4 years. Sharkey wants a payment every six months. The rate is consistent with what Sharkey charges all its borrowers, 24%. How much is the payment? To compute your answer, refer to the present value of an annuity tables, which you can find at `www.flexstudy.com/demo/demopdf/96019_appendix.pdf`.

Determining Return on Investment (ROI)

933–936

933. The Butchers Hair Salon has three shops in a city. The owner wants to compare the performance of the shops on the basis of ROI. The shop in the trendy neighborhood has an ROI of 8% and an operating income of $43,000. The shop in the downtown office building has an ROI of 9% and an operating income of $35,000. The shop in the suburbs has an ROI of 4% and an operating income of $47,000. Which shop is performing the best?

934. Little Falls Bandage Company wants to evaluate performance for the year. It began the year with $12,000 in operating assets. During the year the company expanded and bought another machine for $3,000. Operating income for the year was $1,080. Calculate ROI.

935. Management of It'll Heal Medical Company are evaluating the performance of three divisions of the company. The Booboo Division had operating profit of $499 and on average used assets with a book value of $6,238. The Splint Division had operating profit of $350 and used average assets of $3,889. The Intensive Care Division had operating profit of $570 and average assets of $9,500. Which division is performing the best?

936. Vegan Steaks had the best year ever, with sales of $4,500,000 and operating profit of $950,000. The balance sheet at the beginning of the year showed assets used in production with a cost of $20,000,000 and accumulated depreciation of $5,000,000. The company didn't buy any assets during the year but did have depreciation expense of $1,000,000. Calculate the ROI for the year.

Recognizing the Two Different Components of ROI

937–940

937. Charlie Gross, the owner of Gross Products, is evaluating performance of the company. The financial gurus have given him the following information:

- Net sales: $3,000,000
- Profit margin: 3.92%
- Asset turnover: 1.5

Calculate the company's ROI.

938. The DuPont model evaluates business performance using a combination of two ratios. What ratios does the model use and how does it use them?

939. Goody Picnic Tables had sales of $351,000 last year and operating income of $98,000. Average assets for the year were $234,000. Calculate the profit margin, the asset turnover, and ROI for the company.

940. The following information is taken from Lily Valley Drain Tiles:

- Sales: $85,300
- Cost of goods sold: $31,000
- Fixed costs: $27,300
- Operating profit: $27,000
- Average assets used during the year: $101,000

Calculate the profit margin, the asset turnover, and ROI for the company.

Distinguishing between Return on and Return of Investment

941–944

941. Brinky's Liquors began business in the current year and received $140,000 in proceeds from the sale of common stock. The results for the year are shown in the income statement:

Brinky's Liquors Income Statement For the current year	
Net sales	48,560
Cost of goods sold	35,551
Gross profit	13,009
Operating expenses	5,700
Operating income	7,309
Other expenses	6,950
Income before tax	359
Tax expense	144
Net income	215

Brinky's paid out dividends of $280. How much of the dividends was a return of investment to stockholders?

942. Brinky's Liquors began business in the current year and received $140,000 in proceeds from the sale of common stock. The results for the year are shown in the income statement:

Brinky's Liquors Income Statement For the current year	
Net sales	48,560
Cost of goods sold	35,551
Gross profit	13,009
Operating expenses	5,700
Operating income	7,309
Other expenses	6,950
Income before tax	359
Tax expense	144
Net income	215

Brinky's paid out dividends of $280. How much of the dividends was income to the stockholders?

943. Brinky's Liquors began the current year with retained earnings of $40. The results for the year are shown in the income statement:

Brinky's Liquors Income Statement For the current year	
Net sales	48,560
Cost of goods sold	35,551
Gross profit	13,009
Operating expenses	5,700
Operating income	7,309
Other expenses	6,950
Income before tax	359
Tax expense	144
Net income	215

Brinky's paid out dividends of $280. How much of the dividends was income to the shareholders?

944. Brinky's Liquors began the current year with retained earnings of $40. The results for the year are shown in the income statement:

Brinky's Liquors Income Statement For the current year	
Net sales	48,560
Cost of goods sold	35,551
Gross profit	13,009
Operating expenses	5,700
Operating income	7,309
Other expenses	6,950
Income before tax	359
Tax expense	144
Net income	215

Brinky's paid out dividends of $280. How much of the dividends was a return of investment?

Configuring the Average Annual RIO over Multiple Years

945–948

945. Maralyn invests $10,000 in Cleaner Pools, Inc. Six years later, she sells the investment for $11,000. During the time she held the stock, she received a total of $2,000 in dividends. Calculate the average annual ROI.

946. Naoya invests $50,000 in Frugal Lifestyles Publications. He receives a 2% dividend each of the 10 years he owns the stock. At the end of the 10 years, he sells his stock for $100,000. Calculate the average annual ROI.

947. Aaron invests $20,000 in Rubber Bullets Corporation. Each year he receives $1,000 in dividends. After 8 years, he sells half of his stock for $10,000. Calculate the average annual ROI.

948. Dana invests in a new restaurant called the Dessert Factory. She pays $50 per share and buys 1,000 shares. The first year, Dana receives dividends of $1 per share. In years 2, 3, and 4, the dividends are $2 per share. In year 5, the dividends are $3 per share, and on December 31 of that year, Dana sells all her stock for $55 per share. Calculate the average annual ROI.

Having Fun with the Rule of 72

949–952

949. Glenda Goodwich invests $5,000 in Red Wing Shoes. The company promises an 8% return over time. Using the rule of 72, estimate the number of years it will take for the investment to double in value.

950. Hugh Wolverine invests $20,000 in a risky nail file venture that promises to pay a 15% return. Using the rule of 72, calculate how long it will take him to double his investment.

951. Kim Kashan invests $100,000 in a publishing company that produces a popular magazine. The expected return is 10%. Using the rule of 72, calculate how long it will take for her to double her investment.

952. Sheldon Cooper has $40,000 to invest for 10 years. He wants to double his money in that time. Using the rule of 72, calculate the rate he'll need to earn to achieve that goal.

Building on Imputed Cost of Capital

953–956

953. Wacky Corporation has $1,000,000 in long-term debt and is paying 6% interest on it. The shareholders of Wacky have invested $1,000,000 and demand an 8% return. What is the weighted average cost of capital for Wacky?

954. The following information is taken from the records of Goodbye Puppy Co.:

Financing	Rate
$2,000,000 mortgage	6.25%
$1,000,000 bonds payable	7%
$1,500,000 preferred stock	10%
$2,000,000 common stock	12%

Calculate the weighted average cost of capital for the company.

955. The following information is taken from the records of Manga Counting Service:

Financing	Rate
$575,000 mortgage	3.5%
$20,000 long-term debt	7%
$150,000 bonds payable	12%
$1,000,000 common stock	12%

Calculate the weighted average cost of capital for the company.

956. The following information is taken from Open Wide Dental Instruments:

Financing	Rate
$2,000,000 mortgage	4.25%
$10,000,000 bonds payable	5%
$150,000 preferred stock	10%
$200,000,000 common stock	12%

Calculate the weighted average cost of capital for the company.

Determining Present Value, Net Present Value, and Future Value

957–959

957. Happy Bird Feeders is trying to decide whether to invest in new technology for its manufacturing process. The cost is $450,000 and will return cash flows of $150,000 per year for 4 years. The company has a required rate of return of 10%. Calculate the NPV of the investment opportunity. To compute your answer, refer to the present value of annuity tables, which you can find at `www.flexstudy.com/demo/demopdf/96019_appendix.pdf`.

958. Happy Bird Feeders is trying to decide whether to invest in new technology for its manufacturing process. The cost is $500,000 and will return cash flows of $200,000 per year for 3 years. The company has a required rate of return of 10%. Should the company invest in the new technology? Why or why not? You can find the present value of annuity tables at `www.flexstudy.com/demo/demopdf/96019_appendix.pdf`.

959. Happy Bird Feeders is deciding between investing in two machines. The first machine costs $100,000 and will provide annual cash flows of $15,000 for 20 years. The second machine costs $75,000 and will provide annual cash flows of $15,000 for 10 years. The company has a required rate of return of 10%. Which machine should the company purchase and why?

Solving for the IRR (Internal Rate of Return)

960–961

960. Bebebanana is considering an investment in new technology for the customer care department. The cost is $500,000. The new system will save the company $80,000 per year for the next 10 years. The company is only taking on new investments that provide an internal rate of return greater than 8%. Should Bebebanana invest in the new technology? Why or why not?

961. Edible Fungus Mushroom Farms is considering an investment in machinery that will harvest the mushrooms. The cost is $75,000 and will save the company $10,000 per year for 9 years. What is the IRR for the investment in the machinery?

Chapter 14

Financial Statement Analysis

Accountants are responsible for generating financial statements. However, an accountant should also know how to perform analysis on those statements. Financial analysis helps any business make intelligent decisions. This chapter discusses financial ratios that verify profitability and how efficiently management uses assets and equity. The chapter also reviews turnover ratios. These ratios determine how quickly a company sells its product and collects cash from customers.

The Problems You'll Work On

In this chapter, you see problems on these accounting topics:

- Understanding earnings per common share (EPS)
- Distinguishing between liquidity ratios and solvency ratios
- Using accounts receivable turnover and inventory turnover to assess a company's operating cycle
- Investigating a borrower's times interest earned to determine the risk of lending money to a business
- Using the price-earnings ratio to determine the value of common stock

What to Watch Out For

Don't let common mistakes trip you up. Some of the following suggestions may be helpful:

- Companies that generate earnings are not required to pay a dividend to shareholders.
- *Liquidity* refers to a firm's ability to generate sufficient current assets to pay all current liabilities.
- *Solvency* refers to a company's ability to raise capital and generate profits over the long term.
- Firms can raise money by issuing stock or debt. Some companies operate with no debt and raise all their capital from stock (equity) issuance. Other firms only issue debt.

Usefulness of Ratios

962–971

962. Which of the following ratios is useful for evaluating whether a company is able to comfortably pay its current bills?

A. current ratio

B. debt to assets ratio

C. earnings per share

D. price-earnings ratio

E. payout ratio

963. Which of the following ratios would be useful in analyzing the profitability of a company for a given time period?

A. current ratio, receivables turnover, and inventory turnover

B. free cash flow, times interest earned, and cash debt coverage

C. return on equity, return on assets, and earnings per share

D. debt to assets ratio, times interest earned, and current ratio

E. average collection period, days in inventory, and free cash flow

964. Amanda is retiring and looking to invest in a stock that will provide income in the form of dividends. What ratio would be particularly useful in her analysis?

965. Antisocial Security Company had an accounts receivable turnover of 10 last year and 11.5 this year. What can you conclude from that information?

966. Which of the following situations is best addressed by analyzing liquidity ratios?

A. a city trying to decide which company is more likely to be in business and still employing citizens in 30 years

B. an investor who is looking for a profitable company

C. a bank looking at the ability of a company to take on more debt

D. a supplier trying to determine whether a customer is creditworthy

E. a stockholder analyzing her return

967. Identify three solvency ratios that are used to evaluate the ability of a company to survive over a long period of time.

968. Which of the following ratios measures how well a company uses its assets to produce sales?

A. asset turnover

B. earnings per share

C. payout ratio

D. debt to assets ratio

E. inventory turnover

969. The following information is available from the records of Fiber Palace:

- Last year's current ratio: .87
- This year's current ratio: .90

What conclusion can you draw from this information?

970. BebeBanana has a debt to assets ratio of 78%. The industry average is 49%. What conclusion can you draw from this information?

971. Southern North Bank is looking at the financial statements attached to a company's loan application. Information on the ratios:

- Times interest earned: 5.8 and industry average is 19.6
- Debt to assets ratio: 81% and industry average is 49%
- Current ratio: .89 and industry average is .70

Would you look favorably on this application based on the limited information?

Solvency and Liquidity Analysis

972–981

972. Trendy Royal Coaches has these comparative balance sheets:

	2015	2014
Cash	150	100
Accounts receivable	70	60
Inventory	60	50
Plant assets, net	200	180
	480	390
Accounts payable	50	60
Mortgage payable	100	100
Common stock	120	120
Retained earnings	210	110
	480	390

Calculate the current ratio for 2015.

973. Trendy Royal Coaches has these comparative balance sheets:

	2015	2014
Cash	150	100
Accounts receivable	70	60
Inventory	60	50
Plant assets, net	200	180
	480	390
Accounts payable	50	60
Mortgage payable	100	100
Common stock	120	120
Retained earnings	210	110
	480	390

Credit sales were $475 in 2015, and returns were $25. Calculate accounts receivable turnover.

974. Trendy Royal Coaches has these comparative balance sheets:

	2015	2014
Cash	150	100
Accounts receivable	70	60
Inventory	60	50
Plant assets, net	200	180
	480	390
Accounts payable	50	60
Mortgage payable	100	100
Common stock	120	120
Retained earnings	210	110
	480	390

From the statement of cash flows, cash provided by operating activities was $350 in 2015 and $270 in 2014. Calculate current cash debt coverage for 2015.

975. Closet Queen Organizers has the following financial statements:

Balance Sheet		
	2015	2014
Cash	25	10
Accounts receivable	30	80
Inventory	136	135
Plant assets, net	710	400
	901	625
Accounts payable	112	42
Long-term loan payable	450	100
Common stock	300	300
Retained earnings	39	183
	901	625

Selected information from the 2015 financial statements:

- Interest expense: $8
- Tax expense: $10
- Net income: $20
- Cash dividends paid: $164
- Capital expenditures: $310
- Net cash provided by operating activities: $35

Calculate times interest earned in 2015.

976. Closet Queen Organizers has the following financial statements:

Balance Sheet		
	2015	2014
Cash	25	10
Accounts receivable	100	80
Inventory	136	135
Plant assets, net	1,090	500
	1,351	725
Accounts payable	562	142
Long-term loan payable	450	100
Common stock	300	300
Retained earnings	39	183
	1,351	725

Selected information from the 2015 financial statements:

- Interest expense: $8
- Tax expense: $10
- Net income: $20
- Cash dividends paid: $164
- Net cash provided by operating activities: $35

Calculate cash debt coverage for 2015 and interpret the ratio as compared to a competitor's ratio of .17.

977. Closet Queen Organizers has the following financial statements:

Balance Sheet		
	2015	2014
Cash	25	10
Accounts receivable	30	80
Inventory	136	135
Plant assets, net	710	400
	901	625
Accounts payable	112	42
Long-term loan payable	450	100
Common stock	300	300
Retained earnings	39	183
	901	625

Selected information from the 2015 financial statements:

- Interest expense: $8
- Tax expense: $10
- Net income: $20
- Cash dividends paid: $164
- Capital expenditures: $310
- Net cash provided by operating activities: $550

Calculate free cash flow for 2015.

978. Closet Queen Organizers has the following financial statements:

Balance Sheet		
	2015	2014
Cash	25	10
Accounts receivable	30	80
Inventory	136	135
Plant assets, net	710	400
	901	625
Accounts payable	112	42
Long-term loan payable	450	100
Common stock	300	300
Retained earnings	39	183
	901	625

Selected information from the 2015 financial statements:

- Interest expense: $8
- Tax expense: $10
- Net income: $20
- Cash dividends paid: $164
- Capital expenditures: $310
- Net cash provided by operating activities: $35

Calculate times interest earned and comment on its relationship to the industry average of 19.6.

979. Trendy Royal Coaches has these comparative balance sheets:

	2015	2014
Cash	150	100
Accounts receivable	70	60
Inventory	60	50
Plant assets, net	200	180
	480	390
Accounts payable	50	60
Mortgage payable	100	100
Common stock	120	120
Retained earnings	210	110
	480	390

Credit sales were $475 in 2015, and returns were $25. Cost of goods sold was $285 in 2015. Calculate inventory turnover for 2015.

980. Trendy Royal Coaches has these comparative balance sheets:

	2015	2014
Cash	150	100
Accounts receivable	70	60
Inventory	60	50
Plant assets, net	200	180
	480	390
Accounts payable	50	60
Mortgage payable	100	100
Common stock	120	120
Retained earnings	210	110
	480	390

Credit sales were $475 in 2015, and returns were $25. Calculate the average collection period.

981. Closet Queen Organizers has the following financial statements:

Balance Sheet		
	2015	2014
Cash	25	10
Accounts receivable	30	80
Inventory	136	135
Plant assets, net	710	400
	901	625
Accounts payable	112	42
Long-term loan payable	450	100
Common stock	300	300
Retained earnings	39	183
	901	625

Selected information from the 2015 financial statements:

- Interest expense: $8
- Tax expense: $10
- Net income: $20
- Cash dividends paid: $164
- Capital expenditures: $310
- Net cash provided by operating activities: $35

Calculate the debt to assets ratio in 2014 and 2015 and indicate whether the company's solvency is improving.

Profitability Analysis

982–991

982. The following information is taken from the annual report of Little Falls Bandages:

	2015	2014
Assets	8,192	6,753
Liabilities	2,828	1,784
Contributed capital	1,000	1,000
Retained earnings	4,364	3,969
Net sales	14,727	10,639
Cost of goods sold	7,598	5,334
Gross profit	7,129	5,305
Operating expenses	5,500	4,182
Other expense	59	33
Tax expense	600	400
Net income	970	690

Cash dividends paid to common stockholders amounted to $575. Calculate the ROE or return on common stockholders' equity.

983. The following information is taken from the annual report of Little Falls Bandages:

	2015	2014
Assets	8,192	6,753
Liabilities	2,828	1,784
Contributed capital	1,000	1,000
Retained earnings	4,364	3,969
Net sales	14,727	10,639
Cost of goods sold	7,598	5,334
Gross profit	7,129	5,305
Operating expenses	5,500	4,182
Other expense	59	33
Tax expense	600	400
Net income	970	690

Cash dividends paid to common stockholders amounted to $575. Calculate profit margin or return on sales for 2015.

984. The following information is taken from the annual report of Little Falls Bandages:

	2015	2014
Assets	8,192	6,753
Liabilities	2,828	1,784
Contributed capital	1,000	1,000
Retained earnings	4,364	3,969
Net sales	14,727	10,639
Cost of goods sold	7,598	5,334
Gross profit	7,129	5,305
Operating expenses	5,500	4,182
Other expense	59	33
Tax expense	600	400
Net income	970	690

Cash dividends paid to common stockholders amounted to $575. The company had 1,000 shares of common stock outstanding in both 2014 and 2015. Calculate earnings per share for 2015.

985. The following information is taken from the annual report of Little Falls Bandages:

	2015	2014
Assets	8,192	6,753
Liabilities	2,828	1,784
Contributed capital	1,000	1,000
Retained earnings	4,364	3,969
Net sales	14,727	10,639
Cost of goods sold	7,598	5,334
Gross profit	7,129	5,305
Operating expenses	5,500	4,182
Other expense	59	33
Tax expense	600	400
Net income	970	690

Cash dividends paid to common stockholders amounted to $575. Calculate the payout ratio for 2015.

986. The following information is taken from the annual report of Little Falls Bandages:

	2015	2014
Assets	8,192	6,753
Liabilities	2,828	1,784
Contributed capital	1,000	1,000
Retained earnings	4,364	3,969
Net sales	14,727	10,639
Cost of goods sold	7,598	5,334
Gross profit	7,129	5,305
Operating expenses	5,500	4,182
Other expense	59	33
Tax expense	600	400
Net income	970	690

Cash dividends paid to common stockholders amounted to $575. Calculate return on assets for 2015.

987. The following information is taken from the annual report of Little Falls Bandages:

	2015	2014
Assets	8,192	6,753
Liabilities	2,828	1,784
Contributed capital	1,000	1,000
Retained earnings	4,364	3,969
Net sales	14,727	10,639
Cost of goods sold	7,598	5,334
Gross profit	7,129	5,305
Operating expenses	5,500	4,182
Other expense	59	33
Tax expense	600	400
Net income	970	690

Cash dividends paid to common stockholders amounted to $575. Calculate asset turnover for 2015.

988. Boys Corporation had a dividend payout ratio of 23% in 2015. Girls Company, a direct competitor, had a payout ratio of 55%. If you are looking for an investment in a company that has high growth, which investment do you prefer, and why?

989. The following information is taken from the annual report of Little Falls Bandages:

	2015	2014
Assets	8,192	6,753
Liabilities	2,828	1,784
Contributed capital	1,000	1,000
Retained earnings	4,364	3,969
Net sales	14,727	10,639
Cost of goods sold	7,598	5,334
Gross profit	7,129	5,305
Operating expenses	5,500	4,182
Other expense	59	33
Tax expense	600	400
Net income	970	690

Cash dividends paid to common stockholders amounted to $575. The company had 1,000 shares of common stock outstanding in both 2014 and 2015. The price of the company stock was $22.31 at the end of 2015. Calculate the price-earnings ratio for 2015.

990. The following information is taken from the annual report of Little Falls Bandages:

	2015	2014
Assets	8,192	6,753
Liabilities	2,828	1,784
Contributed capital	1,000	1,000
Retained earnings	4,364	3,969
Net sales	14,727	10,639
Cost of goods sold	7,598	5,334
Gross profit	7,129	5,305
Operating expenses	5,500	4,182
Other expense	59	33
Tax expense	600	400
Net income	970	690

Cash dividends paid to common stockholders amounted to $575. Calculate the return on sales or profit margin in both 2014 and 2015 and comment on the trend.

991. The following information is taken from the annual report of Little Falls Bandages:

	2015	2014
Assets	8,192	6,753
Liabilities	2,828	1,784
Contributed capital	1,000	1,000
Retained earnings	4,364	3,969
Net sales	14,727	10,639
Cost of goods sold	7,598	5,334
Gross profit	7,129	5,305
Operating expenses	5,500	4,182
Other expense	59	33
Tax expense	600	400
Net income	970	690

Cash dividends paid to common stockholders amounted to $575. Calculate the gross profit rate for 2014 and 2015 and comment on the trend.

Cash Flow Analysis

992–1,001

992. The following information was taken from the 2015 year-end records of Cloud Glasses Co.:

- Net change in cash: $6,500
- Cash from operating activities: $10,900
- Average current assets: $15,000
- Average total assets: $35,000
- Average current liabilities: $17,000
- Average long-term debt: $5,000
- Average stockholders' equity: $13,000

Calculate current cash debt coverage for 2015.

993. Cold Pack Athletic Gear, Inc. had the following information in its 2015 annual report:

- Net change in cash: $135,000
- Net cash provided by operating activities: $63,500
- Net cash used by investing activities: $30,000, including $27,300 spent on capital improvements
- Cash dividends paid on preferred stock: $8,000
- Cash dividends paid on common stock: $10,000

Calculate free cash flow.

994. Perfect Bag, Inc. reports the following in its 2015 annual report:

- Balance in the cash account, 12/31/15: $589,100
- Net increase in cash: $56,700
- Net cash provided by operating activities: $101,500
- Average current assets: $95,000
- Average total assets: $995,000
- Average current liabilities: $59,100
- Average long-term debt: $600,000

Calculate the cash debt coverage.

995. Travel Fridge, Inc. has the following information:

Balance Sheet 12/31/2015		
	2015	2014
Current assets	12,000	8,000
Noncurrent assets	14,000	15,000
Total assets	26,000	23,000
Current liabilities	1,000	5,000
Long-term debt	3,000	2,000
Stockholders' equity	22,000	16,000
	26,000	23,000

Income Statement Year ended 12/31/2015	
Net sales	53,000
Cost of goods sold	20,000
Profit margin	33,000
Operating expenses	15,000
Income from operations	18,000
Other expenses	8,000
Income before taxes	10,000
Tax expense	4,000
Net income	6,000

Statement of Cash Flows Year ended 12/31/2015		
Net cash provided by operating activities	4,000	
Net cash used by investing activities	(1,000)	
Net cash provided by financing activities	1,000	
Net change in cash	4,000	

Calculate current cash debt coverage.

996. Travel Fridge, Inc. has the following information:

Balance Sheet 12/31/2015		
	2015	2014
Current assets	12,000	8,000
Noncurrent assets	14,000	15,000
Total assets	26,000	23,000
Current liabilities	1,000	5,000
Long-term debt	3,000	2,000
Stockholders' equity	22,000	16,000
	26,000	23,000

Income Statement Year ended 12/31/2015	
Net sales	53,000
Cost of goods sold	20,000
Profit margin	33,000
Operating expenses	15,000
Income from operations	18,000
Other expenses	8,000
Income before taxes	10,000
Tax expense	4,000
Net income	6,000

Statement of Cash Flows Year ended 12/31/2015		
Net cash provided by operating activities	4,000	
Net cash used by investing activities	(1,000)	
Net cash provided by financing activities	1,000	
Net change in cash	4,000	

Calculate cash debt coverage.

997. Easy Add Calculators has net cash provided by operating activities of $13,100. The cash balance at year-end is $25,000. Average current assets for the year equal $130,000. Average current liabilities for the year are $17,000, and average total liabilities are $43,000. Calculate cash debt coverage.

998. Perfect Bag, Inc. reports the following in its 2015 annual report:

- Net increase in cash: $176,00
- Current cash debt coverage: 3.7
- Average current assets: $47,000
- Average current liabilities: $27,000
- Average total liabilities: $35,000

Calculate cash debt coverage for 2015.

999. Easy Add Calculators has net cash used by operating activities of $13,100. The cash balance at year-end is $25,000. Average current assets for the year equal $30,000. Average current liabilities for the year are $17,000, and average total liabilities are $43,000. The company paid cash dividends of $2,300 and bought equipment for $4,000. Calculate the free cash flow for the year.

1,000. Perfect Bags, Inc. has a cash debt coverage of .18 and $46,000 in current assets at year-end, of which $10,000 is cash. Travel Nut Luggage Company has a cash debt coverage of .25 and $37,000 in current assets, of which $12,000 is cash at year-end. Which company is more solvent, and why?

1,001. Easy Add Calculators has net cash used by operating activities of $13,100. The cash balance at year-end is $25,000. Average current assets for the year equal $130,000. Average current liabilities for the year are $17,000, and average total liabilities are $43,000. Calculate current cash debt coverage.

Part II
The Answers

1,001 Answers

web extras

Go to www.dummies.com/cheatsheet/1001accounting to access the Cheat Sheet created specifically for *1,001 Accounting Practice Problems For Dummies.*

In this part . . .

Here you get answers and explanations for all 1,001 problems. As you read the solutions, you may realize that you need a little more help. Lucky for you, the *For Dummies* series (published by Wiley) offers several excellent resources. I recommend checking out the following titles, depending on your needs:

- *Accounting For Dummies,* by John A. Tracy
- *Cost Accounting For Dummies,* by Ken Boyd
- *Financial Accounting For Dummies,* by Maire Loughran
- *Managerial Accounting For Dummies,* by Mark P. Holtzman

Visit `www.dummies.com` for more information.

Chapter 15
Answers and Explanations

1. Each business entity is treated as a separate entity for accounting purposes.

For accounting purposes, businesses are treated separately from their owners. They are separate entities and need to be recognized as such.

2. sole proprietorship

A sole proprietorship is the only business type that has only one owner. Corporations and partnerships have multiple owners, and there are no business types called limited liability proprietorships or sole partnerships.

3. partnership

A *partnership* is a business formed by two or more individuals (partners) and allows access to additional resources or skills.

4. A sole partnership is not one of the ways of legally organizing a business because a partnership requires more than one owner. Therefore, it cannot be "sole."

There is no business entity type called a sole partnership. If it is "sole" then it is a proprietorship. Partnership implies more than one partner.

5. corporation

A corporation provides liability protection for its owners. However, it is more difficult to establish than the other forms of business because it has to be registered with the state.

6. assets = liabilities + owners' equity

The accounting equation states that assets (what the business owns) are the same as the sum of its liabilities and owners' equity.

7. Assets are resources of economic value owned by a business.

Assets are the resources that a business owns and that possess economic value.

8. A vehicle purchased with a loan is an example of an asset because the car has economic value to the company and is expected to provide future benefits.

A car purchased by a business is a resource owned by that business. The car possesses economic value. Therefore, it is an asset. It does not matter how the company paid for it. When a loan is obtained, the company must also record the loan as a liability. Regardless of the method of payment, the company now has a car that will provide future benefit and has economic value.

9. Liabilities are claims resulting from credit extended to a business.

Liabilities represent what the business owes to others — that is, the claims to the business resulting from credit that was extended by other entities.

10. Money owed to a bank is a liability because it represents what the business owes to others.

Money owed to another entity is a debt and therefore a liability. It represents a financial obligation of the company.

11. The company pays for it by obtaining a loan or credit that must be paid back.

Purchasing something *on account* or *on credit* means the company did not pay for it at the time of purchase but instead made a promise to pay for it at a later time.

12. A loan from a bank is not an asset because it represents an obligation to pay the loan back.

A loan from a bank is a liability because the company must pay back the loan to the bank. The cash received from the loan is an asset, but the loan is an obligation or a liability.

13. Office equipment is a resource with monetary value.

Office equipment is an asset. The company purchased the equipment intending to use it for an extended period of time and derives a benefit from it.

14. assets

Assets are defined as economic resources owned by a business that have material value.

15. \$90,000

The basic accounting equation is assets = liabilities + owners' equity.

$$135{,}000 = 45{,}000 + \text{equity}$$

$$135{,}000 - 45{,}000 = 90{,}000$$

16. $500,000

The basic accounting equation is assets = liabilities + owners' equity.

$$\text{assets} = 345,700 + 154,300$$
$$\text{assets} = 500,000$$

17. $796,000

The basic accounting equation is assets = liabilities + owners' equity.

$$1,450,000 = \text{liabilities} + 654,000$$
$$1,450,000 - 654,000 = \text{liabilities}$$
$$796,000 = \text{liabilities}$$

18. $331,000

The basic accounting equation is assets = liabilities + owners' equity.

$$576,000 = 245,000 + \text{equity}$$
$$576,000 - 245,000 = \text{equity}$$
$$331,000 = \text{equity}$$

You can always double-check your answer by going back to the original equation assets = liabilities + owners' equity. In this example, the sum of liabilities of $245,000 and owners' equity of $331,000 is $576,000. This corresponds to the given amount of total assets, so you know your answer is right.

19. $2,518,000

You know that the basic accounting equation is assets = liabilities + owners' equity. In this example, you are given the dollar amount of liabilities and owners' equity and need to calculate the assets. Using the basic accounting equation, you need to find the sum of the liabilities of $142,000 and the owners' equity of $2,376,000 for a total of assets of $2,518,000.

20. The business has experienced losses.

Equity reflects the earnings of a business, along with owners' investment. Retained earnings are part of equity and represent the accumulation of the earnings from the start of the business. Negative retained earnings means the business has not been generating profits.

21. Assets increase by $25,000, and liabilities increase by $25,000.

Assets go down by $5,000, the amount of cash paid, and go up by $30,000, the cost of the truck. The net effect is an increase of $25,000. The loan will increase liabilities by $25,000.

22. an increase in assets and a corresponding decrease in assets

Inventory is an asset, so when a company purchases inventory, it increases its assets. When a company pays for the purchase with cash, it also decreases its assets.

23. an increase in assets and an increase in liabilities

A delivery truck is an asset. Therefore, a purchase increases assets. Obtaining a loan increases the company's liabilities. The accounting equation is still in balance because both assets and liabilities increased.

24. a $20,000 decrease in assets and a corresponding decrease of $20,000 in liabilities

When a company makes a payment on an amount owed to a supplier, the debt decreases. If a debt decreases, then liabilities decrease, and the cash decreases as a result of the payment. This means that assets decrease.

25. an increase in assets and an increase in owners' equity

The owner contributes a delivery truck instead of cash. That contribution increases equity. A delivery truck is an asset that will be used by the company, which increases assets.

26. an increase in assets and an increase in owners' equity

The cash received from the sale increases the balance of cash (assets), and the revenue earned increases profits and therefore increases equity.

27. a decrease in assets and a decrease in owners' equity

The cash used to pay for utilities decreases the balance of cash (assets), and the office expenses decrease profits and therefore decrease equity.

28. The business has a high ratio of debt to equity.

Leverage is the amount of debt a company has in relation to its total capitalization (debt + equity). The term *leverage* refers to the fact that the owners' equity is used as the basis for borrowing.

29. $150,000

You need to go back to the basic accounting equation: assets = liabilities + owners' equity. Step one is to determine total owners' equity, which has two parts — the investment by owners and the losses that the business experienced during the first year of operations. Investment by owners is $1,000,000. So, the total owners' equity is $700,000:

$$1{,}000{,}000 + (-300{,}000) = 700{,}000.$$

Now you can use the basic accounting equation to calculate total liabilities at the end of the year:

850,000 = liabilities + 700,000
850,000 − 700,000 = 150,000
liabilities = 150,000

30. profit of $100,000

The starting point to figure this out is the basic accounting equation: assets = liabilities + owners' equity. The question provides you with the total assets and total liabilities, but you need to calculate equity. Equity has two components: capital/investment from owners and retained earnings, or the profit/loss accumulated since the company's inception. In this example, you are given the capital invested but need to calculate the profit/loss. Rewrite the basic equation in detail:

assets = liabilities + owners' equity + profit
350,000 = 200,000 + 50,000 + profit
350,000 − 200,000 − 50,000 = 100,000
profit = 100,000

31. Cash-basis accounting posts income and expenses solely based on cash inflows and cash outflows.

Cash-basis accounting records all transactions based on when cash exchanges hands, so it focuses on keeping track of all cash inflows and cash outflows.

32. Accrual-basis accounting records revenues when earned and expenses when they occur.

Accrual-basis accounting varies from cash accounting in that it records revenues and expenses when they occur and not when cash exchanges hands.

33. total profit

Cash-basis accounting determines profit by calculating the difference between cash inflows and cash outflows. Accrual-basis accounting measures profit differently because it records revenues when earned and expenses when they occur.

34. individuals

Cash-basis accounting focuses on the daily cash balance, and it is used primarily by individuals to keep track of their checkbook balances.

35. corporations

Large businesses, primarily corporations, use accrual-basis accounting because it provides more complete information required to run the business.

36. because large businesses need additional information not provided by cash-basis accounting

Accrual-basis accounting keeps track of all assets and liabilities as well as all inflows and outflows of cash. All this information is needed to run a large business.

37. Transactions are recorded when they occur, not when cash is paid or received.

The main difference between cash-basis and accrual-basis accounting is when transactions are recorded. Under accrual-basis accounting, they are recorded when they occur, regardless of whether cash exchanged hands.

38. August 1

Under accrual-basis accounting, revenues are recorded when the goods or services are delivered to the customer, regardless of whether the customer has paid for them. This distinguishes accrual-basis accounting from cash-basis accounting, where the revenues are not recorded until the customer pays for the goods or services. Although the company received an order for the ice cream on July 31, delivery didn't happen until August 1.

39. August 10

Cash-basis accounting records revenue when the cash is received from the customer.

40. none

Under cash-basis accounting, revenue is recorded when the cash is received, which is August 1 in this situation. No cash is received in September, so no revenue is recorded.

41. The income statement for May will show $759 in utility expense.

Accrual-basis accounting requires all expenses to be recorded when they are incurred (when the obligation is created), regardless of when they are paid. Because the electricity was used in May, creating an obligation to pay for it, the expense appears on the May income statement.

42. cash-basis accounting

The company has recorded the entire fuel expense in the month in which the cash was paid. That is cash-basis accounting. If the company had used accrual-basis accounting, the $1,000,000 of expense would have been spread out from January 1 to July 1.

43. $750,000

Under cash-basis accounting, revenues are recorded when the customer pays for the products purchased. In this example, you know that cash receipts from sales were $750,000. This amount is recorded as revenues when it's received from customers. None of the other numbers provided are relevant to cash-basis revenues.

44. $700,000

Under cash-basis accounting, expenses equal the amount of cash paid for products, services, and other expenses. Therefore, adding cash payments for purchases of products of $325,000 plus the cash payments for other expenses of $375,000 equals $700,000.

45. $50,000 profit

Under cash-basis accounting, profit is determined as the difference between the cash inflow and cash outflow. In this case, cash receipts of $750,000 minus the cash payments of $700,000 gives the cash-basis profit of $50,000.

46. $905,000

Under accrual-basis accounting, revenues are recorded when they are earned. Revenues include not only the cash collected from customers ($750,000) but also the amount the customers promise to pay in the form of receivables ($155,000). Thus, in this case, total revenues under the accrual basis are the sum of the amount collected from customers and the receivables.

$$750{,}000 + 155{,}000 = 905{,}000$$

47. $205,000

The cost of goods sold includes the beginning inventory value plus the amount of cash paid for purchases of products minus the balance of products still unsold at the end of the year.

$$325{,}000 - 120{,}000 = 205{,}000$$

48. $825,000

Under accrual-basis accounting, expenses are recorded when they are incurred. Therefore, they include not only the cash payment of $375,000 but also the liability for unpaid expenses of $450,000 for a total of $825,000.

49. $125,000 loss

You calculate accrual profit as revenues less cost of goods sold and other expenses. Accrual-based revenues are equal to the cash received from customers plus the amounts owed for sales during the year.

$$750{,}000 + 155{,}000 = 905{,}000$$

Accrual-based cost of goods sold is equal to the beginning inventory value plus the cash paid for inventory less the unsold inventory still on hand.

$$325{,}000 - 120{,}000 = 205{,}000$$

Accrual-based other expenses are equal to the cash paid for those expenses plus any amounts for expenses incurred but unpaid.

$$375{,}000 + 450{,}000 = 825{,}000$$

Revenue minus cost of goods sold minus other expenses equals the profit or loss for the year. A negative result indicates a loss.

$$905{,}000 - 205{,}000 - 825{,}000 = -125{,}000$$

50. $9,000

Under cash-basis accounting, revenues are recorded when cash is collected. Therefore, both cash sales ($6,000) and the amount collected for goods to be delivered in the future ($3,000) are cash-basis revenues.

51. $3,000

Under cash-basis accounting, expenses are recorded when they are paid. In this case, expenses include the amount paid in 2013 for utilities ($2,000) and the amount paid in advance for services to be used in the future ($1,000) for a total of $3,000.

52. $2,000

Cash-basis revenues are equal to all cash received from customers. The cash received for future delivery of goods is not revenue in 2015.

$$6{,}000 + 3{,}000 = 9{,}000$$

Under accrual-basis accounting, revenues are recorded when they are earned. In this case, both sales on account ($5,000) and cash sales ($6,000) should be included in accrual-basis revenues for a total of $11,000.

$$11{,}000 - 9{,}000 = 2{,}000$$

53. income statement

The income statement calculates net profit or loss by summarizing the company's revenues, other income, expenses, and losses.

54. profit and loss statement

The income statement can also be called the profit and loss statement, or P&L. Deducting expenses from revenue leads to the bottom line, which is the net profit or loss for the period.

55. income statement

Income statements deduct expenses from revenue and calculate the profit or loss generated by the business during a period.

56. income statement

An income statement summarizes all revenues, gains, and other income of a business during a period of time. It also shows expenses and losses.

57. losses

In addition to revenues and expenses, an income statement includes all gains and losses. The income statement is sometimes called the profit and loss (or P&L) statement.

58. income statement

Revenue is listed as the first item on an income statement. The borrower will provide the banker income statements for the last few years to substantiate the revenue growth.

59. An income statement presents revenues and expenses for a specific period of time.

An income statement is prepared for a period of time (month, quarter, or year), and it summarizes the revenues earned and expenses incurred during that time.

60. loss on the sale of equipment

An income statement summarizes all revenues, expenses, gains, and losses of a business during a period of time, and it calculates the net income or loss for that period. Deferred revenue is a liability and appears on the balance sheet.

61. interest expense and income tax expense

One of the requirements of income statement preparation is that the interest expense and income tax expense are reported separately.

62. $27,000

You calculate gross margin (also known as gross profit) by subtracting the cost of goods sold from sales revenues.

$$47{,}000 - 20{,}000 = 27{,}000$$

63. $10,000

Operating income/earnings includes all operating revenues and expenses but excludes the interest revenue and income tax expense.

$$47,000-20,000-14,000-3,000=10,000$$

64. $11,200

Income tax expense is presented as a separate line item on the income statement, and the line just before that expense is called "income before income taxes." It includes all revenues, gains, expenses, and losses except tax expense.

$$47,000-20,000-14,000-3,000+1,200=11,200$$

65. $2,600,000

You calculate gross profit as the difference between sales revenues and cost of goods sold.

$$15,000,000-12,400,000=2,600,000$$

66. $1,150,000

You calculate operating earnings as gross profit less selling, general, and administrative expenses. You calculate gross profit as sales revenues less the cost of goods sold.

$$15,000,000-12,400,000=2,600,000$$

Then deduct selling, general, and administrative expenses from cost of goods sold to calculate operating earnings.

$$2,600,000-1,450,000=1,150,000$$

67. $750,000

To calculate earnings before income taxes, all non-income tax expenses are deducted from all revenues.

$$15,000,000-12,400,000-1,450,000-125,000-275,000=750,000$$

68. $550,000

The formula to calculate net income is to subtract all expenses from all revenues.

$$15,000,000-12,400,000-1,450,000-125,000-275,000-200,000=550,000$$

69. $240,000

Net income is the final number on the income statement. You calculate it by subtracting income taxes from earnings before income taxes. However, in this example, you need to determine the amount of the income tax expense. Because earnings before income taxes and net income are provided, your formula should be earnings before the income tax of $420,000 minus the unknown tax expense equals net income of $180,000.

$$420{,}000 - x = 180{,}000$$
$$420{,}000 - 180{,}000 = x$$
$$x = 240{,}000$$

70. $6,000,000

Gross margin is equal to the difference between sales revenue and cost of goods sold.

$$8{,}000{,}000 - x = 2{,}000{,}000$$
$$8{,}000{,}000 - 2{,}000{,}000 = x$$
$$x = 6{,}000{,}000$$

71. $1,350,000

You calculate selling, general, and administrative expenses as the difference between gross margin and operating earnings.

$$2{,}000{,}000 - x = 650{,}000$$
$$2{,}000{,}000 - 650{,}000 = x$$
$$x = 1{,}350{,}000$$

72. $230,000

Interest expense is presented on the income statement after operating earnings and before earnings before income taxes. Thus, you calculate it as the difference between operating income and earnings before income taxes.

$$650{,}000 - x = 420{,}000$$
$$650{,}000 - 420{,}000 = x$$
$$x = 230{,}000$$

In this case, you need to take operating earnings of $650,000 less earnings before income tax of $420,000, which equals $230,000.

73. balance sheet, income statement, and statement of cash flows

The three primary financial statements are balance sheet, income statement, and the statement of cash flows.

Answers 1–100

74. statement of financial position

A balance sheet can also be called a *statement of financial position.*

75. balance sheet

The balance sheet shows the assets, liabilities, and equity of a company at a point in time.

76. $275,000

Assets include cash, amounts owed by customers (accounts receivable), and cost of unsold product (inventory).

$$110{,}000 + 75{,}000 + 90{,}000 = 275{,}000$$

77. $155,000

Liabilities include amounts owed for unpaid purchases and expenses (accounts payable), notes payable to the bank, and unearned revenues.

$$72{,}000 + 73{,}000 + 10{,}000 = 155{,}000$$

78. $120,000

The basic accounting equation is assets = liabilities + owners' equity. You can calculate equity from this equation by subtracting liabilities from assets.

Assets include cash, amounts owed by customers (accounts receivable), and cost of unsold product (inventory).

$$110{,}000 + 75{,}000 + 90{,}000 = 275{,}000$$

Liabilities include amounts owed for unpaid purchases and expenses (accounts payable), notes payable to the bank, and unearned revenues.

$$72{,}000 + 73{,}000 + 10{,}000 = 155{,}000$$

$$275{,}000 = 155{,}000 + x$$

$$275{,}000 - 155{,}000 = x$$

$$120{,}000 = x$$

79. The statement of cash flows because it provides information about cash inflows and outflows.

The statement of cash flows provides information about the sources of a company's cash and how the cash is used. If the company can generate cash from operations, as opposed to selling off assets, the company is more likely to be able to make the loan payments.

80. operating activities

The statement of cash flows breaks down cash inflows and outflows into operating, financing, and investing activities.

81. cash flows from investing activities

The statement of cash flows classifies the purchase of fixed assets as investing activities.

82. as a financing activity

Paying off loans is a financing activity.

83. as a cash inflow of $30,000

Proceeds from sales of operating assets are an investing activity on the statement of cash flows. The cash inflow is measured as the amount of cash received.

84. increase of $20,000

You calculate the net increase in cash as the sum of cash flow from operating, investing, and financing activities.

$$(-50{,}000) = 20{,}000 + 50{,}000 = 20{,}000$$

85. ($115,000)

You calculate the net increase in cash as the sum of cash flow from operating, investing, and financing activities. However, in this example, you are given the net decrease in cash and need to calculate the cash flow from investing activities.

$$50{,}000 + 25{,}000 + x = (-40{,}000)$$
$$50{,}000 + 25{,}000 + 40{,}000 = x$$
$$115{,}000 = x$$

86. $12,000

You calculate the net increase in cash as the sum of cash flow from operating, investing, and financing activities. However, in this example, you are given the net increase in cash and need to calculate the cash flow from financing activities.

$$6{,}000 + (-5{,}000) + x = 13{,}000$$
$$x = 13{,}000 - 6{,}000 - (-5{,}000)$$
$$x = 12{,}000$$

87. $110,000

You calculate the net increase in cash as the sum of cash flow from operating, investing, and financing activities. However, in this example, you are given the beginning and ending cash balance and must calculate the change. Then, you use that number to determine cash flows from operating activities. Cash increased by $100,000.

$$370{,}000 - 270{,}000 = 100{,}000$$

Now, the sum of the cash flows from operating, investing, and financing activities must equal 100,000.

$$x + 45{,}000 + (-55{,}000) = 100{,}000$$
$$x = 100{,}000 - 45{,}000 - (-55{,}000)$$
$$x = 110{,}000$$

88. net cash outflow of $85,000

Investing activities include investments in financial markets and investments in capital assets. In the example, investing activities include the cash received from the sale of old equipment and the cash paid to purchase the new equipment.

$$(-130{,}000) + 45{,}000 = (-85{,}000)$$

89. net cash inflow of $45,000

Financing activities are activities that raise capital and repay investors. After reviewing the information provided in the example, you should note that financing activities include the proceeds from the new debt and proceeds from the issuance of stock less the amount paid for dividends.

$$20{,}000 + (-40{,}000) + 65{,}000 = 45{,}000$$

90. $11,300

Net cash increase/decrease is the sum of all cash inflows and outflows or the sum of cash flows from financing, investing, and operating activities. Cash flows from financing activities include the sale of stock, the payment of dividends, and the proceeds from the new loan.

$$20{,}000 + (-40{,}000) + 65{,}000 = 45{,}000$$

Cash flows from investing activities include the cash paid for new equipment and the proceeds from the sale of old equipment.

$$(-130{,}000) + 45{,}000 = (-85{,}000)$$

The net change in cash for the year combines the cash flows from financing, investing, and operating activities.

$$45{,}000 + (85{,}000) + 45{,}000 = 5{,}000$$

The cash balance increased by $5,000 during the year.

$$6{,}300 + 5{,}000 = 11{,}300$$

91. balance sheet, statement of cash flows, and income statement

The three primary financial statements are the balance sheet, the statement of cash flows, and the income statement. When a company presents financial statements, it should always present these three together because these statements are what decision-makers need to see.

92. balance sheet

The balance sheet summarizes assets, liabilities, and owners' equity at the end of a period. This statement is prepared as of a specific date. The balance sheet does not reflect a period of time.

93. income statement

The income statement summarizes the profit-making transactions during a period of time. This statement is the first one prepared because it's needed to prepare the other statements. It shows all the revenues, expenses, and net income for the period.

94. statement of cash flows

The statement of cash flows summarizes a business's cash transactions during a period of time. This statement shows how cash was generated and used during an accounting period.

95. generating a profit

Businesses are formed primarily to make a profit by generating sales and minimizing expenses.

96. purchasing inventory

When inventory is sold to a customer, the seller increases cost of goods sold.

97. selling services to customers

Selling services to customers generates revenue for a business; thus, it's a profit-making activity.

98. purchasing a new machine for a factory

Purchasing new machinery or equipment is a way of investing in the business.

99. obtaining a loan from a bank

Obtaining a loan is a financing activity.

Answers 101–200

100. recording of the transactions in the accounting records

Accountants capture business transactions, determine the financial effect of those transactions, record them in the accounting records, and then prepare the financial statements. Auditors then audit the financial statements for accuracy.

101. cash, accounts receivable, inventory, and fixed assets

Most businesses that sell products show cash, accounts receivable, inventory, and fixed assets on their balance sheets. Those assets are the fundamental assets of a business selling products.

102. operating liabilities

Operating liabilities are short term and do not bear interest.

103. Cash increased to $175,000, and owners' invested capital increased to $170,000.

The $50,000 cash contribution increased the cash balance and the owners' invested capital balance.

$$125{,}000 + 50{,}000 = 175{,}000$$
$$120{,}000 + 50{,}000 = 170{,}000$$

104. Cash increased to $225,000, and interest-bearing liabilities increased to $260,000.

Taking out a loan gives the company cash, so it increases cash and liabilities because the company now has to pay the loan back to the bank.

$$125{,}000 + 100{,}000 = 225{,}000$$
$$160{,}000 + 100{,}000 = 260{,}000$$

105. Cash increased to $150,000, and accounts receivable decreased to $125,000.

The $25,000 received from a customer decreases the customer's receivables balance and increases the cash balance.

$$125{,}000 + 25{,}000 = 150{,}000$$
$$150{,}000 - 25{,}000 = 125{,}000$$

106. Cash decreased to $45,000, and interest-bearing liabilities decreased to $80,000.

The principal payment decreased cash and decreased the loan balance. Subtracting the payment of $80,000 from the starting balance of $125,000 gives a new balance of $45,000. Subtracting the payment of $80,000 from the $160,000 starting balance of the loan gives a new balance $80,000.

107. Cash decreased to $115,000, and owners' retained earnings decreased to $365,000.

The $10,000 distribution to owners decreased the cash balance and decreased retained earnings. The company started with $125,000 cash and subtracted the distribution of $10,000 to give $115,000. The retained earnings that started at $375,000 decreased by $10,000 because of the distribution to give a final amount of $365,000.

108. Cash decreased to $120,000; property, plant, and equipment increased to $350,000; and interest-bearing liabilities increased to $175,000.

This transaction increased the balance of equipment and the balance of liabilities and also decreased the balance in cash.

$$330{,}000 + 20{,}000 = 350{,}000$$
$$160{,}000 + 15{,}000 = 175{,}000$$
$$125{,}000 - 5{,}000 = 120{,}000$$

109. Operating liabilities decreased to $135,000, and inventory decreased to $185,000.

This transaction decreased the inventory balance and the operating liabilities (accounts payable) balance by $15,000.

$$150{,}000 - 15{,}000 = 135{,}000$$
$$200{,}000 - 15{,}000 = 185{,}000$$

110. increase sales, decrease expenses, or a combination of both

Profit is measured as the difference between sales revenue and expenses.

111. profit

Profit is sometimes also called *net income.* You calculate profit by taking all revenues and deducting all expenses.

112. cash sales

Only cash sales increase both assets and revenue when the cash is received. A credit sale increases assets and revenue when the sale is made, not when the cash is received. An advance payment sale increases liabilities and assets when the cash is received.

113. customer deposit

Customer deposits occur when the customer pays for the product or service before the product or service is actually delivered to the customer. An example of a customer deposit is a magazine subscription. Customers pay for the subscription in advance and then receive their magazines later. The publisher has an obligation to send out the magazines and can record the revenue as magazines are delivered.

114. cash sale

Cash sales occur when a customer pays for a product or service at the same time the product or service is delivered. Paying for groceries with cash is an example of a cash sale.

115. credit sale

Credit sales occur when a customer pays for a product or service some time after the product or service is delivered. An example of a credit sale is when a customer agrees with the company that the customer will pay for the sale in the next 30 days.

116. customer deposit

Customer deposits for products or services increase cash but do not increase profit until the goods or services are provided to the customer. Customer deposits represent an obligation of the company to provide goods or services in the future. As such, they are recorded as liabilities until the product or service is delivered to the customer.

117. customer deposit

Although the cash is received, the airline has not earned the revenue until the ticket is used. A customer deposit creates an obligation for the airline to provide a service to the purchaser of the ticket.

118. Cash increased by $17,100,000, operating liabilities increased by $1,710,000, and owners' retained earnings increased by $15,390,000.

Cash is received, so cash is increased. If 90% of the orders were filled, then the company can record the revenue for that amount, and that will increase owners' retained earnings.

$$17{,}100{,}000 \times .9 = 15{,}390{,}000$$

The remaining 10% of orders that were not filled represent an operating liability — a customer deposit.

119. $60

Magazine deliveries started in January and continued for 12 months. At the end of June, only 6 issues have been delivered, leaving 6 issues yet to be delivered. Total price of $120 divided by 12 months gives you $10, which is the monthly price of the magazine. It's also the revenue the magazine publisher receives each month. Because there are 6 remaining undelivered issues, you multiply the 6 issues by the $10 cost of production to get $60. Thus, $60 remains as the unearned revenue as of June 30.

120. income statement

Income statements summarize revenues and expenses and calculate the net profits of businesses.

121. $43,000

This example emphasizes that an expense is recorded, or matched, with the revenue it generates. In this case, even though the company paid $47,000 for inventory, less than that was sold, only $43,000. The products are bought and paid for before they are sold to customers but are only recorded as an expense when the sale is made.

122. throughout the time the company uses the building

Businesses buy long-term assets and charge the cost as an expense through depreciation, which is taken over the useful life of the asset.

123. Cash decreased by $277,500; property, plant, and equipment net decreased by $7,500; operating liabilities increased by $2,000; and owners' retained earnings decreased by $287,000.

It's easiest to start with the liabilities and owners' equity: $287,000 in expenses decreased owners' retained earnings by that amount. But, on that same side of the accounting equation, operating liabilities increased by $2,000. The net effect is a decrease in total liabilities and owners' equity of $285,000.

$$2{,}000+(-287{,}000)=-285{,}000$$

Total assets, then, must also go down by $285,000. The depreciation expense decreased total assets by $7,500, so the remaining amount must be expenses that were paid in cash.

$$285{,}000-7{,}500=277{,}500$$

124. $6,000

The company paid $24,000 for 12 months of insurance coverage. This means that the monthly cost was $24,000 divided by 12 months, or $2,000. As of December 31, the company benefited from 3 months of coverage. Therefore, the expense should be the monthly $2,000 cost multiplied by the 3 months of benefit received, for a total of $6,000.

125. $600

The $3,600 covers 3 years of coverage, or 36 months. That makes the cost of the insurance $100 per month. The insurance was in force from July 1 through the end of the year, so 6 months of expense would be $600.

126. $90,000

Total liabilities and owners' equity decreased by $95,000 if the company had that amount in expenses. On the asset side, the depreciation expense decreased assets by $5,000. The remaining $90,000 must have been expenses paid in cash, which reduces total assets.

127. $130,100

Total expenses are $141,000. Depreciation expense is a non-cash item. The increase in accounts payable means that $2,400 of the expense was posted to a liability account, not paid in cash.

Cash payments are $141,000 – $8,500 – $2,400 = $130,100.

128. $489,000

Total expenses of $500,000, less the increase in wages payable of $3,500 and less the depreciation expense of $7,500, equals $489,000.

$500,000 – $3,500 – $7,500 = $489,000

129. $113,400

$139,000 in total expenses is reduced by $9,000 in depreciation expense. Depreciation is a non-cash item. Also, wages payable and sales tax payable did not use cash. Cash paid for expenses equals:

$139,000 – $9,000 – $12,000 – $4,600 = $113,400

Inventory increases and prepaid rent increases do not impact expenses.

130. $1,180,000

The total increase to cash should be calculated as $480,000 (collections of credit sales) plus $500,000 (customer deposits) and $200,000 (cash sales), for a total increase in cash of $1,180,000.

131. Receivables increased by $720,000.

The total impact on receivables is $1,200,000 (credit sales) minus $480,000 (collections), giving a total increase of $720,000.

132. Operating liabilities increased by $250,000.

You calculate the total impact to operating liabilities as the increase of $500,000 (when the customer deposits were made) minus the $250,000 decrease (when 50% of the products/services were provided) to give a total increase of $250,000.

133. Retained earnings increased by $1,650,000.

First, you must identify the transactions that influence retained earnings (revenues and expenses), and then you must calculate the net income (or impact to retained earnings). In this example we have only revenues. The revenues include credit sales of $1,200,000, delivery of $250,000 of advance sales (calculated as 50% of the $500,000 of advance sales), and cash sales of $200,000 for a total of $1,650,000.

134. Total assets increased by $1,900,000.

You must first determine which transactions affect assets and whether they increase or decrease the assets.

Credit sales of $1,200,000 increase accounts receivable. Cash sales of $200,000 increase cash by this amount because cash is received.

Customer deposits of $500,000 increase cash by this amount because the company receives the cash in advance of the sale (deposit).

Amount of credit sales collected ($480,000) increases cash but decreases receivables, so there is no net impact to assets.

The percentage of customer deposits delivered later in the year (50%) does not impact assets. When those products are delivered, the liability is decreased and revenue is increased.

$$1{,}200{,}000 + 200{,}000 + 500{,}000 = 1{,}900{,}000$$

135. Property, plant, and equipment decreased by $10,000.

First, you need to identify the transactions that impacted property, plant, and equipment. In this case, the purchases of assets and the depreciation expense are the only transactions that impacted property, plant, and equipment. Thus, purchases of $5,000 (increase in property, plant, and equipment) less depreciation of $15,000 (decrease in property, plant, and equipment) equals a decrease in property, plant, and equipment of $10,000.

136. Retained earnings decreased by $300,000.

Retained earnings refer to the net income (or revenues minus expenses). In this case, you are told that total expenses were $300,000, so you know that this is the amount by which retained earnings decreased.

137. Total assets decreased by $275,000.

Remember that assets are equal to liabilities plus owners' equity. In this case, owners' equity includes only retained earnings or expenses that decreased by $300,000. Liabilities increased by $25,000. Thus, you calculate the net impact on total liabilities and owners' equity as a decrease of $300,000 (equity) plus an increase of $25,000 (liabilities) for a total decrease of $275,000. Looking back at the accounting equation, if equity plus liabilities decreased by $275,000, then the change in assets must also be a decrease of $275,000 in order to maintain a balance in the accounting equation.

138. Total liabilities and owners' equity decreased by $275,000.

You are told in the problem that expenses (retained earnings or owners' equity) decreased by $300,000, and liabilities increased by $25,000. Thus, the total change is the $300,000 decrease in equity plus the $25,000 increase in liabilities for a total decrease of $275,000.

139. Cash decreased by $310,000.

The starting point for this question is the basic accounting equation (assets equal liabilities plus owners' equity). In this example, assets include cash (unknown amount), inventory (increase of $45,000), and property, plant, and equipment (decrease of $10,000) for a total increase of assets (excluding cash) of $35,000. Liabilities are an increase of $25,000. Equity (retained earnings) is a decrease of $300,000, for a total decrease in liabilities and equity of $275,000. Now you know that assets (excluding cash) increased by $35,000, and liabilities plus equity decreased by $275,000. Because the basic accounting equation must stay in balance, you can find the cash amount by taking the $275,000 decrease in liabilities plus equity and subtracting the $35,000 increase in assets (excluding cash) to get a cash decrease of $310,000.

140. revenues – expenses

You calculate profit as the difference between revenues and expenses.

141. interest-bearing liabilities and owners' invested capital

Interest-bearing liabilities and owners' invested capital accounts on the balance sheet are not affected by any revenue or expense transactions. Interest-bearing liabilities are only impacted by debt payments, which are balance sheet transactions. Owners' invested capital is impacted by contributions from owners and distributions to owners, transactions that do not impact profit.

142. Assets increased by $11,000, and total liabilities and owners' equity increased by $11,000.

Cash increased by $53,000 from sales and decreased by $42,000, for a net change of $11,000. This translates into a net increase of $11,000 in total assets. Owners' equity increased by the amount of sales and decreased by the amount of expenses, so the net change is an increase of $11,000, which translates into an increase in total liabilities and owners' equity of $11,000.

143. retained earnings

Retained earnings are the earnings/profit kept by a business since its inception. They represent earnings the company can invest back into the business.

144. Assets increased by $12,000, and total liabilities and owners' equity increased by $12,000.

Accounts receivable increased by $35,000 from sales and decreased by $33,000 from collections. Cash increased by $33,000 from collections and decreased by $23,000 from the payment of expenses, for a net increase in assets of $12,000. Owners' equity increased by the amount of sales and decreased by the amount of expenses, so the net change is an increase of $12,000, which translates into an increase in total liabilities and owners' equity of $12,000.

145. Operating liabilities increased by $2,500,000.

The transactions affecting operating liabilities include unearned revenue and accounts payable.

$$2,000,000 + 500,000 = 2,500,000$$

146. Total assets increased by $1,700,000.

Solving this problem is based on the understanding that total assets must equal total liabilities and owners' equity. It's easier to figure out the change in total liabilities and owners' equity. Operating liabilities increased by $2,500,000 as a result of increased unearned revenue and increased accounts payable. Owners' retained earnings increased by the amount of sales, $3,200,000, and decreased by the amount of expenses, $4,000,000. The net effect on the liability and owners' equity side is an increase of $1,700,000.

$$2,000,000 + 500,000 + 3,200,000 - 4,000,000 = 1,700,000$$

That means that assets must have also increased by $1,700,000.

147. Net loss is $800,000.

The only relevant information is the amount of sales and expenses.

$$3,200,000 - 4,000,000 = -800,000$$

The unearned revenue has no effect on sales, and the increase in accounts payable and inventory has no effect on expenses.

148. Cash decreased by $1,900,000.

Solving this problem is based on the understanding that total assets must equal total liabilities and owners' equity. It's easier to figure out the change in total liabilities and owners' equity. Operating liabilities increased by $2,500,000 as a result of increased unearned revenue and increased accounts payable. Owners' retained earnings increased by the amount of sales, $3,200,000, and decreased by the amount of expenses, $4,000,000. The net effect on the liability and owners' equity side is an increase of $1,700,000.

$$2,000,000 + 500,000 + 3,200,000 - 4,000,000 = 1,700,000$$

That means that assets must have also increased by $1,700,000. Accounts receivable increased by $1,200,000, and inventory increased by $2,500,000. Property, plant, and equipment net decreased by $100,000.

$$1,200,000 + 2,500,000 - 100,000 = 3,600,000$$

The net effect of these changes is an increase of $3,600,000. However, the total increase in assets is only $1,700,000, so cash must have decreased by $1,900,000.

149. Accounts hold the historical record of transactions for a category of activities.

Accounts are used to record data by category. This data is later used to create financial reports. Companies are free to set up their own accounts, and there's no standard that should be followed.

150. Contra accounts record the negative side of certain accounts.

Contra accounts can be used for various purposes and are basically the negative side of certain accounts. For example, accumulated depreciation is a contra account to a fixed asset account. Sales returns and allowances is a contra account to a revenue account.

151. accumulated depreciation

Accumulated depreciation is a contra account because it offsets the fixed asset account. When depreciation is recorded and the asset value is decreased, the decrease is recorded in the accumulated depreciation account instead of the fixed asset account.

152. information needed to prepare financial statements

When first establishing a chart of accounts, you should consider the information needed for the tax return, for management reports, and to prepare financial statements. There are no standard or recommended charts of accounts. Also, a chart of accounts should be as detailed as necessary.

153. an index of all accounts

A *chart of accounts* is a listing of all accounts that the business uses. It doesn't show the balances of the accounts. You can think of it as a file cabinet with empty files (accounts).

154. asset accounts

In the United States, most companies begin their charts of accounts with asset accounts.

155. account number and account name

A chart of accounts is a listing of account numbers and account names. It doesn't include amounts or balances, and the classification is determined by the numbering scheme. For example, a company may decide that accounts starting with 1 are cash accounts and accounts starting with 5 are revenue accounts.

156. rent expenses

Expense for renting warehouse space would be recorded in a rent expenses account.

157. sales revenue and accounts receivable

Sales should be recorded in a sales revenue account, and amounts sold to customers on account should be recorded in an accounts receivable account.

158. cash and unearned revenue

If a sale is made and the cash is received before the product or service is delivered, the company has an obligation to provide it in the future. That liability is called *unearned revenue*.

159. asset accounts, liability accounts, and equity accounts

Real accounts (permanent accounts) are balance sheet accounts that include asset, liability, and equity accounts.

160. revenue and expense accounts

Revenue and expense accounts (income statement accounts) are called *nominal* or *temporary* accounts. They're temporary because they're zeroed out at the end of the year.

161. balance sheet accounts

Real accounts are balance sheet accounts. They're permanent accounts that show balances at a point in time based on activity accumulated since the inception of the business.

162. Nominal accounts are reported on the income statement.

Nominal accounts are income statement accounts. They're temporary accounts that show activity during a period of time.

163. Nominal accounts are closed to reset all the balances to zero for the next year.

Income statement accounts (nominal accounts) are closed at the end of an accounting period to zero out all revenues and expenses for the year and start the next year with zero balances.

164. rent expense

Rent expense is an expense account. Therefore, it's a nominal (temporary) account.

165. interest income

Interest income is a revenue account. Therefore, it's a nominal (temporary) account.

166. inventory

Inventory is an asset account or a balance sheet account. Therefore, it's a real (permanent) account.

167. unearned revenue

Unearned revenue is a liability account or a balance sheet account. Therefore, it's a real (permanent) account.

168. owners' capital

Owners' capital is an equity account or a balance sheet account. Therefore, it's a real (permanent) account.

169. the debit side

The left side of an account is the debit side, and the right side is the credit side.

170. the credit side

The right side of an account is the credit side, and the left side is the debit side.

171. a visual way of showing the basic form of an account

T accounts aren't actual accounts where accounting records are maintained. Instead, they're just a visual way of presenting the basic form of an account.

172. asset and expense accounts

Assets and expenses increase on the debit side. Liabilities, equity, and revenue accounts all increase on the credit side. This allows the accounting equation to stay balanced.

173. liabilities, equity, and revenue accounts

Liabilities, equity, and revenue accounts all increase on the credit side. Asset and expenses increase on the debit side. This allows the accounting equation to stay balanced.

174. as debits

Double-entry accounting uses debits and credits to record transactions. Liabilities decrease on the debit side and increase on the credit side.

175. as credits

Double-entry accounting uses debits and credits to record transactions. Revenues increase on the credit side.

176. the side that increases the account's balance

Normal account balance depends on the account type, but it's always the side (debit or credit) that increases the account's balance.

177. assets, expenses, and dividends

Assets, expenses, and dividends are debit balance accounts because they increase on the debit side. Therefore, they each have a normal debit balance.

178. liabilities, revenues, and retained earnings

Liabilities, revenues, and retained earnings are credit balance accounts because they increase on the credit side. Therefore, they have normal credit balances.

179. a debit to an asset account for $2,000 and a credit to another asset account for $2,000

Collection of outstanding receivables increases cash by $2,000 and decreases accounts receivable by $2,000. Therefore, an asset account (cash) should be debited (increased) $2,000, and another asset account (accounts receivable) should be credited (decreased) $2,000.

180. asset accounts

Asset accounts are increased on the debit side. Therefore, they have a normal debit balance.

181. recording an amount on the right side of an account

Crediting an account means recording an amount on the right side of an account.

182. credit to another account for $800

The company has a debit of $1,000 and a credit of $200, so the entry doesn't balance. If you take the debit of $1,000 less the credit of $200, you can see the entry is off by a credit of $800. To make the entry balance, the company needs to record another credit of $800 and such a credit could be recorded to another account. The account could be a balance sheet or income statement account.

183. the total debits exceed the total credits

A debit balance reflects that the total of debits is greater than the total of credits. An account with a normal debit balance is an account that increases on the debit side but could still have a credit balance.

184. recording journal entries

Posting is the process of recording journal entries.

185. the date of the transaction, the account numbers, account names, and amounts to be debited and credited

A *journal entry* is a record of transactions that includes the date of the transaction, the account numbers, account names, and amounts to be debited and credited.

186. expense journal

Examples of specialized journals include sales journals, payroll journals, cash receipts journals, and disbursement journals.

187. non-routine accounting entries

The general journal is reserved for non-routine transactions as well as those that don't occur often and closing entries.

188. The company made a $5,000 cash sale.

Debit to cash increases cash. Therefore, cash was received. Credit to revenues increases revenues, so a sale was made.

189. The company sold $5,000 of product and recorded a decrease in inventory and an increase in cost of goods sold.

Credit to inventory decreases the balance and a debit to an expense (cost of goods sold) increases the amount of the expense. Thus, the company sold $5,000 of its inventory.

190. debit cash and credit accounts receivable

A payment received from a customer increases the cash balance (debit to cash) and decreases the receivable balance (credit to receivable).

191. debit inventory $12,000 and credit accounts payable $12,000

Purchase of inventory increases the balance of inventory. Therefore, the inventory account needs to be debited. Purchasing something on account means that the supplier extended credit; thus the proper account is accounts payable.

192. debit accounts payable and credit cash

A payment on an outstanding balance owed to a supplier decreases cash and decreases the amount owed (accounts payable). Therefore, accounts payable must be debited, and cash must be credited.

193. debit cash $100,000 and credit bank loan $100,000

The bank loan increases the cash balance and increases the bank loan liability. Both accounts must be increased by $100,000. Cash is increased as a debit, and a liability is increased as a credit. The interest isn't recorded until the end of the accounting cycle, when it has actually been incurred.

194. debit cash and credit owners' invested capital $25,000

Owners' cash investment increases cash (debit to cash) and increases the owners' invested capital equity account (credit). The retained earnings account isn't impacted by this transaction because retained earnings relate to the profit and loss generated by the business.

195. debit salary expenses $8,000 and credit cash $8,000

Payment of salaries decreases cash (credit) by $8,000 and increases the salary expenses (debit).

196. debit loan payable and credit cash

Payment on a loan decreases cash (credit to cash) and decreases the loan payable account (debit to loan payable).

197. debit prepaid rent $1,500 and credit cash $1,500

Payment of rent decreases cash (credit) by $1,500 and increases (debit) the prepaid rent by the same amount.

198. debit equipment $20,000, credit cash $10,000, and credit loan payable $10,000

Purchase of a truck for $20,000 increases the equipment account by $20,000 (debit). The purchase was paid for 50% with cash and 50% with a loan. Thus, the amount of cash paid was ($20,000) (50%) = $10,000, and cash needs to decrease (credit) by that amount, and a new loan liability must increase (credit) by $10,000.

199. $4,900

Cash is recorded at the net amount because the credit card fee is automatically deducted from the amount of cash the seller receives. In this case, total sales were $5,000, but you need to deduct the $100 of fees for a net amount of cash of $4,900.

200. receives cash equal to the amount of sale less any credit card fees

When a company accepts credit card payments, it must pay a fee. Therefore, the amount of cash it receives is the amount of the sale less the amount of the fee.

201. increase sales, because customers enjoy the convenience of credit cards

Customers demand the convenience of paying with a credit card, so sellers don't have a choice but to pay the fee.

202. $625

In this question, a company had $25,000 of credit card sales and was required to pay a 2.5% fee to the credit card processor. Thus, the total fee amount is 2.5% multiplied by $25,000 to give a total of $625.

203. debit cash $40,000 and sales revenue $40,000

Cash sales increase cash (debit) by $40,000 and increase sales revenues (credit) by $40,000.

204. $2,940

The credit card fee is 2% times the amount of credit card sales ($3,000), giving a total of $60. The amount of the sale is $3,000, but out of this amount, $60 is the credit card fee. Thus, the seller will receive the amount of the sales minus the fee, which gives $2,940.

205. debit cash $49,000, debit credit card expenses $1,000, and credit sales revenues $50,000

Credit card sales of $50,000 result in a credit (increase) to sales revenues of $50,000. The credit card fee equals ($50,000) (0.02) = $1,000 and should be recorded as a debit (increase) to credit card expense. The amount of cash received is the amount of the sales ($50,000) less the credit card fee ($1,000) and should be debited (increase) to cash.

206. debit accounts receivable $20,000 and credit sales revenue $20,000

Credit sales (sales on account) increase accounts receivable (debit) and increase sales revenues (credit). Thus, the journal entry needs to debit (increase) accounts receivable by $20,000 and credit (increase) sales revenues by the same amount.

207. cash $115,800 and credit card fees $4,200

The amount of the credit card fee is calculated as the amount of credit card sales ($120,000) multiplied by the percentage fee (0.035), totaling $4,200. The next step is to calculate the amount of cash received. Do this by taking the amount of credit card sales ($120,000) less the amount of the fee ($4,200), totaling $115,800. Therefore, an entry needs to be recorded to increase cash (debit) $115,800 and to increase (debit) credit card fees $4,200.

208. $10,000

Sales revenue is recorded as the gross amount or the total amount of the sale before the credit card fee is considered.

209. liability income

Sales revenue, service revenue, interest income, and investment income are all examples of income. There is no such thing as liability income.

210. Investment income is reported on the income statement separately from sales revenues.

Investment income is reported on the income statement separately from sales revenues.

211. It decreases the amount of sales revenues.

Sales returns are recorded by debiting an account called *sales returns and allowances.* This account is a contra revenue account, and it records decreases in total revenues.

212. debit sales returns and allowances $3,000 and credit cash $3,000

When cash is refunded to the customer, a credit to cash needs to be recorded. Returns are recorded by debiting sales returns and allowances.

213. revenue for the full sales amount before the credit card fee amount

When customers pay with credit cards, the sellers record revenue at the full amount of the sale.

214. debit inventory $1,000 and credit cost of goods sold $1,000

When inventory is returned, it needs to be recorded back on the books by debiting (increasing) the inventory balance. Also, the previously recorded cost of goods sold needs to be reversed and removed from the accounting records by crediting it.

215. debit cash $500 and credit interest income $500

The $500 of cash received as interest should be recorded as a debit (increase) to cash, and the credit should be recorded to interest income to reflect the increase in revenue.

216. debit cash $31,630, debit accounts receivable $32,500, debit credit card fee $370, and credit sales revenue $64,500

First determine the amount of cash. Calculate cash from credit card sales by taking the total credit card sales ($18,500) and subtracting the credit card fee of 2% of $18,500 ($370), for a total of $18,130. Thus, total cash includes cash sales of $13,500 and cash from credit card sales of $18,130, for a total of $31,630. Record cash of $31,630 as a debit. The next debit is to accounts receivable from credit sales, which equal $32,500. Record the credit card fee of $370 as a debit (increase) to credit card fees. Finally, total revenue is the sum of cash sales of $13,500 plus credit sales of $32,500 plus credit card sales of $18,500, or a total of $64,500, and should be recorded as a credit to sales revenue.

217. $45,000

Revenue is calculated as sales on account of $20,000 plus the cash sales of $10,000 plus credit card sales of $15,000, totaling $45,000.

218. $24,700

Cash recorded for the day includes cash received from the credit card sales and cash sales. First you should calculate cash received from credit card sales. Credit card sales were $15,000, but the company has to pay a 2% fee to the bank. Thus, (.02) ($15,000) = $300 is the fee, so the company receives only the net amount, or $15,000 less $300 for a total of $14,700 from credit card sales. Now you're ready to calculate the total cash recorded. This includes the $14,700 received from credit card plus $10,000 received from credit card sales for a total of $24,700.

219. There is no correct number of expense accounts. Businesses set up their expense accounts based on their own reporting needs.

There is no predetermined number of expense accounts for the chart of accounts. Each business sets up its own chart of accounts based on its reporting needs. Charts of accounts are company-specific, and what works for one company may not work for another.

220. decreasing assets

Expenses can be recorded by either decreasing assets (for example, decreasing cash when an expense is paid) or by increasing liabilities (for example, by increasing accounts payable).

221. increasing liabilities

Expenses can be recorded by either increasing liabilities (for example, by increasing accounts payable) or by decreasing assets (for example, decreasing cash when an expense is paid).

222. assets or liabilities

When expenses are recorded (debited), balance sheet accounts such as assets or liabilities are credited. For example, when a company pays its employees their wages, the company records a debit (increase) to payroll expense and a credit (decrease) to cash.

223. cost of goods sold

When cost of goods sold is recorded (debited/increased), inventory is credited (decreased).

224. accounts receivable

When bad debt expense is recorded (debited), the uncollectible accounts receivable are credited to remove them from the accounting records.

225. It causes assets to decrease.

When expenses are paid with cash, cash decreases. Therefore, assets decrease.

226. Expenses decrease owners' equity.

Expenses are recorded on the income statement, and as such, they decrease net income, so they decrease retained earnings (owners' equity).

227. debit utilities expense $550 and credit cash $550

When expenses are paid with cash, cash decreases and so it must be credited. Expenses increase as debits, and therefore, a debit must be recorded to utilities expense.

228. debit rent expense $2,500 and credit cash $2,500

When expenses are paid with cash, cash decreases and so it must be credited. Expenses increase as debits, and therefore, a debit must be recorded to rent expense.

229. debit salary expense $25,000 and credit cash $25,000

When expenses are paid with cash, cash decreases and so it must be credited. Expenses increase as debits, and therefore, a debit must be recorded to salary expense.

230. a contra asset account

Accumulated depreciation decreases the value of the fixed asset. Therefore, it's a contra asset account.

231. debiting depreciation expense and crediting accumulated depreciation

Depreciation is a rational method of allocating the costs of the asset into future periods. As such, it increases expense and decreases the value of the asset. The entry to record it is a debit to depreciation expenses and a credit to accumulated depreciation (contra account).

232. debit cost of goods sold $12,000 and credit inventory $12,000

When inventory is sold, two entries must be recorded: one to record the sale and one to record the cost of goods sold. The cost of goods sold is recorded as a debit (increase) to cost of goods sold and a credit (decrease) to inventory for the amount of the cost of the sold inventory, or $12,000 in this case.

233. debit bad debt expense $100,000 and credit accounts receivable $100,000

When accounts receivable are determined to be uncollectible, they should be written off. They're written off by crediting (decreasing) accounts receivable and debiting (increasing) bad debt expense.

234. It's the negative side for fixed assets.

Accumulated depreciation is a contra account to fixed assets. That means that the depreciation amounts are recorded in the accumulated depreciation account instead of the fixed asset account.

235. debit depreciation expense $6,500 and credit accumulated depreciation $6,500

Recording depreciation increases depreciation expense (debit) and increases accumulated depreciation (credit).

236. vacation accrual

Vacation and sick pay benefits build up in accounts over time as employees earn them throughout the year. The liability associated with those benefits (vacation accrual) continues to increase until time off is actually taken. The expense is recorded when the liability is built up, not when the vacation time is taken.

237. debit consulting services expense $5,000 and credit accounts payable $5,000

Consulting services expense should be increased (debit) because the expense was already incurred when the services were performed. The invoice won't be paid until it's due; therefore, the credit should be recorded to accounts payable to increase the liability.

238. pension expenses and pension obligation

Accounting for retirement benefits can be complex, as it requires specialists to determine the annual cost of defined benefit pension plans. The two primary issues revolve around the amount of pension obligation/liability and the expense.

239. Set-up and follow-up transactions take place before or after revenues and expenses are recorded.

Set-up and follow-up transactions support the profit-making transaction of the business, and as such, they take place either before or after revenues and expenses are recorded.

240. paying for office supplies in advance

Paying for office supplies in advance is an example of a set-up and follow-up transaction.

241. processing sales returns

Processing sales returns isn't an example of a set-up and follow-up transaction.

242. collecting receivables

Collecting receivables is an example of a set-up and follow-up transaction.

243. asset

Asset accounts are prepaid because they reflect expenses that have been paid in advance, thereby providing a future benefit to the business.

244. prepaid rent

Prepaid rent is an asset because the company will receive a future benefit as a result of paying for rent early.

245. debit prepaid insurance $22,000 and credit cash $22,000

When a payment is made in advance (covering six months of insurance premiums), it's considered prepaid. Therefore, prepaid insurance should be increased (debited), and cash should be decreased (credited) for the amount of the payment.

246. expenses that are paid before they're used

Prepaids are expenses that are paid in advance, and the expense has not been incurred or used yet.

247. debit supplies inventory and credit cash $2,000

The shipping supplies are an asset to the company until they're used to package and ship a product. The company must debit (increase) the asset account supplies inventory and then credit (reduce) cash for the amount paid.

248. debit prepaid insurance and credit cash $120,000

The insurance is an asset when it is purchased because it will provide benefits to the company in the future. The insurance coverage doesn't become an expense until time passes. When insurance is purchased for future coverage, an asset account, prepaid insurance, is increased with a debit. Cash is decreased with a credit.

249. purchase of inventory with cash

Purchase of inventory with cash increases inventory and decreases cash, both of which are asset accounts.

250. debit accounts payable $10,000 and credit cash $10,000

The original purchase was recorded as a debit to inventory and a credit to accounts payable for $20,000. When a 50% payment is made, the entry should credit (decrease) cash and debit (decrease) accounts payable. The amount of the payment is calculated as ($20,000) (.5) = $10,000.

251. the balance sheet because purchases of inventory are recorded as assets until they're sold

Inventory is an asset until it's sold, when it becomes part of cost of goods sold, an expense. Assets are on the balance sheet.

252. debit prepaid expenses $90,000 and credit accounts payable $90,000

Because the paper will be used over the next three months, it's a prepaid (or could be considered inventory). Therefore, a debit (increase) to a prepaid should be recorded, along with a corresponding credit (increase) to accounts payable because the purchase was made on account.

253. debit printing expense $30,000 and credit prepaid expenses $30,000

When the paper is used, the company needs to move $30,000 from the prepaid account to an expense account. This is done by crediting (decreasing) the prepaid and debiting (increasing) an expense account.

254. debit cash $88,200, debit sales discounts $1,800, and credit accounts receivable $90,000

When the sale was first recorded, the full amount ($90,000) was recorded in accounts receivable (regardless of the discount offered). When the payment is received, the full amount ($90,000) must be credited (decreased) from accounts receivable. Because the customer paid on time and took the discount, the amount of the cash received is decreased by the discount, which can be calculated as

$$90{,}000 - (.02 \times 90{,}000) = 88{,}200$$

255. debit accounts payable $10,000 and credit prepaid expense $10,000

The entry recorded by the textbook publisher (customer) is to decrease (credit) the previously recorded prepaid expenses and to decrease (debit) accounts payable.

256. $30,000

The company uses $30,000 worth of paper a month. In two months, it will use $60,000, leaving $30,000 in the prepaid expenses account.

257. $20,000

The expense for the third month is the amount remaining. In the first month the company used $30,000 and returned $10,000, leaving $50,000 worth of paper. In the second month it used another third of the amount purchased, or $30,000. That leaves $20,000 of paper in the third month.

258. only short-term loans due within one year

Liabilities due within one year or the operating cycle (whichever is longer) are considered short-term liabilities.

259. covenants

Covenants are restrictions placed on companies by the debt holders (banks).

260. acquisition of patents

Acquisition of patents is an investing activity because it's an acquisition of (or investment in) intangible assets.

261. capital expenditures

Purchases of long-term assets to be used in the operations of the business are often called *capital expenditures.*

262. property, plant, and equipment

When fixed assets are presented on a balance sheet, they're referred to as *property, plant, and equipment.* They're also frequently abbreviated as PP&E.

263. either selling them, exchanging them for a new asset, or scrapping them

Fixed assets can be disposed of by sale, exchange, or scrapping.

264. financing

Financing transactions include borrowing money, repaying borrowed money, raising capital from shareholders, and returning invested capital to owners.

265. debit property, plant, and equipment $2,000,000; credit cash $1,000,000; and credit loan payable $1,000,000

Property, plant, and equipment increases as a result of the purchase, so it should be debited. Cash decreases, so it should be credited, and the company has a loan, a liability, that is increased.

266. debit property, plant, and equipment $200,000 and credit loan payable $200,000

The interest on the loan isn't recorded until the end of the accounting period. Therefore, when the loan is first initiated, the company has to record a credit to loans payable for the face value of the loan, or $200,000, and debit the equipment for $200,000.

267. debt and equity capital

Debt capital is one of the two sources of capital. The second source is equity capital. The two sources differ and are not similar.

268. as a $2,000,000 asset and a $2,000,000 liability on the balance sheet

The new building is an asset listed under property, plant, and equipment on the balance sheet. Interest-bearing debt is a liability and is reported as such on the balance sheet.

269. debit retained earnings and credit cash $250,000

Both cash and retained earnings are reduced. The debit is to retained earnings and the credit is to cash.

270. buying a piece of land to be used in constructing a new factory

Capital expenditures is another term used to describe purchases of fixed assets.

271. debt

Debt has no impact on revenues. However, it's used to finance purchases of fixed assets. Lines of credit can be used to finance operating cash needs. Bonds can be issued to raise capital and to finance the short-term cash needs of a business.

272. inventory

Inventory is an asset held for sale and not a capital expenditure. Capital expenditures are purchases of long-term operating assets.

273. $87,000

The following cash amounts are recorded to cash: $2,000 (purchase of computers with cash), $15,000 (down payment on machinery), and $70,000 (down payment on building) for a total of $87,000.

274. The transactions result in credits to accounts payable totaling $35,000.

As a result of these transactions, a credit to accounts payable is recorded for $5,000 for the purchase of office furniture, and a credit to accounts payable is recorded for $30,000 for the purchase of inventory. Thus, the total credit is the sum of $5,000 and $30,000, or $35,000.

275. credit to loans payable $315,000

There are two loans in this example: loan for machinery and the building loan. The machinery loan amount is 70% of the $50,000 purchase price, or $35,000. The loan for the building is 80% of the $350,000 purchase price, or $280,000. Thus, the total credit to loans payable is the sum of those two loan amounts, or $35,000 plus $280,000 for a total of $315,000.

276. $407,000

Total fixed assets include office furniture, computers, machinery, and building. Thus, $5,000 (office furniture) plus $2,000 (computers) plus $50,000 (machinery) plus $350,000 (building) equals $407,000.

277. Financing and investing transactions are not as frequent as other types of business transactions.

The majority of business transactions are sales, expenses, and set-up and follow-up transactions.

278. statement of cash flows

Financing and investing activities are reported on the statement of cash flows. The statement of cash flows includes operating, financing, and investing activities.

279. employees

Equity capital normally comes from institutions, banks, venture capitalists, or individuals.

280. equity on the balance sheet

Equity capital is part of the equity section of the balance sheet.

281. debit cash $1,000,000 and credit owners' invested capital $1,000,000

As a result of the owner investing in the business, the cash increases (debit) by $1,000,000, and owners' invested capital increases (credit).

282. debit retained earnings $500,000 and credit cash $500,000

Dividends are paid out of retained earnings and are not an expense. Cash decreases (credit) when dividends are paid.

283. debit dividends $500,000 and credit cash $500,000

In the two-entry approach, the first entry decreases cash (credit) and increases dividends (debit).

284. debit retained earnings $500,000 and credit dividends $500,000

In the two-entry approach, the second entry credits dividends and debits retained earnings to show that dividends are being paid out of retained earnings.

285. common and preferred

Companies can issue either preferred or common stock.

286. debit cash and credit owners' invested capital

When a company issues stock it receives cash. Thus, cash is increased as a debit and owners' invested capital is credited.

287. operating

Paying operating liabilities is an operating activity because it's part of the day-to-day transactions.

288. ownership capital

Equity is the ownership capital of a business. It's the residual interest in assets of a business after deducting all liabilities.

289. assets less liabilities

The basic accounting equation states: assets = liabilities + owners' equity. Owners' equity includes invested capital and retained earnings. Thus, equity can equal either invested capital plus retained earnings or assets less liabilities.

290. Total equity equals $2,000,000.

Total equity is the difference between assets and liabilities; therefore total equity must be $2,000,000. It's possible for the company to have a retained earnings loss. For example, if assets are $5,000,000, liabilities are $3,000,000, and invested capital is $4,000,000, then retained earnings would have to be a loss of $2,000,000 to keep the accounting equation in balance. Also, it's possible for the company to just start operations and have no retained earnings. In this case, the invested capital would be $2,000,000.

291. net worth

The net worth of a business can be determined by looking at total assets and deducting total liabilities. Total assets less total liabilities is also called *owners' equity.*

292. issuing shares of stock

Companies can generate capital by issuing equity such as issuing shares of stock. Issuing debt, obtaining a loan, and issuing bonds are all examples of debt capital. Paying a dividend is a distribution of profit.

293. common stock

Companies frequently raise capital by issuing stock. The two main types of stocks are common stocks and preferred stocks. However, common stock, as the name suggests, is the most frequently issued stock.

294. Common stockholders have voting rights.

One of the advantages of common stock is that common stockholders have voting rights when it comes to certain company matters. Common stock doesn't guarantee an annual dividend, and common stockholders are the last to get paid in case of a bankruptcy. Common stock of a publicly traded company is available to everyone.

295. Preferred stockholders receive a dividend before common stockholders do.

Preferred stockholders have a preference to receive a dividend first before the common stockholders, but dividends are not guaranteed.

296. zero

This transaction is a financing activity. The borrowing does not increase revenue, even though the company receives cash. The sale of stock does not increase revenue, even though the company receives cash. Revenue is increased by the sale of products and services.

297. accountants

Year-end financial statements are prepared by a company's accountants and reviewed by management and the board of directors.

298. Adjusting entries are recorded at year-end to make sure all expenses, revenue, and income entries are recorded accurately.

Adjusting entries are part of the accounting process and are necessary to make sure all revenues, expenses, and income entries are recorded in the financial statements.

299. to make final entries for the year and ensure that financial statements are accurate and complete

Adjusting entries are necessary to record final year-end entries. These entries ensure the completeness and accuracy of the year-end financial statements. They're part of the normal end-of-period accounting process.

300. debit cost of goods sold $20,000 and credit inventory $20,000

Because the sale portion of the transaction was already recorded, the only portion that still needs to be recorded is the decrease to inventory and increase to cost of goods sold. The cost of the inventory was $20,000; therefore, the cost of goods sold needs to be debited (increased) $20,000, and inventory needs to be credited (decreased) $20,000.

301. debit utility expense $500 and credit accounts payable $500

The bill hasn't been received, but the expense relates to December. Therefore, the company must record the estimated amount by increasing (debiting) utility expense and crediting (increasing) accounts payable.

302. An adjustment entry is necessary to correct the amount from $12,540 to $12,450 and to record the purchase as inventory instead of equipment.

It appears that digits were transposed when the transaction was recorded, an error that should be fixed with an adjusting entry. Also, the purchase was incorrectly recorded as equipment, and it should be posted to inventory.

303. debit accounts receivable $40,000 and credit sales revenues $40,000

Because the cost of the transaction was already recorded, the only missing entry is the entry to record sales. Sales revenues need to be increased (credited) by $40,000, and accounts receivable need to be increased (debited) by the same amount.

304. debit salary expense $2,000 and credit cash $2,000

Because an entry was forgotten, an additional expense of $2,000 needs to be recorded to salary expense (debit). Because the salaries were already paid, the credit needs to be recorded to cash to decrease the balance.

305. debit sales revenue $5,000 and credit accounts receivable $5,000

The original transaction recorded a credit to sales revenue for $60,000 instead of $55,000. Therefore, a sales revenue debit of $5,000 is needed to correct the transaction. Similarly, the original transaction recorded a debit to accounts receivable of $60,000 instead of $55,000, so an accounts receivable credit of $5,000 is needed to correct the balance.

306. debit accounts payable $900 and credit consulting services $900

The company mistakenly recorded consulting services of $2,140 and accounts payable of $2,140. However, the invoice amount was only $1,240, which is $900 less than the amount recorded. Therefore, an adjusting entry is necessary to decrease the consulting services expense by $900 (credit) and decrease accounts payable by the same amount (debit).

307. controller

In the United States, the chief accountant responsible for the financial statements is known as the *controller*. This person is the top-level accounting officer in an organization.

308. A controller is usually the one who makes the year-end adjusting entries.

A controller is ultimately responsible for the year-end adjustments and is involved in reviewing them. Adjustments are typically posted by staff-level accountants.

309. Bookkeeping is the process of accumulating, organizing, storing, and accessing financial data. Accounting is the analysis of the data and financial reporting.

Bookkeeping and accounting are not the same. Bookkeeping has a much narrower scope and focuses on recording the transactions, while accounting focuses on analyzing the transactions and preparing the financial statements.

310. to allocate the cost of a fixed asset over the years of its useful life

Depreciation is not related to the value of an asset. Instead, it's the process of spreading the cost of an asset over its useful life.

311. Estimated lives of fixed assets are estimates determined by each company.

The only standards for depreciation of estimated lives are set by the Internal Revenue Code for tax purposes, but they're not required for financial accounting. Useful lives are usually determined for each category of assets such as buildings, trucks, or computers, and they're estimated by each company.

312. The straight-line depreciation method allocates the same amount of depreciation to each year of useful life of an asset.

Companies are not required to use the straight-line depreciation method for their fixed assets, but most companies prefer it because it allocates the same amount of depreciation to each year the asset is in use.

313. debit depreciation expense–machinery $1,500 and credit accumulated depreciation–machinery $1,500

Annual depreciation is calculated as the cost of an asset divided by its useful life. In this case, the machinery was purchased for $90,000 and has a useful life of 5 years. Thus, the annual amount of depreciation should be $90,000 (purchase price of the machine) divided by 5 years, or $18,000 per year. In this example, the company already recorded 11 months of depreciation and needs to record only one more month. So, you need to find the monthly depreciation, which you calculate by dividing the annual depreciation of $18,000 by 12 months, or $1,500 per month. The adjusting entry should be recorded as a debit to depreciation expense and a credit to accumulated depreciation for $1,500, or one month's worth of depreciation.

314. debit depreciation expenses–equipment $5,000 and credit accumulated depreciation–equipment $5,000

Annual depreciation is calculated as the cost of an asset divided by its useful life. In this case, the truck was purchased for $25,000 and has a useful life of 5 years. Thus, the amount of depreciation should be $25,000 (purchase price of the truck) divided by 5 years, or $5,000 per year. The annual entry to record the depreciation should be a debit to depreciation expense and a credit to accumulated depreciation.

315. $2,000

Because the equipment was purchased on October 1, the company has only had it for 3 months of the year (October, November, and December), and it needs to depreciate it only for the 3 months — or one-fourth of the year. You calculate quarterly depreciation as the purchase price of the equipment ($24,000) divided by the useful life (3years) and then multiply that number by one-fourth:

$$\frac{24,000}{3} \times \frac{1}{4} = 2,000$$

316. debit accumulated depreciation $10,000 and credit fixed asset $10,000

When a fully disposed asset is retired, it needs to be removed from the financial record. The amount needs to credit fixed assets and debit accumulated depreciation to essentially reverse the previously recorded entry to purchase the asset and to record the depreciation.

317. $10,000

Annual depreciation is calculated as the purchase price less the salvage value divided by the useful life. In this case, the building was purchased for $450,000 and had an estimated salvage value of $50,000, meaning only $400,000 needs to be depreciated. Thus, the annual depreciation is

$$\frac{450,000 - 50,000}{40} = 10,000$$

318. Income before tax will be overstated by $40,000.

If depreciation expense is not recorded, then income before taxes will be too high by the amount of that expense. The depreciation expense that should have been recorded is

$$\frac{450{,}000-50{,}000}{10}=40{,}000$$

319. Total assets decrease because accumulated depreciation, a contra asset account, is increased.

The correct entry to record depreciation expense includes a debit to depreciation expense and a credit to accumulated depreciation. Accumulated depreciation is a contra asset account that reduces the property, plant, and equipment account. That reduction produces a decrease in assets.

320. they have no physical substance

Intangible assets can't be touched because they have no physical substance.

321. capitalized equipment

Capitalized equipment has physical substance; thus, it's a physical fixed asset and not an intangible asset.

322. amortization

Amortization is the process of allocating the cost of intangible assets over their useful lives.

323. Amortization is recorded as a debit to amortization expense and a credit to the intangible asset account.

Recording amortization is not done via a contra account. Instead, it's recorded directly as a credit to the asset account. The debit is recorded as amortization expense.

324. intangible assets

Examples of intangible assets include trademarks, patents, copyrights, and customer lists.

325. $48,000

Annual amortization is calculated as the purchase price of an intangible asset divided by the estimated life. Thus, in this case you should take the purchase price of $240,000 and divide it by 5 years to come up with $48,000 as the annual amortization.

326. debit franchise amortization $5,000 and credit franchise $5,000

The amount paid as a franchise fee was correctly classified as an intangible asset called a *franchise*. The amount now needs to be amortized. Annual amortization is calculated as the purchase price divided by the useful life. In this case, you divide the purchase price of $40,000 by the useful life of 8 to arrive at an annual amortization of $5,000. Amortization is recorded as a debit to amortization expense and a credit directly to the asset account for $5,000.

327. $100,000 each year for 5 years

The cost of the intangible asset is allocated to the time period it's used by the company, or 5 years:

$$\frac{500,000}{5} = 100,000$$

328. Total assets remain the same because cash decreases and intangible assets increase by $1,000,000.

A current asset, cash, decreases by $1,000,000, and an intangible asset, patent, increases by $1,000,000, resulting in no change in total assets.

329. Income is overstated by $100,000, and assets are overstated by $100,000.

Recording annual amortization decreases income through amortization expense and reduces assets. Annual amortization is calculated as the purchase price divided by useful life. In this case, you divide the purchase price of $1,000,000 by the life of 5 years to get to an annual amortization of $200,000. However, the patent was purchased on July 1, so the company used it for only half a year. Therefore, the company needs to amortize it only for 6 months. To calculate the amount of amortization for 6 months, you take the annual amortization of $200,000 and divide it by 2 to arrive at $100,000.

330. to analyze the receivables based on how old they are and estimate the amount of uncollectible receivables

An *aging analysis* categorizes receivables based on how old they are. In general, the more past due the receivable, the less likely it is to be collected. Therefore, an aging analysis is used primarily to estimate how much of a company's receivable balance is uncollectible.

331. allowance method

The allowance method is based on estimates, and it records the estimated bad debt in the same accounting period as the revenue. This is the method that is required by accounting standards.

332. debit bad debt expense $50,000 and credit allowance for doubtful accounts $50,000

The company is using the allowance method because it estimated the amount of uncollectible receivables. Under the allowance method, the bad debt expense is increased (debited), and allowance for doubtful accounts is also increased (credited).

333. debit bad debt expense $10,000 and credit accounts receivable $10,000

Because the company identified the specific uncollectible accounts receivable, it's probably using the direct write-off method. The company needs to write off the uncollectible accounts immediately. The proper entry is to debit (increase) the bad debt expense and to credit (decrease) the specific accounts receivable accounts.

334. debit interest receivable $500 and credit interest income $500

Under accrual accounting, interest must be recorded when earned. Because the interest earned hasn't been received yet, the company has a receivable and should record it as a $500 debit to interest receivable and a $500 credit to interest income.

335. an accrual

Expenses that have been incurred but not paid must be recorded as accruals.

336. debit property tax expense $3,000 and credit property tax payable $3,000

The invoice must be accrued when received because it relates to 2015. The proper entry is to increase (debit) the property tax expense $3,000 and increase (credit) the property tax payable $3,000. This will ensure that the property tax expense is properly recognized in 2015.

337. debit legal expense $3,000 and credit accounts payable $3,000

The company knows it incurs approximately $1,000 of legal services each month, and the last quarter's invoice hasn't been received. An entry should be posted to accrue the last three months of legal services:

$$1{,}000 \times 3 = 3{,}000$$

A debit should be recorded to legal expense for $3,000 and a credit to accounts payable for the same amount.

338. debit interest expense and credit interest payable

When a company has an outstanding loan, it must pay interest in accordance with the terms of the agreement. Also, interest must be accrued in the period to which it relates, regardless of when it's paid. The accrual is recorded as an increase (debit) to interest expense and an increase (credit) to interest payable.

339. recording inventory purchases

Inventory purchases should be recorded on a regular basis as they occur and don't typically require a year-end adjusting entry.

340. expenses paid for in cash and recorded as assets before they're used

Prepaids are expenses that have been paid but have not been incurred. They're paid ahead of time.

341. insurance

Insurance is a great example of a prepaid because it's usually paid ahead of time. Companies frequently prepay insurance for 6 or 12 months in advance.

342. debit insurance expense $10,000 and credit prepaid insurance $10,000

The company purchased the policy on March 1 and used 10 months of the policy (March through December) as of the end of the year, so it needs to record the equivalent of 10 months of expenses as of the end of the year. You calculate this by taking the total annual policy amount of $12,000 and dividing it by 12 months in a year to get $1,000 as the monthly expense. Then, to determine 10 months, you just take the $1,000 monthly amount times 10 months to find $10,000. This amount must be recorded as a decrease (credit) to prepaid insurance and an increase (debit) to insurance expense.

343. Total assets remain unchanged because one asset, cash, is decreased and another asset, prepaid insurance, is increased for the same amount.

When the purchase of three years of insurance is recorded, cash is decreased and prepaid insurance is increased. Both of those accounts are assets, resulting in no change in total assets.

344. recording the adjusting entry for insurance expense for 2016

In 2015, only 10 months of insurance coverage will be an expense for the year, resulting in an asset decrease of $2,500. In 2016, though, the company will adjust for a whole year of coverage, or $3,000. The asset, prepaid insurance, will decrease by that amount.

345. All revenue and all expense accounts are closed.

Closing entries must be recorded to close out all revenue and expense accounts to get them ready for the next accounting period.

346. to transfer profit or loss to retained earnings

Closing entries must be done at the end of each accounting period to zero out the income statement accounts and transfer the profit or loss to retained earnings on the balance sheet.

347. zero out all revenue and expense accounts so they can be available for the next accounting period

Closing entries must be done at the end of each accounting period to zero out the income statement accounts and transfer the profit or loss to retained earnings on the balance sheet.

348. all temporary or nominal accounts

Income statement accounts are called *temporary accounts* or *nominal accounts* and must be closed out each year.

349. closing entries

Closing entries are recorded at the end of the year to zero out the income statement accounts and prepare them for the next year.

350. retained earnings

***Retained earnings* is an account on the balance sheet that records all profit and loss accumulated since the inception of the business. The profit and loss from the income statement must be transferred to retained earnings at the end of the year.**

351. revenue account

Revenue accounts are credit balance accounts, so they have to be debited to be zeroed out.

352. service revenue

Service revenue is a revenue account; thus, it needs to be closed at the end of the year. The remaining accounts provided are balance sheet accounts (assets and liabilities); thus, they remain open.

353. prepaid insurance

Prepaid insurance is an asset account and a permanent account. Therefore, it's not closed. The remaining accounts provided are income statement accounts and should be closed.

354. depreciation expense

Only income statement accounts are closed out at the end of the year, and this results in zero balances. Out of the accounts listed, only depreciation expense is an income statement account.

355. debit sales revenue and credit income summary

The closing entry zeros out the balance in the accounts. Because sales revenue is a credit account, a debit needs to be recorded to zero it out. So, the closing entry is a debit to the sales revenue account and a credit to the income summary.

356. zero balances

The purpose of the closing entries is to zero out the temporary accounts. Therefore the temporary accounts have zero balances after the closing entries are recorded.

357. credit expense accounts

The closing entries zero out the balances in the accounts. Because expenses are debit balance accounts, a credit must be recorded to zero out the accounts.

358. cost of goods sold

Cost of goods sold is an expense account, and it needs to be closed at the end of the year.

359. debit retained earnings and credit income summary

Net loss is recorded as a debit to retained earnings. Revenues are closed as debits and expenses are closed as credits. Net loss occurs when expenses exceed revenues. In such a case, the credits to close out expenses exceed the debits to close out revenues. Therefore, an additional debit is needed to balance the entry. This debit is made to retained earnings.

360. $30,000 to sales revenues

The balance in the sales revenues account is $30,000, and it's a credit account. Therefore, a debit must be recorded to zero it out.

361. profit of $6,000

Net income is calculated as total revenues less total expenses. In this example, total revenues are known to be $30,000, and you calculate total expenses by simply adding them up: cost of goods sold ($20,000) plus salary expense ($1,950) plus office expense ($2,000) plus income tax expense ($50) for a total of $24,000. Therefore, net income is $30,000 (total revenues) less $24,000 (total expenses), or $6,000.

362. $24,000

When the expense accounts are closed out at the end of the year, the account balances are zeroed out. To determine the total amount of credits to be recorded, you need to find the total balances in the expense accounts. Thus, cost of goods sold ($20,000) plus salary expense ($1,950) plus office expenses ($2,000) plus income tax ($50) gives a total of $24,000.

363. credit retained earnings $6,000

The amount recorded to retained earnings as a result of the year-end closing entry is net income. Net income is calculated as total revenues less total expenses. In this example, total revenues are known to be $30,000, and you calculate total expenses by simply adding them up: cost of goods sold ($20,000) plus salary expense ($1,950) plus office expenses ($2,000) plus income tax expense ($50) for a total of $24,000. Therefore, net income is $30,000 (total revenues) less $24,000 (total expenses), or $6,000, and it needs to be credited to retained earnings.

364. immaterial errors

Errors occur in all accounting systems, but internal controls should be in place to detect and correct any material errors. Financial statements should be free of material errors for the financial information to be useful and reliable to the decision-makers.

365. management

Internal controls involve everyone in a business, including management.

366. Internal controls are in place to protect and safeguard a company's assets.

The purpose of internal controls is to protect a company's assets.

367. a company's management and accounting department

Internal controls are designed by the company's management and accounting department.

368. to make financial statements look better

Fraud includes intentional actions and not errors, and the main reason management commits fraud is to make the financial statements look better.

369. potential for fraud

Strong internal controls call for an additional level of approval for cash disbursements over a certain amount. This ensures that larger disbursements have another person reviewing them.

370. cash

Cash is the account that is most vulnerable to fraud because of its immediate value.

371. on a monthly basis

Bank statement reconciliation should be completed every month and should be done by someone other than the person who handles the recording of cash.

372. management

Accounting fraud or financial statement fraud is a type of fraud that is usually committed by management to make a company's financial statements appear more profitable. Employee fraud probably occurs more frequently, but it does not involve financial statement fraud.

373. collusion

Collusion occurs when two or more people conspire together to bypass controls. Internal controls can't prevent collusion.

374. requiring all adjusting entries to be recorded before the books are closed

Recording adjusting entries is part of the accounting cycle and not related to internal controls.

375. assets

Organizations have internal controls in place to protect their assets.

376. theft

Controls protect from theft, embezzlement, and fraud.

377. accepting only cash payments

Accepting only cash payments is not a good control because cash is easily stolen. A good control would be not to accept cash at all.

378. bank charges

Bank charges would be recorded by the bank but not by the company because the company usually finds out about them when doing the reconciliation.

379. separation of duties

Separation of duties requires different persons to be responsible for each step in the process. It's the fundamental principle of internal controls because it makes it difficult for one individual to approve and execute a transaction by himself.

380. requiring a second signature on checks over a certain amount

Requiring a second signature on large checks is a common control in the payment cycle. Doing so ensures that two people look at the payment, thus making fraud more difficult.

381. Profit is the difference between revenues and expenses.

Profit is determined by summing up all revenues and subtracting all expenses.

382. Generally Accepted Accounting Principles

Generally Accepted Accounting Principles, or GAAP, is the set of standards that govern financial accounting in the United States.

383. selling products or services

Profit is generated by selling products or services. Companies can try to decrease costs to improve profits, but ultimately, if there are no sales, there will be no profit.

384. Sales revenues increase assets.

When a company sells a product to a customer, the customer is expected to either pay for it immediately with cash or pay for it in accordance with the terms of the agreement (accounts receivable). Thus, sales revenues increase either cash or accounts receivable. So an asset is increased when sales revenues are recorded.

385. Assets increased $300,000.

This question requires you to look at the basic accounting equation: assets = liabilities + owners' equity. If net income increased by $550,000, that means equity increased by $550,000. The decrease in liabilities is $250,000. All you need to do is plug in those numbers to the equation and solve for assets. Thus, assets equal the decrease in liabilities of $250,000 plus the increase in equity of $550,000, which equals $300,000 (note that liabilities are negative because they decreased).

386. revenues, expenses, and profit

The objective of the income statement is to report profit or net income. *Net income* is the difference between revenues and expenses, and those are also on the income statement.

387. total revenues and total expenses

The single-step income statement only reports the totals for revenues and expenses and doesn't provide any additional subtotals.

388. gross margin

Gross margin is the difference between sales revenues and cost of goods sold, and it appears only on the multi-step income statement.

389. cost of goods sold

Every company that sells a product has an expense of cost of goods sold. This expense reflects the cost to the company of the product that it sold during the period.

390. assets

Assets are reported on the balance sheet.

391. single-step format and multi-step format

The multi-step format is one of the formats of the income statement. Multi-step is the format more commonly used because it provides more detail to the users of financial statements. The less common format is called the *single-step format*.

392. Gross margin is the difference between sales revenues and cost of goods sold.

Gross margin is calculated as total revenues less cost of goods sold.

393. income statement

The income statement allows users to analyze a company's historical performance and develop expectations for future performance. It allows the users to compare performance between companies.

394. operating earnings

Operating earnings are characteristic of the multi-step income statement.

395. Earnings before income tax are reported only on the multi-step income statement.

Earnings before income tax are one of the fundamental measures of profit reported on the multi-step income statement format.

396. rent expense

Rent expenses are an operating expense, while the other expenses listed are non-operating.

397. income tax expense

Income tax expense is reported below operating income and is not an operating expense.

398. will not be reported

The single-step income statement doesn't report gross profit; it only reports total revenues and expenses.

399. sales revenues

Sales revenues are one of the fundamental pieces of the income statement and are reported on the income statement regardless of the format used.

400. single-step income statement

The single-step income statement provides only one bottom line profit number, and it does so by summing up all expenses and deducting them from total revenues. There is no other detail provided on the single-step income statement.

401. the SEC

The Securities and Exchange Commission regulates financial disclosures only for publicly traded companies.

402. confidentiality

Companies want to make sure they don't disclose too much information. Sometimes the information is just considered private, and sometimes companies don't want to disclose it for competitive reasons.

403. materiality

The concept of *materiality* means that the focus should be only on amounts that are significant enough to impact a decision.

404. practicality

Practicality refers to the fact that putting too much information on the income statement may not be practical and may make it too busy and too difficult to read. Sometimes less is more.

405. materiality, confidentiality, regulations, and practicality

Materiality, confidentiality, regulations, and practicality are the main considerations when deciding on income statement disclosures.

406. Net income from the income statement is transferred to the balance sheet as retained earnings.

The income statement is the first financial statement prepared, and the net income is necessary to calculate the retained earnings that are reported on the balance sheet.

407. cash

Cash from the balance sheet is also reported on the statement of cash flows.

408. the balance sheet and the statement of cash flows

The balance sheet, income statement, and statement of cash flows are interconnected, and activity on the income statement impacts both the balance sheet and the statement of cash flows.

409. increase cash, increase accounts receivable, and decrease inventory

Sales can be either cash sales or credit sales, meaning that either cash or accounts receivable will increase on the balance sheet. Inventory doesn't decrease by the amount of sales but by the amount of cost of goods sold.

410. They increase cash for the amount of cash sales.

Cash increases as a result of cash sales; therefore, cash would be increased on the statement of cash flows.

411. Net worth is the difference between total assets and total liabilities.

Profit increases retained earnings. This increases owners' equity. *Owners' equity* is a type of equity that is also called *net worth.* Owners' equity is the difference between total assets and total liabilities.

412. Revenues increase.

Accounts receivable increase as a result of sales on account. Sales increase sales revenue.

413. debit accounts receivable

Increases to sales revenue increase cash or accounts receivable, as that is how customers pay for the product. Receivables increase as debits.

414. credit inventory

Cost of goods sold is an expense that reflects the cost of the product sold. Cost of goods sold essentially moves the cost from inventory (by crediting inventory) and puts it in cost of goods sold as an expense.

415. credit accrued expenses $400

The total interest expense was $600, and only $200 was paid with cash. The difference between the expense of $600 and the amount paid of $200 is $400, and it represents an unpaid liability called *accrued expenses.* Because liabilities are credit accounts, the $400 should be a credit to accrued expenses.

416. credit $2,000

Accounts payable related to inventory purchases increased $2,000, and liabilities increase as credits.

417. selling and general expenses

Accumulated depreciation is recorded with depreciation expense. Depreciation expense is included on the income statement in selling and general expenses.

418. decrease of $400

Prepaids represent expenses paid ahead of time. In this case, the prepaid increased by $400, meaning an expense was paid early and cash decreased by the amount of the expense.

419. cost of goods sold

The cost of goods sold entry records the decrease in inventory.

420. credit cash $8,000

The company purchased $10,000 of inventory; however, accounts payable increased only by $2,000. The difference between the purchases of $10,000 and the accounts payable increase of $2,000 is $8,000. It implies that $8,000 of purchases was paid with cash, causing a cash decrease (credit) of $8,000.

421. credit cash $200

The problem states that the company paid $200 for interest. Because interest was paid, it decreased cash; therefore, cash needs to be credited for $200. The amount of interest expenses is not relevant because the entire amount wasn't actually paid.

422. debit $3,000

The company purchased $10,000 of inventory but recorded only $7,000 of costs of goods sold. This implies that the difference between the $10,000 purchased and the $7,000 sold, which is $3,000, still remains in inventory. Inventory is an asset account. Therefore, the remaining balance is a debit of $3,000 in inventory.

423. credit accrued expenses $1,500

You were told that accrued expenses increased $1,500. Accrued expenses are a liability, so they increase as credits. Thus, to record an increase, the account should be credited.

424. credit cash $700

Based on the facts provided, the debits to the summary entry are debit to selling and general expense $5,000 and to prepaid expenses $400. Those debits total $5,400. Then you need to identify the credits based on the facts provided. The credits to the entry are accounts payable $2,000, accrued expenses $1,500, and accumulated depreciation $1,200, totaling $4,700. In summary, there are debits of $5,400 and credits of $4,700, so the entry doesn't balance by $700. Because the debits are larger than the credits, you need a credit to cash of $700.

425. credit $8,000

The company purchased $10,000 of inventory; however, accounts payable increased only by $2,000. The difference between the purchases of $10,000 and the accounts payable increase of $2,000 is $8,000. It implies that $8,000 of purchases was paid with cash, causing a cash decrease (credit) of $8,000.

426. It prohibits people from divulging financial information.

A confidentiality agreement is frequently signed by parties outside of a company when they're given access to confidential financial information. It prohibits the signers of the agreement from divulging financial information.

427. balance sheet, income statement, statement of cash flows, and footnotes

The four essential elements of an annual financial report are the balance sheet, the income statement, the statement of cash flows, and the footnotes.

428. It provides additional assurance that the financial statements are materially correct.

A company may obtain an audit of its financial statements that provides additional credibility as to the accuracy of the financial statements. Only publicly traded companies must be audited every year. Private companies may be required by their lenders to obtain an audit.

429. horizontal or vertical format

There is no presentation format called *combination.* Balance sheets are most commonly presented using the horizontal (landscape) or vertical (portrait) format.

430. Presenting a balance sheet in a portrait format allows a business to keep it on one page.

When a balance sheet is presented in a portrait format, it can fit on one page.

431. assets, liabilities, and equity of a business

A balance sheet summarizes the assets, liabilities, and equity of a business. It follows the basic accounting equation of assets equal liabilities plus equity.

432. profit, profit margin, total cash, and the overall financial condition of the business

Deciding to purchase an existing business is a very complex decision, and a buyer should consider the company's profit, profit margin, total cash, and the overall financial condition, among other aspects of the business.

433. a statement of financial condition

A balance sheet summarizes the assets, liabilities, and equity of a business and is sometimes also referred to as the *statement of financial condition.*

434. Liabilities reflect claims against the assets of a business.

Liabilities are obligations of a business and represent claims against the assets of the business.

435. excess of assets over liabilities

Assets less liabilities equal the owners' equity, so owners' equity is the excess of assets over liabilities.

436. profit earned and retained by a business and capital invested by the owners

The sources of owners' equity include capital invested by the owners and the profit earned and retained by a business.

437. as retained earnings

Profits retained by a business are called *retained earnings,* and they're part of equity on the balance sheet.

438. The balance sheet is not presented for a period of time. It is reported at a point in time.

All financial statements except for the balance sheet are presented for the end of the period. The balance sheet is presented at a point in time or at the close of business on the last day of the period. The balance sheet is sometimes referred to as a *snapshot* because it's reported at that point only.

439. if it has had consecutive profitable years

Information about profits of a business can be found only on the income statement. Information about cash and liabilities can be found on the balance sheet.

440. operating, financing, and investing activities

The three basic transaction types that make up the balance sheet are operating activities, financing activities, and investing activities.

441. investment of capital in a company by its owners

Financing transactions finance the operations of a business and include the investment of capital in the business by its investors, as well as the return of capital to the owners and distribution to the owners from profits.

442. transactions related to expenses

Operating activities are the day-to-day operations of a business. They include all profit-making activities of the business, as well as sales, expenses, and other income and losses.

443. the purchase of intangible assets

Investing activities are investments in a business such as the purchase and construction of long-lived assets utilized in the operations of the business, the purchase of intangible assets, and the disposal of operating assets.

444. the return of capital to its owners

Financing transactions finance the operations of a business and include the investment of capital in the business by its investors, as well as the return of capital to the owners and distribution to the owners from profits.

445. the purchase of long-lived assets used in the operations of a business

Investing activities are investments in a business such as the purchase and construction of long-lived assets utilized in the operations of the business, the purchase of intangible assets, and the disposal of operating assets.

446. the profit-making activities of a company

Operating activities are the day-to-day operations of a business. They include all profit-making activities of the business, as well as sales, expenses, and other income and losses.

447. accounts receivable

Accounts receivable are a result of sales transactions, which are operating activities.

448. inventory

When a company either purchases items to resell or manufactures product for sale, it records the transaction as inventory on its balance sheet.

449. short-term notes

Short-term notes reflect short-term borrowing and would not be presented if the company did not borrow any money.

450. inventory

If a company only provides services and does not sell any product, then it would not report inventory balances on its balance sheet. Inventory represents the product the company has for sale.

451. the amount of money borrowed

The total amount of money borrowed is a short-term or long-term debt and is recorded as a liability on a balance sheet.

452. $28,000

In the problem presented, total liabilities include accounts payable, accrued expenses, short-term notes, and long-term notes. To calculate the total liabilities, you need to add them up as follows: accounts payable of $5,000 plus accrued expenses of $6,000 plus short-term note of $7,000 plus long-term notes of $10,000 equals total liabilities of $28,000.

453. $52,000

In the problem presented, total equity includes capital stock and retained earnings. To calculate the total equity, you need to add them up as follows: capital stock of $40,000 plus retained earnings of $12,000 to give a total equity of $52,000.

454. $80,000

In the problem presented, total assets include cash; accounts receivable; inventory; prepaid expenses; and property, plant, and equipment minus accumulated depreciation. To calculate the total assets, you need to add them up as follows: cash of $10,000 plus accounts receivable of $20,000 plus inventory of $14,000 plus prepaid expenses of $3,000 plus property, plant, and equipment of $35,000 less accumulated depreciation of $2,000 equals total assets of $80,000.

455. $47,000

In the problem presented, current assets include cash, accounts receivable, inventory, and prepaid expenses. To calculate the total of current assets, you need to add them up as follows: cash of $10,000 plus accounts receivable of $20,000 plus inventory of $14,000 plus prepaid expense of $3,000 equals total current assets of $47,000.

456. The business has retained $12,000 of its cumulative net income since inception.

The amount of net income retained by the business is presented as retained earnings. Thus, the $12,000 in retained earnings means the company has retained this amount of its cumulative net income since the inception of the business.

457. $18,000

In the problem presented, current liabilities include accounts payable, accrued expenses, and short-term notes. To calculate the total current liabilities, you need to add them up as follows: accounts payable of $5,000 plus accrued expenses of $6,000 plus short-term notes of $7,000 equals total current liabilities of $18,000.

458. accounts receivable

Accounts receivable is used to record credit sales; therefore, if a company only had cash sales, it would not report accounts receivable on its balance sheet.

459. merchandiser only

The company lists inventory on its balance sheet. This means it sells products, so the company is a merchandiser.

460. Customers either pay immediately with cash or the company extends them credit.

The company's balance sheet shows cash and accounts receivable. This implies that some customers pay with cash immediately, while others use extended payment terms.

461. The company pays some of its expenses in advance and some after they've been incurred.

The company's balance sheet presents prepaid expenses, meaning the company pays some of its expenses in advance. In addition, the balance sheet presents accounts payable and accrued expenses, which implies that some expenses are paid after they've been incurred.

462. $33,000

Property, plant, and equipment is $35,000, and accumulated depreciation is $2,000. Thus, the net amount is the gross amount of property, plant, and equipment of $35,000 less the accumulated depreciation of $2,000 for a total of $33,000.

463. The company incurred expenses for which it has not yet been invoiced.

Accrued expenses represent expenses that have been incurred by the company but the company has not yet received an invoice for them.

464. current asset

Accounts receivable are generated as a result of making sales to customers on credit. They're collected within a company's operating cycle; therefore, they're a current asset.

465. 2.5

Current ratio is calculated as current assets divided by current liabilities. In this case, the company has current assets of $500,000 and current liabilities of $200,000. Therefore, you divide $500,000 by $200,000 to give a current ratio of 2.5.

466. cash plus cash equivalents divided by current liabilities

Quick ratio is the ratio of cash and cash equivalents divided by current liabilities.

467. inventory

Only inventory is a current asset. Accounts payable is a current liability. Notes receivable and long-term investments are non-current assets. Retained earnings is an equity account.

468. property, plant, and equipment

Property, plant, and equipment are long-term assets because companies invest in those assets for the long term.

469. long-term asset

Land is a long-term asset because it's not converted to cash within an operating cycle.

470. current assets divided by current liabilities

The *current ratio* compares the current assets to current liabilities to help determine a company's ability to pay its current obligations.

471. bonds payable

Bonds payable are long-term or non-current liabilities because they're not paid off within an operating cycle.

472. 1 or more

There's no rule as to what a healthy company's current ratio should be. However, most analysts regard a current ratio of at least 1 to be the minimum.

473. inventory

Inventory is held for sale; thus, it's turned into cash within one operating cycle. Therefore, it's a current asset.

474. a company's ability to pay its long-term debts on time

Liquidity is a company's ability to pay its short-term obligations, while *solvency* refers to the ability to pay long-term debts.

475. a company's efficiency at using its assets in creating revenues

The asset turnover ratio is calculated as annual sales revenues divided by total assets. This ratio measures how well a company uses its assets to create its revenues.

476. A capital-intensive business requires a significant amount of assets to generate sales.

When a business is said to be *capital-intensive,* it requires a lot of assets to generate sales. Examples of such businesses are power plants and airlines. Capital-intensive companies have very low asset turnover ratios because, after they invest in the assets, they keep them long term.

477. Most assets are recorded on the balance sheet at their historical cost.

Most assets are reported at historical values. However, the accounting method selected impacts the values recorded.

478. forward-looking

Valuation of a business is an estimate and can be very complex. Financial statements of a company provide a backward look at its financial performance, while business valuation has a forward-looking focus.

479. future cash flow estimates

Historical performance of a company is not a guarantee of future performance. Therefore, though historical performance is reviewed during a business valuation, it's not one of the primary factors used for valuing a business. Instead, business valuation focuses on forward-looking analysis, primarily estimated future cash flows of the business.

480. The values of assets on the balance sheet in most cases are based on the original transaction when the asset was first recorded.

Some assets are reviewed for impairment on an annual basis. However, appreciation of assets is not recorded (except for some investments). Instead, the value of assets on the balance sheet usually reflects the value of the original transaction when the asset was first recorded.

481. 2.0

The current ratio is calculated as current assets divided by current liabilities. In this case, the company has current assets of $600,000 and current liabilities of $300,000. Therefore, you divide $600,000 by $300,000 to get a current ratio of 2.0.

482. 1.0

The quick ratio is calculated as cash and cash equivalents divided by current liabilities. In this case, the company has cash of $100,000, cash equivalents of $200,000, and current liabilities of $300,000. Therefore, you first add cash of $100,000 and cash equivalents of $200,000 to get a total of $300,000. Then, you divide that $300,000 by the current liabilities of $300,000 to arrive at a quick ratio of 1.0.

483. 2.4

The asset turnover ratio is calculated as revenues divided by assets. In this case, the company has revenues of $2,400,000 and assets of $1,000,000. Therefore, you divide $2,400,000 by $1,000,000 to get an asset turnover ratio of 2.4.

484. increase

The current ratio would increase as a result of the payment. You calculate the current ratio by comparing current assets to current liabilities. Here's an example: If current assets are $120,000 and current liabilities are $100,000, then the current ratio is $120,000 divided by $100,000, or 1.2. If a payment is made of $20,000, then cash decreases by $20,000, causing current assets to decrease from $120,000 to $100,000 and accounts payable to decrease, causing current liabilities to decrease from $100,000 to $80,000. You calculate the new current ratio as $100,000 of current assets divided by $80,000 of current liabilities, or 1.25, an increase in the current ratio.

485. collection of accounts receivable

Collection of accounts receivable doesn't impact the current ratio, because the transaction impacts only the current asset. The transaction decreases and increases current assets, resulting in a net impact of zero. Cash is received (increased), and receivables are decreased when they're paid.

486. It reflects how much one might pay for a business.

Business valuation can be very complex and relies on estimates. It does consider some of the data in the financial statements and historical performance, but those are only pieces of the required information. Accountants prepare financial statements, but they don't perform business valuations. Business valuations are needed to determine how much an interested party might pay for the business.

487. The future earnings potential of a business is a major factor in business valuation.

Business valuation is most commonly based on the future earnings potential of a business. Businesses are acquired because of the earnings they may generate in the future, not because of the earnings they have generated in the past.

488. It does not consider the values in the balance sheet.

The earnings multiple valuation method is a simple calculation that only looks at current earnings and doesn't consider any values on the balance sheet.

489. No adjustment is necessary.

When stock is exchanged among investors, no entries are recorded on the company's books. Therefore, the price paid for the business is the buyer's private transaction and is not reflected in the financial statements of the business.

490. total liabilities

Depreciation methods impact depreciation expenses and, thus, net income. They also impact the net book value of the assets. Therefore, they impact total assets and accumulated depreciation. They don't have any impact on total liabilities.

491. on two separate pages

The income statement and the balance sheet are not reported together; they're usually presented on two separate pages.

492. $750,000

You know from the data provided that the balance in accounts receivable is 3 weeks of sales. You also know that total annual sales are $13,000,000. So the next step is to figure out 3 weeks of sales. To do that you should take total sales of $13,000,000 and divide by total weeks in a year, or 52 weeks. This gives you weekly sales of $250,000. Now multiply that total by 3 to get $750,000 as the balance of receivables representing 3 weeks of sales.

493. $1,100,000

You know from the information provided that inventory balance at the end of the year is 8 weeks of cost of goods sold. You also know that cost of goods sold for the year is $7,150,000. The next step is to figure out 8 weeks of cost of goods sold. To do that you should take the total cost of goods sold of $7,150,000 and divide by total weeks in a year, or 52 weeks. This gives you weekly cost of goods sold of $137,500. You need 8 weeks of cost of goods sold, so multiply $137,500 by 8 to get $1,100,000 as the inventory balance.

494. $550,000

You know from the information provided that the balance in accounts payable related to inventory purchases is 4 weeks of cost of goods sold for the year. The next step is to figure out 4 weeks of cost of goods sold. To do that you should take the total cost of goods sold of $7,150,000 and divide by total weeks in a year, or 52 weeks. This gives you weekly cost of goods sold of $137,500. You need 4 weeks of cost of goods sold, so multiply $137,500 by 4 to get $550,000 as the accounts payable from inventory purchases balance at the end of the year.

495. $189,000

You calculate interest expense as the average amount of debt times the average annual interest rate. In this example, the average amount of debt is $3,600,000, and the average annual interest rate is 5.25%. Therefore, the average amount of debt of $3,600,000 times the average annual interest rate of 5.25% equals $189,000.

496. benchmarks for a particular company

Normative ratios are the benchmarks or norms for a particular company.

497. interest expense

When interest expense is unpaid but incurred, it increases the accrued payables balance on the balance sheet.

498. net income

The net income from the income statement is added to the previous balance of retained earnings on the balance sheet.

499. accounts receivable

Accounts receivable is an asset account that is debited at the time of a sale on credit.

500. credit accounts receivable

Accounts receivable decreases when cash is collected; thus, a credit needs to be recorded.

501. based on the terms of the agreement with a particular customer

Almost all companies have credit sales, and they should be collected according to the terms of the agreement.

502. debit accounts receivable and credit sales revenue

Sales transactions increase sales revenue and either cash or accounts receivable. Therefore, accounts receivable (or cash) must be debited, and sales revenue must be credited.

503. debit cost of goods sold and credit inventory

The cost of sale is recorded as an increase (debit) in cost of goods sold and a decrease (credit) in inventory.

504. when sales transactions occur

Accrual accounting is required by GAAP, and it disregards when cash exchanges hands. Instead, it records revenues when sales are made.

505. It increases the cash flow.

When accounts receivable decrease, that means that outstanding balances were collected, and thus, cash increased. If cash increased, then the cash flow increased.

506. the amount of sales revenues that has not yet been converted to cash

The balance in receivables reflects the sales that have been recorded but not yet collected; therefore, they have not yet been converted to cash.

507. debit accounts receivable $25,000 and credit sales revenues $25,000

Both accounts receivable and sales revenues increase $25,000 as a result of the sale. The expected collection pattern doesn't impact how the original sale is recorded. Therefore, both accounts receivable and sales revenues need to be increased by a debit to accounts receivable and a credit to sales revenues.

508. debit cash $3,000, debit accounts receivable $27,000, and credit sales revenue $30,000

The company makes a sale of $30,000 and receives a down payment of 10%. First, you need to calculate the amount of the down payment by taking the total sale of $30,000 and multiplying by the percentage of down payment, or 10%. Based on that, the down payment amount is $3,000. This is the amount of cash the company receives, so it should be recorded as a debit to cash for $3,000.

Next, you need to determine the outstanding balance. You calculate the balance due as the total sale amount of $30,000 less the amount of the down payment of $3,000, to give $27,000. The outstanding balance of $27,000 represents accounts receivable and should be recorded as a debit to accounts receivable. Now you have a debit to cash of $3,000 and a debit to accounts receivable of $27,000. To make the entry balance you need a credit of $30,000, and it should be recorded to sales revenue to record the revenue earned on the transaction.

509. cost of goods sold

Businesses that sell physical products record the cost of product in an account called *cost of goods sold.*

510. the cost of the product sold

Cost of goods sold is the expense account that records the cost of the product sold.

511. inventory

Inventory reflects assets held for resale.

512. The cost of the sold product is transferred to cost of goods sold.

At the time of the sale, the cost of the inventory sold is removed from inventory and transferred to cost of goods sold.

513. the cost of the items held for sale and waiting to be sold

The inventory balance on the balance sheet is the purchase cost of the items a company has available for sale.

514. on the income statement as a deduction from sales revenues

Cost of goods sold is reported near the top of the income statement as a deduction from sales revenues.

515. It's the difference between revenues and cost of goods sold.

Gross margin applies only to companies that sell a physical product. It's reported on the income statement as the difference between revenues and cost of goods sold.

516. cars at a car rental facility

Cars at a rental facility are held to be leased and not to be sold; thus, they're not inventory.

517. the time that a product is shipped to a buyer

The sale is complete when the product is exchanged for cash or a promise to pay. Then, the company should record the sale (sales revenue and cash or accounts receivable), increase (debit) cost of goods sold, and credit inventory.

518. Net income would be overstated by $90,000.

The company recorded cost of goods sold of $10,000 instead of $100,000. You calculate the amount of difference as the correct amount of cost of goods sold of $100,000 less the incorrectly recorded amount of $10,000, which equals $90,000. Because the amount incorrectly recorded was less than it should've been, the company understated its cost of goods sold expense by $90,000. If expenses are understated, then net income is overstated.

519. used in operations

Fixed assets are assets that are held by a company and used in the operations of the business.

520. inventory held for sale

Inventory is not a fixed asset, because it's held for sale. *Fixed assets* are assets that are held by a company and used in the operations of the business.

521. the allocation of the cost of an asset over its useful life

Depreciation doesn't address the value of an asset; it's simply a methodology for allocating the cost of the asset over the useful years of its life.

522. depreciable cost of an asset divided by the estimated useful life

The straight-line depreciation method takes the depreciable cost of an asset — usually the original purchase cost less salvage value — and divides it by the asset's estimated useful life.

523. as an increase to accumulated depreciation

Depreciation is recorded as a debit to expense and a credit to accumulated depreciation. Accumulated depreciation is an asset contra account, so a credit increases its balance.

524. increases expenses and decreases assets

Depreciation is an expense that is increased when recorded. Also, the value of the asset is decreased by recording accumulated depreciation.

525. equipment held for resale by an equipment dealer

If equipment is held for sale, then it's not a fixed asset. Instead, the equipment dealer would consider it inventory.

526. to allocate the cost of an asset to the period it's used to generate revenue

Depreciation allocates the cost of an asset to the years the asset will be used in the operations.

527. allocates the cost of the building over the time it's used through depreciation expense on the income statement

Depreciation is the process of spreading or allocating the cost of a fixed asset over its useful life.

528. Fixed assets and retained earnings will be too high on the balance sheet, expenses will be too low on the income statement, and net income will be too high on the income statement.

The company forgot to record an expense and accumulated depreciation. If the expense is too low, then net income is too high. If net income is too high, then retained earnings are too high. If the accumulated depreciation account isn't increased, then fixed assets are too high on the balance sheet.

529. lack of physical substance

Intangible assets are assets that lack physical substance. They can't be handled in a tactile way.

530. amortization

Amortization is a rational process of allocating the cost of an intangible asset to expense.

531. delivery vehicle

Vehicles are examples of a fixed asset because they have physical substance and are held by a company.

532. intangible asset

Patents are intangible assets; they can't be handled in a tactile way.

533. Amortization is the methodology used to allocate the cost of an intangible asset to expense over its useful life.

Amortization is similar to depreciation, but it's used for intangible assets, whereas depreciation is used for fixed assets. *Amortization* is the process of allocating the cost of an intangible asset to expense over its useful life.

534. increases expenses

Amortization is the process of transferring a partial cost of an intangible from the asset account to expenses, which increases expenses.

535. customer lists

Customer lists are examples of intangible assets because the names lack physical substance.

536. Only purchased intangible assets may be recorded as intangible assets.

Internally developed intangible assets can't be recorded as intangible assets; only purchased assets can be recorded as intangible assets.

537. as a debit to the intangible asset account

Purchases of intangibles increase the intangible asset account, so the intangible asset account must be debited when the assets are first purchased.

538. It decreases the intangible asset account, thereby decreasing assets.

Amortization of intangibles is recorded directly in the asset account, so amortization decreases the intangible asset account and decreases assets.

539. magazine subscription received

Magazine subscription received is unearned revenue because the company received the money for the subscription but still has to provide the product.

540. current assets

Prepaid expenses are usually current assets because they are prepayments that will be utilized in the next year.

541. at the time of payment

Prepaid expenses are assets because the cash is paid upfront for a benefit to be provided in the future. They're recorded as soon as they're paid.

542. A portion of the cost of the prepaid is transferred to an expense account in the period the expense contributes to the production of revenue.

Prepaid expenses, such as insurance, cover various periods and may overlap different years. In every accounting period, a portion of the cost of the prepaid is moved to an expense account to show the amount of expense incurred in that particular period.

543. after the period in which the expenses were incurred

Operating expenses are usually incurred and recorded before they're paid.

544. accounts payable

Accounts payable are unpaid expenses — an obligation.

545. current liability

Accounts payable are a current liability, so they're always short-term liabilities.

546. to allocate the expense costs to the period in which the expense produces revenues

Prepaid expenses are recorded on the balance sheet at the time they're paid; then, their cost is allocated to the appropriate periods.

547. accrued expenses

Accrued expenses is a liability account used to record unpaid costs for which the invoices have not been received.

548. Current liabilities will be too low and income will be too high.

The company should record an expense for an estimate of the electricity bill and set up a current liability to pay in the future when the bill arrives.

549. informal agreement

Debt is a formal credit instrument that allows a company to borrow money on a basis of interest-bearing notes.

550. due in one year or sooner

Short-term debt is debt that is payable within one year or the operating cycle, whichever is shorter.

551. Debt is frequently needed to finance the growth or operations of a business.

Companies usually obtain debt to finance their business. This includes financing growth and operations.

552. Debt requires regular payments of principal and interest.

Monthly payments must be made on debt, regardless of other circumstances.

553. as an other expense not part of operating income

Operating earnings are earnings from operating a business. *Business-wide expenses,* such as interest expense, are excluded and reported in the section of other revenues, expenses, gains, and losses following operating income.

554. when an interest expense is incurred

Interest expenses are recorded when they're incurred. This is usually done monthly.

555. assets and liabilities

When a company obtains debt, liabilities increase because the company now has an obligation to pay back the debt. Also, cash increases because the company receives the cash from the financing.

556. additional infusion of equity

Owners can choose to contribute additional capital at any time; however, if a business is defaulting on its debt, then it's unlikely that owners would be interested in investing more.

557. combined with accrued expenses

Interest payable can be presented on the balance sheet combined with accrued expenses unless the amount is large, in which case it should be presented separately.

558. 5.74%

Annual interest of $175,000 divided by total debt of $3,050,000 equals 5.74%.

559. income tax payable

The amount due is a liability or a payable. The account representing the amount due to the IRS is called *income tax payable.*

560. as income tax payable

Income tax payable is the liability account that includes the unpaid portion of income tax.

561. income reported to the IRS

The actual taxable income isn't reported on the income statement and varies from earnings before income tax because of complexities of IRS regulations.

562. Income tax payable is usually smaller than the income tax expense.

A significant portion of income taxes is usually paid before the end of the year, so the amount owed at the end of the year is usually significantly smaller than the income tax expense.

563. Income tax payable is a result of delaying tax payments because of different tax accounting rules.

Companies don't borrow money from the IRS, but they usually defer payment as long as legally possible. This causes a payable.

564. increases both retained earnings and owners' equity

Net income increases retained earnings and therefore increases owners' equity because retained earnings are part of owners' equity.

565. Dividends are usually paid quarterly.

Dividends are usually paid on a quarterly basis. Because dividends are discretionary payments, there's no requirement as to how often they should be paid.

566. Income tax expense decreases net income, while dividends have no impact on net income.

Dividends aren't an expense, so they don't impact the income statement. Income tax expense is an expense, and it decreases net income.

567. both income tax and interest expenses

Operating income is income from operations, and it excludes business-wide expenses, such as income tax and interest expenses. Dividends aren't an expense, so there's no such item as dividends expense.

568. decrease retained earnings and have no impact on net income

Dividends are distributions to owners, and they're paid out of retained earnings. This decreases retained earnings. Dividends aren't an expense, so they don't impact the net income at all.

569. balance sheets and income statements

Every sales transaction impacts the income statement as sales/revenues are recorded and also the balance sheets as cash or accounts receivable are recorded.

570. equity

Net income from the income statement is included in retained earnings that are part of equity on the balance sheet.

571. $350,000

You calculate net worth as total assets minus total liabilities. In this case, total assets equal $1,200,000. You calculate total liabilities as current liabilities of $500,000 plus long-term liabilities of $350,000 for a total of $850,000. When you know total liabilities, you can go back to the original equation and take total assets of $1,200,000 less total liabilities of $850,000 for a total net worth of $350,000.

572. cumulative losses over time

Negative net worth is possible and usually occurs either as a result of losses over time or very large losses in one year.

573. $1,500,000

Total assets are $2,500,000, and you calculate total liabilities by adding current liabilities of $800,000 and long-term liabilities of $200,000 for a total of $1,000,000. Then, you simply take total assets of $2,500,000 less total liabilities of $1,000,000 to get equity of $1,500,000. In this problem, there are no cash dividends and no new stock issued. As a result, the entire equity balance is due to net income.

574. Cash dividends decrease net worth, and owners' capital contributions increase net worth.

Cash dividends paid decrease net worth, and owners' capital contributions increase net worth.

575. $395,000

You usually calculate total net income as total revenues less total expenses. However, from the balance sheet you can also calculate net income as total net worth plus cash dividends less issued stock. First, you calculate net worth as total assets minus total liabilities. In this case, total assets equal $1,200,000. You calculate total liabilities as current liabilities of $500,000 plus long-term liabilities of $350,000 for a total of $850,000. When you know total liabilities, you can go back to the original equation and take total assets of $1,200,000 less total liabilities of $850,000 to get a total net worth of $350,000. Then, you simply take the calculated net worth of $350,000 and add the cash dividends of $45,000 to get net income of $395,000. There was no stock issued in this example.

576. $320,000

You usually calculate total net income as total revenues less total expenses. However, from the balance sheet you can also calculate net income as total net worth plus cash dividends less issued stock. First, you calculate net worth as total assets minus total liabilities. In this case, total assets equal $1,200,000. You calculate total liabilities as current liabilities of $500,000 plus long-term liabilities of $350,000 for a total of $850,000. When you know total liabilities you can go back to the original equation and take total assets of $1,200,000 less total liabilities of $850,000 to get a total net worth of $350,000. Then, you simply take the calculated net worth of $350,000 and subtract the issued stock of $30,000 to get net income of $320,000. There were no dividends paid.

577. $440,000

You usually calculate total net income as total revenues less total expenses. However, from the balance sheet you can also calculate net income as total net worth plus cash dividends less issued stock. First, you calculate net worth as total assets minus total liabilities. In this case, total assets equal $800,000. You calculate total liabilities as current liabilities of $200,000 plus long-term liabilities of $100,000 for a total of $300,000. When you know total liabilities you can go back to the original equation and take total assets of $800,000 less total liabilities of $300,000 to get total net worth of $500,000. Then, you simply take the calculated net worth of $500,000 and subtract the issued stock of $80,000, and then add the dividends paid of $20,000 to get a net income of $440,000.

578. $1,700,000

You can determine net income from the balance sheet by taking total assets less total liabilities plus cash dividends less issued stock. In this case, total assets are $2,500,000, and you calculate total liabilities by taking current liabilities of $800,000 plus long-term liabilities of $200,000 for a total of $1,000,000. Then, you simply take total assets of $2,500,000 less total liabilities of $1,000,000 plus cash dividends of $200,000 to get net income of $1,700,000.

579. statement of cash flows

The statement of cash flows is a required financial statement. It provides information not available elsewhere, so financial statement users, such as investors, find it important and useful.

580. operating activities

The first section of the statement of cash flows is operating activities, followed by financing activities and investing activities in any order.

581. The purchase of the new equipment and the sale of the old delivery trucks are investing activities.

Investing activities involve more than just buying investments in another company. More commonly, companies invest in themselves by buying fixed assets and disposing of old ones. The sale of a company's own stock is not an investing activity; it's a financing activity.

582. cash outflow under investing activities of $570,000

If the fixed asset account increased, then the company must have acquired more assets. Because it didn't take on any more debt, the purchase must have been made with cash. Cash purchases of fixed assets are investing activities.

583. the $300,000 sale of stock and the payment of $30,000 in dividends

Financing activities include the sale of the company's common stock and the payment of dividends. The sale of investments and the receipt of dividends from those investments are investing activities.

584. The direct method presents sales and expenses on a cash basis.

The indirect method adjusts accrual-basis net income to cash basis, while the direct method disregards net income and simply determines sales and expense on a cash basis.

585. net income

Net income is reported on the income statement and on the indirect method statement of cash flows. However, it's not used in the direct method.

586. collections from sales

Collections from sales appear as a line item on the direct method statement of cash flows under the operating cash section.

587. The indirect method is preferred but not required.

There is no requirement to use the direct method or the indirect method. A reconciliation of net income to cash from operating activities is required if the indirect method is used, but not with the direct.

588. only the operating section

The operating section is the only section that differs between the two methods. The total cash from operating activities is the same regardless of the method selected.

589. The indirect method is used by almost all companies.

Almost all companies use the indirect method.

590. indirect method

The indirect method starts with net income and adjusts for non-cash transactions. This process only applies to cash flow from operating activities.

591. depreciation expense

Depreciation expense is a non-cash expense, meaning it impacts net income but doesn't impact cash flows. Thus, under the indirect method, depreciation expense is an adjustment to net income.

592. Cash flow from operating activities will be exactly the same under either method.

The financing and investing activities sections of the statement of cash flows are exactly the same under both the direct and indirect methods. The only difference is in the presentation of the operating activities. However, the net cash flow from operating activities will be the same regardless of which method is used.

593. by eliminating non-cash transactions from the net income

The method is called *indirect* because instead of just looking at the cash collected or paid, it starts with net income and eliminates non-cash transactions.

594. accrued liabilities

Accrued liabilities is an operating liability account.

595. as an addition to net income in the operating activities section

The indirect method starts with net income and adjusts it for non-cash transactions to get to cash from operating activities. Decreases in current assets, such as inventory and accounts receivable, are added to net income in the adjustment process.

596. added to net income

Decreases in current assets (such as accounts receivable) are added to net income to determine cash from operating activities.

597. subtracted from net income

Increases in current assets are deducted from net income to determine cash from operating activities.

598. decreases operating cash flow

An increase in receivables implies that a business generated more credit sales during the year than it collected. Therefore, it decreases operating cash flow.

599. long-term loans

Operating liabilities are current liabilities and include liabilities that will be paid within a year. Those liabilities include accounts payable, accrued expenses payable, income tax payable, and salaries payable. Long-term loans aren't operating liabilities because they aren't paid within a year.

600. It increases cash flow from operations.

When income taxes payable increase, it means that the company did not pay out as much as it recorded as an expense, so the expense was higher than the cash paid.

601. $25,000

The increase in accounts payable must be added to net income to calculate cash from operating activities. Thus, the net income of $20,000 plus the increase in accounts payable of $5,000 equals $25,000 of cash provided by operating activities.

602. $43,000

The increase in accounts receivable and the decrease in accounts payable must be deducted from net income. Therefore, the net income of $50,000 less the increase in accounts receivable of $5,000 less the decrease in accounts payable of $2,000 equals $43,000 of cash provided by operating activities.

603. $104,000

The increase in accounts receivable must be deducted from the net income, and the increase in accrued liabilities must be added to the net income to determine cash from operating activities. Therefore, the net income of $100,000 less an increase in accounts receivable of $8,000 plus an increase in accrued liabilities of $12,000 equals cash provided by operating activities of $104,000.

604. Depreciation expense does not impact cash.

Depreciation is a non-cash expense because it doesn't impact cash.

605. added to net income

Depreciation is a non-cash expense. Therefore, it must be added to net income to determine cash from operating activities.

606. ignored

The indirect method starts with net income and adjusts non-cash expenses, such as depreciation. The direct method determines cash paid and cash received and doesn't adjust net income to cash basis; thus, it ignores depreciation.

607. $175,000

Depreciation expenses must be added back to net income to determine cash from operating activities. Also, the increase in accounts receivable must be deducted, and the increase in accounts payable must be added to net income to determine cash from operating activities. Therefore, net income of $155,000 plus the depreciation expense of $35,000 less the increase in accounts receivable of $25,000 plus the increase in accounts payable of $10,000 equals cash provided by operating activities of $175,000.

608. $90,000

Both the depreciation expense and amortization expense must be added back to net income to determine cash from operating activities. Also, the decrease in accounts receivable must be added to net income to determine cash from operating activities. Therefore, net income of $80,000 plus depreciation expense of $5,000 plus amortization expense of $2,000 plus accounts receivable decrease of $3,000 equals cash provided by operating activities of $90,000. The proceeds from the sale of bonds are in the financing section and aren't operating activities.

609. total assets

Total assets are reported on the balance sheet and not on the statement of changes in stockholders' equity. The statement of changes in stockholders' equity includes only items that impact equity, such as investments by owners, capital returned to owners, dividends, and earnings.

610. shareholders

Shareholders are the primary users of the statement of shareholders' equity because it shows the changes in their accounts.

611. income tax statement

There is no statement called the income tax statement. Companies are required to file an annual tax return, but that's not a financial statement.

612. statement of cash flows, income statement, statement of changes in equity, and balance sheet

The four primary financial statements are the balance sheet, the income statement, the statement of cash flows, and the statement of changes in equity.

613. proceeds from the sale of bonds

A net loss is treated similar to net income on the statement of changes in stockholders' equity, except it's a deduction from retained earnings. The sale of common stock and all dividend payments are also reflected in the statement of changes in stockholders' equity because they involve changes in equity accounts. The proceeds from the sale of bonds, though, don't involve a change in any equity accounts and therefore aren't included in the statement of changes in stockholders' equity.

614. It increases owners' equity.

Net income increases retained earnings and therefore increases equity.

615. companies that only report profit in their equity accounts

Companies that have profit as the only equity transaction are not required to present a statement of changes in owners' equity because the information about profit is already available on the income statement.

616. It summarizes the activity impacting the equity accounts.

The statement of changes in owners' equity summarizes the activity in all equity accounts over a period of time. Equity accounts include the retained earnings and invested capital accounts.

617. as a detailed roll forward schedule, showing types of accounts as columns and a description of activities in the rows

The statement of changes in owners' equity looks like a big worksheet, showing beginning balances for each account in columns and the detailed activity in each row. This type of presentation is usually referred to as a *roll forward,* as it rolls the balance from the beginning balance to the ending balance by showing what transactions occurred in between.

618. owners' personal expenses

Owners' personal expenses should be recorded in the owners' personal financial statements, not in the business's financial statements.

619. payment of cash dividend

Cash dividends are paid out of retained earnings, so they decrease retained earnings.

620. special gains and losses, which are recorded in equity and not on the income statement

Accumulated other comprehensive income are special gains and losses that are recorded through equity and not included in the income statement in the calculation of profit/loss.

621. bottom of income statement or in the statement of changes in owners' equity

Accumulated other comprehensive income can't be presented on the bottom of the balance sheet. It can be presented on the bottom of the income statement or in the statement of changes in owners' equity.

622. debt issued

Debt issued is an obligation reported as a liability on the balance sheet.

623. realized gains and losses from certain types of securities

Realized gains and losses are included in the calculation of profit and are reported on the income statement.

624. when earnings are the only equity transaction

When a company does not have any equity transactions besides earnings, it doesn't need to present the statement of changes in owners' equity, because the only change is available on the income statement.

625. net income divided by owners' equity

Return on equity is a ratio that is calculated by taking net income and dividing it by owners' equity.

626. 28%

Return on equity is calculated as net income divided by owners' equity. Thus, net income of $5,000,000 should be divided by owners' equity of $18,000,000 to get a return on equity of 27.78%, or rounded to 28%.

627. debt divided by equity

The debt-to-equity ratio is calculated as total debt divided by total equity.

628. The higher the debt-to-equity ratio, the more profit the company has recorded.

The higher the debt-to-equity ratio, the higher the debt balance. Profit increases retained earnings and equity. Therefore, a higher profit would actually decrease this ratio.

629. corn

Fungible goods are indistinguishable from one another. Kernels of corn are identical. Artwork, such as original oil paintings, hand-woven tapestries, or designer jewelry, is unique and therefore not fungible. New cars are also unique and are identified by an identification number.

630. hand-painted portraits of kings and queens of England

Works of art are unique; one can't be substituted for another. Items that are unique are not fungible.

631. Are the goods interchangeable or unique?

The business must determine the nature of the inventory before it can decide how to record the cost of goods sold expense. If the items are unique, then the business will use specific identification to record cost of goods sold. If not, then other options are available to the business. The key characteristic is the uniqueness of the item that makes it difficult to substitute one item for another. While printers may have unique serial numbers, within the same model the customer doesn't notice the substitution of one printer for another.

632. unique

Specific identification is used by businesses that sell items that are uniquely identifiable. If the goods sold are fungible, specific identification is not necessary because each item is just like every other one.

633. $2,000

Businesses selling non-fungible goods such as artworks keep track of the cost by specific identification. Then, when an item is sold, the cost of that particular item becomes the cost of goods sold expense. In this case, the cost of the small painting of trees is $2,000, and that is the cost of goods sold.

634. the cost of each individual piece of jewelry that was sold during the month

A jeweler who sells designer pieces must keep a record of the cost of each individual piece of jewelry to record the correct cost of goods sold expense when the item is sold.

635. The items are unique and have high value.

Non-fungible goods can be specifically identified and are not substitutable. Common examples are original works of art, designer jewelry, and vehicles. The uniqueness makes it possible to record the cost of goods sold expense using the specific identification method. Fungible goods are indistinguishable. One bushel of corn is identical to another bushel of corn, so it would be impossible to record the cost of a specific bushel of corn when it was sold.

636. because if the goods are non-fungible, the business must keep records of the costs for each individual item

If goods are non-fungible, that means each item is unique, and then cost of goods sold is recorded using specific identification, which is the cost of each individual item in inventory.

637. 2,000 bushels of corn, 2,000 bushels of tomatoes, 2,000 bushels of soybeans

Corn, tomatoes, and soybeans are all fungible goods. Each item is not uniquely identifiable.

638. specific identification

Because vehicles are unique, or non-fungible, the car dealership records the cost of goods sold expense using specific identification.

639. $37

The LIFO method assigns the costs of the most recently acquired inventory to cost of goods sold. That would be the cost of the units acquired on May 12, April 3, and March 10.

$$15 + 12 + 10 = 37$$

640. $13

The LIFO method uses the costs associated with the oldest purchases to value ending inventory. That would be the unit in beginning inventory and the one purchased on February 10.

$$5 + 8 = 13$$

641. $30

The average cost method calculates the cost of all units available for sale during the period.

$$5 + 8 + 10 + 12 + 15 = 50$$

Then, a cost per unit is calculated using the cost of all units available for sale divided by the total number of units available for sale.

$$50 / 5 = 10$$

Then, that cost per unit is multiplied by the number of units sold to arrive at cost of goods sold expense.

$$10 \times 3 = 30$$

642. $23

The FIFO method assigns the cost of the oldest inventory units to cost of goods sold. That would be the unit that was in beginning inventory, the unit purchased on February 10, and the unit purchased on March 10.

$$5 + 8 + 10 = 23$$

643. $20

The average cost method calculates the cost of all units available for sale during the period.

$$5+8+10+12+15=50$$

Then, a cost per unit is calculated using the cost of all units available for sale divided by the total number of units available for sale.

$$50/5=10$$

Then, that cost per unit is multiplied by the number of units remaining to arrive at the value for ending inventory.

$$10\times 2=20$$

644. $27

The FIFO method uses the cost of the most recently purchased inventory to determine the value of ending inventory. That would be the cost of the units purchased on May 12 and April 3.

$$15+12=27$$

645. LIFO

LIFO stands for *last-in, first-out,* meaning the cost of the last inventory items acquired are put into cost of goods sold expense.

646. FIFO

FIFO stands for *first-in, first-out,* meaning the cost of the first inventory items acquired are put into cost of goods sold expense.

647. average cost

The average cost method calculates a cost per unit based on all inventory items available for sale and uses that cost per unit to calculate cost of goods sold expense and ending inventory.

648. average cost

The average cost method calculates a cost per unit based on all inventory items available for sale and uses that cost per unit to calculate cost of goods sold expense and ending inventory.

649. LIFO

LIFO stands for *last-in, first-out,* meaning the cost of the last inventory items acquired are put into cost of goods sold expense, and the oldest costs are left in ending inventory.

650. FIFO

FIFO stands for *first-in, first-out,* meaning the cost of the first inventory items acquired are put into cost of goods sold expense, leaving the cost of the newest inventory purchases in ending inventory.

651. $30,060

You assign the 5,010 units in ending inventory the most recent costs when using FIFO. The last purchase made was at $6, and that purchase included more than 5,010 units. You assign each of the units in ending inventory a $6 cost.

$$5{,}010 \times 6 = 30{,}060$$

652. $3,164

If the company is using FIFO, then you assign the most recent costs to the 14 units in ending inventory. Twelve of the units have a cost of $227 each, and you assign 2 of the units the next most recent cost of $220.

$$(12 \times 227) + (2 \times 220) = 2{,}724 + 440 = 3{,}164$$

653. $354

The company had 52 units available for sale during the year — the beginning inventory plus the purchases.

$$10 + 12 + 15 + 15 = 52$$

If 12 units remain in inventory, that means the company sold 40 units.

$$52 - 12 = 40$$

FIFO uses the oldest costs to determine cost of goods sold. Costs assigned to the sold units include 10 units at $6, because that is the oldest cost in inventory, plus 12 units at $8, which is the next oldest cost, plus 15 units at the next oldest cost of $11, plus 3 more units at the most recent cost of $11. That accounts for 40 units at the oldest costs.

$$(10 \times 6) + (12 \times 8) + (15 \times 11) + (3 \times 11) = 60 + 96 + 165 + 33 = 354$$

654. $132

FIFO uses the newest costs to value ending inventory. You assign the 12 units that are left in inventory a cost of $11 each, the most recent acquisition cost.

$$12 \times 11 = 132$$

655. $5,172,000

The company had 395,000 units available for sale during the year — the beginning inventory plus the purchases:

$$40,000+100,000+50,000+75,000+50,000+80,000=395,000$$

FIFO uses the oldest costs to determine cost of goods sold. Costs assigned to the sold units include 40,000 units at $10 because that is the oldest cost in inventory, plus 100,000 units at $12, which is the next oldest cost, plus 50,000 more units at the next oldest cost of $15, plus 75,000 at $16, plus 50,000 at $18, plus 38,000 at $19. That accounts for 353,000 units at the oldest costs.

$$(40,000\times 10)+(100,000\times 12)+(50,000\times 15)+(75,000\times 16)+(50,000\times 18)+(38,000\times 19)=$$
$$400,000+1,200,000+750,000+1,200,000+900,000+722,000=5,172,000$$

656. $798,000

The beginning inventory plus the purchases determines the goods available for sale during the period in units.

$$40,000+100,000+50,000+75,000+50,000+80,000=395,000$$

If Gray Paints sold 353,000 units, then 42,000 units remain in inventory at the end of the year.

$$395,000-353,000=42,000$$

FIFO uses the most recent costs to value ending inventory. Ending inventory would include 42,000 units with a cost of $19 each, the most recent cost of inventory purchases.

$$42,000\times 19=798,000$$

657. $51,493

The first step is to calculate the number of units sold during the month. Add the units purchased to the number of units in beginning inventory to arrive at the total number of units available during the month.

$$4,251+5,000+7,300=16,551$$

If 5,010 remain in inventory, then the company must have sold 11,541 units.

$$16,551-5,010=11,541$$

FIFO assigns the oldest costs to cost of goods sold.

$$(4,251\times 3)+(5,000\times 5)+(2,290\times 6)=$$
$$12,753+25,000+13,740=51,493$$

658. $10,372

The first step is to calculate the number of units sold during the month. Add the number of units purchased to the number of units in the beginning inventory and then subtract the number left to determine the number of units sold.

$$13+20+18+12=63$$
$$63-14=49$$

Stone Stuff sold 49 units and, if using FIFO, will assign the oldest costs to the 49 units sold and the newest costs to ending inventory.

$$(13\times204)+(20\times210)+(16\times220)=$$
$$2,652+4,200+3,520=10,372$$

659. $1,900,661

The first step is to determine the number of units sold. Core had 43,172 units to start with and bought 67,000 in one purchase, 132,000 in another, 125,000 in another, and 83,000 in the last purchase of the period. It had 450,172 units available for sale during the period.

$$43,172+67,000+132,000+125,000+83,000=450,172$$

At the end of the period, 45,669 units are still in inventory, so Core must have sold 404,503 units.

$$450,172-45,669=404,503$$

If Core uses FIFO, then you assign the oldest costs to cost of goods sold expense. You apply the oldest cost, $2, to the same number of units as was in the beginning inventory, 43,172. Then, you expense the next 67,000 units at $4 each, the next 132,000 at $5, and the next 125,000 also at $5. The remaining units necessary to get to the number of units sold, 37,331, use the cost of $7.

$$(43,172\times2)+(67,000\times4)+(132,000\times5)+(125,000\times5)+(37,331\times7)=$$
$$86,344+268,000+660,000+625,000+261,317=1,900,661$$

660. $319,683

If Core uses FIFO, then you assign the 45,669 units in ending inventory the most recent cost. The last purchase was at $7 per unit and was more than 45,669 units.

$$45,669\times7=319,683$$

661. $16,548

You assign the units in ending inventory the oldest costs when using the LIFO method. Of the 5,010 units in ending inventory, 4,251 are valued at $3. Another 759 units are needed to get to the ending inventory of 5,010 units, and you apply the next oldest cost, $5, to those units.

$$(4{,}251 \times 3) + (759 \times 5) =$$
$$12{,}753 + 3{,}795 = 16{,}548$$

662. $2,862

When using LIFO, you apply the oldest costs to units in ending inventory. Of the 14 units in ending inventory, you can assign 13 a cost of $204 because that is the oldest cost from the beginning inventory. The last unit gets the next oldest cost, $210.

$$(13 \times 204) + (1 \times 210) =$$
$$2{,}652 + 210 = 2{,}862$$

663. $96,332

Core is using LIFO, and that means that the oldest costs are in ending inventory. The ending inventory consists of 45,669 units. Of those, 43,172 can use the oldest price of $2, and you assign the remaining 2,497 units the next oldest cost of $4.

$$(43{,}172 \times 2) + (2{,}497 \times 4) =$$
$$86{,}344 + 9{,}988 = 96{,}332$$

664. $410

If the company uses LIFO, you apply the oldest costs to ending inventory, and the newest costs are in cost of goods sold expense. The first step is to figure out how many units were sold by calculating how many units were available for sale and then deducting the number remaining in inventory to arrive at 40 units sold.

$$10 + 12 + 15 + 15 = 52$$
$$52 - 12 = 40$$

The assign the units sold the most recent costs, beginning with the 30 $11 units and filling in to get to 40 with 10 units at $8.

$$(15 \times 11) + (15 \times 11) + (10 \times 8) =$$
$$165 + 165 + 80 = 410$$

665. $76

You assign the 12 units in ending inventory the oldest costs when using LIFO. Ten of the units are carried at $6 each, and 2 have a cost of $8 per unit.

$$(10\times6)+(2\times8)=$$
$$60+16=76$$

666. $5,546,000

When using LIFO, you apply the most recent costs to cost of goods sold expense. In this problem, the most recent costs are $19, $18, $16, $15, and $12. You can apply the $19, $18, $16, and $15 costs to the same number of units that were purchased. Only 98,000 of the 100,000 units purchased at $12 were sold.

$$(80{,}000\times19)+(50{,}000\times18)+(75{,}000\times16)+(50{,}000\times15)+(98{,}000\times12)=$$
$$1{,}520{,}000+900{,}000+1{,}200{,}000+750{,}000+1{,}176{,}000=5{,}546{,}000$$

667. $424,000

When using LIFO, you apply the oldest costs to units in ending inventory. The first task is to determine the number of units remaining in inventory by calculating the total number available for sale and deducting the number sold.

$$40{,}000+100{,}000+50{,}000+75{,}000+50{,}000+80{,}000=395{,}000$$
$$395{,}000-353{,}000=42{,}000$$

Then you assign the oldest costs to the units in ending inventory, beginning with the $10 cost associated with 40,000 of the units. Assign the next 2,000 units the next oldest cost of $12 per unit.

$$(40{,}000\times10)+(2{,}000\times12)=$$
$$400{,}000+24{,}000=424{,}000$$

668. $65,005

When using LIFO, you assign the most recent costs to the cost of goods sold expense. The first step is to determine the number of units sold by deducting the units remaining in inventory from the total units available for sale. The number of units available for sale is the total of the number in beginning inventory plus all the units purchased.

$$4{,}251+5{,}000+7{,}300=16{,}551$$

Then, if 16,551 units were available for sale, you can calculate the number sold by subtracting the number of units still in inventory.

$$16{,}551-5{,}010=11{,}541$$

Next, assign the most recent costs to the units sold. Apply the most recent cost, $6, to 7,300 units, and $5 to the remaining 4,241 units. This adds up to the 11,541 units sold.

$$(7{,}300\times 6)+(4241\times 5)=$$
$$43{,}800+21{,}205=65{,}005$$

669. $10,674

If the company uses LIFO, then the most recent costs are put into cost of goods sold expense. The first step is to calculate the number of units sold and then apply the most recent costs to those units. Calculate the number of units sold by deducting the units remaining in inventory at the end of the period from the total number of units available for sale during the period. The number of units available for sale includes those in beginning inventory plus all the units purchased during the period.

$$13+20+18+12=63$$

The problem tells you that 14 units are unsold, meaning they're still in inventory. The other units must have been sold.

$$63-14=49$$

Next, you assign the most recent costs to the 49 units sold, beginning with 12 units at $227, 18 units at $220, and 19 units at $210, which makes up the 49 units included in cost of goods sold.

$$(12\times 227)+(18\times 220)+(19\times 210)=$$
$$2{,}724+3{,}960+3{,}990=10{,}674$$

670. $2,124,012

If Core is using the LIFO method, it will assign the most recent costs to the cost of goods sold expense. The first step is to calculate the number of units sold. Beginning with the units on hand at the beginning of the year and adding all the purchases, the total units available for sale is 450,172.

$$43{,}172+67{,}000+132{,}000+125{,}000+83{,}000=450{,}172$$

If Core has 45,669 units left at the end of the year, then the others must have been sold. 404,503 units were sold.

$$450{,}172-45{,}669=404{,}503$$

When using LIFO, you apply the most recent costs to cost of goods sold, beginning with the purchase on November 11.

$$(83{,}000\times 7)+(125{,}000\times 5)+(132{,}000\times 5)+(64{,}503\times 4)=$$
$$581{,}000+625{,}000+660{,}000+258{,}012=2{,}124{,}012$$

671. $3,008.04

Calculating the value of ending inventory using the average cost method requires a cost per unit applied to the number of units remaining in inventory. Calculating cost per unit is a three-step process that results in a weighted average cost per unit. Step 1 is to determine the number of units available for sale during the period. That includes the units in beginning inventory plus the purchases throughout the period.

$$13+20+18+12=63$$

Step 2 is to determine the value of all the goods available for sale during the period by multiplying each group of units by the cost associated with the group and then summing the extensions.

$$13\times204=2,652$$
$$20\times210=4,200$$
$$18\times220=3,960$$
$$12\times227=2,724$$
$$2,652+4,200+3,960+2,724=13,536$$

Step 3 divides the result from Step 2, the value of all goods available for sale during the period, by the result from Step 1, the total number of units available for sale during the period, to get the average cost per unit.

$$\frac{13,536}{63}=214.86$$

Then you assign the average cost per unit to all units in ending inventory.

$$214.86\times14=3,008.04$$

672. $214.86

Calculating cost per unit is a three-step process that results in a weighted average cost per unit. Step 1 is to determine the number of units available for sale during the period. That includes the units in beginning inventory plus the purchases throughout the period.

$$13+20+18+12=63$$

Step 2 is to determine the value of all the goods available for sale during the period by multiplying each group of units by the cost associated with the group and then summing the extensions.

$$13\times204=2,652$$
$$20\times210=4,200$$
$$18\times220=3,960$$
$$12\times227=2,724$$
$$2,652+4,200+3,960+2,724=13,536$$

Step 3 divides the result from Step 2, the value of all goods available for sale during the period, by the result from Step 1, the total number of units available for sale during the period, to get the average cost per unit.

$$\frac{13,536}{63} = 214.86$$

673. $15.11

Calculating cost per unit is a three-step process that results in a weighted average cost per unit. Step 1 is to determine the number of units available for sale during the period. That includes the units in beginning inventory plus the purchases throughout the period.

$$40,000 + 100,000 + 50,000 + 75,000 + 50,000 + 80,000 = 395,000$$

Step 2 is to determine the value of all the goods available for sale during the period by multiplying each group of units by the cost associated with the group and then summing the extensions.

$$40,000 \times 10 = 400,000$$
$$100,000 \times 12 = 1,200,000$$
$$50,000 \times 15 = 750,000$$
$$75,000 \times 16 = 1,200,000$$
$$50,000 \times 18 = 900,000$$
$$80,000 \times 19 = 1,520,000$$
$$400,000 + 1,200,000 + 750,000 + 1,200,000 + 900,000 + 1,520,000 = 5,970,000$$

Step 3 divides the result from Step 2, the value of all goods available for sale during the period, by the result from Step 1, the total number of units available for sale during the period, to get the average cost per unit.

$$\frac{5,970,000}{395,000} = 15.11$$

674. $5,333,830

The average cost flow method uses the weighted average cost per unit and assigns it to all units, both cost of goods sold and ending inventory. The company sold 353,000 units during the year.

$$15.11 \times 353,000 = 5,333,830$$

675. $634,620

The average cost flow method uses the weighted average cost per unit and assigns it to all units, both cost of goods sold and ending inventory. Ending inventory contains 42,000 units.

$$15.11 \times 42,000 = 634,620$$

676. $4.93

Calculating cost per unit is a three-step process that results in a weighted average cost per unit. Step 1 is to determine the number of units available for sale during the period. That includes the units in beginning inventory plus the number of units purchased.

$$43,172 + 67,000 + 132,000 + 125,000 + 83,000 = 450,172$$

Step 2 is to determine the value of all the goods available for sale during the period by multiplying each group of units by the cost associated with the group and then summing the extensions.

$$43,172 \times 2 = 86,344$$

$$67,000 \times 4 = 268,000$$

$$132,000 \times 5 = 660,000$$

$$125,000 \times 5 = 625,000$$

$$83,000 \times 7 = 581,000$$

$$86,344 + 268,000 + 660,000 + 625,000 + 581,000 = 2,220,344$$

Step 3 divides the result from Step 2, the value of all goods available for sale during the period, by the result from Step 1, the total number of units available for sale during the period, to get the average cost per unit.

$$\frac{2,220,344}{450,172} = 4.93$$

677. $225,148.17

Determining the value of ending inventory requires a cost per unit that is assigned to each unit in inventory. Calculating cost per unit is a three-step process that results in a weighted average cost per unit. Step 1 is to determine the number of units available for sale during the period. That includes the units in beginning inventory plus the number of units purchased.

$$43,172 + 67,000 + 132,000 + 125,000 + 83,000 = 450,172$$

Step 2 is to determine the value of all the goods available for sale during the period by multiplying each group of units by the cost associated with the group and then summing the extensions.

$$43{,}172\times 2 = 86{,}344$$
$$67{,}000\times 4 = 268{,}000$$
$$132{,}000\times 5 = 660{,}000$$
$$125{,}000\times 5 = 625{,}000$$
$$83{,}000\times 7 = 581{,}000$$
$$86{,}344 + 268{,}000 + 660{,}000 + 625{,}000 + 581{,}000 = 2{,}220{,}344$$

Step 3 divides the result from Step 2, the value of all goods available for sale during the period, by the result from Step 1, the total number of units available for sale during the period, to get the average cost per unit.

$$\frac{2{,}220{,}344}{450{,}172} = 4.93$$

Next, multiply the cost per unit by the number of units in ending inventory.

$$4.93\times 45{,}669 = 225{,}148.17$$

678. $9.35

Calculating cost per unit is a three-step process that results in a weighted average cost per unit. Step 1 is to determine the number of units available for sale during the period. That includes the units in beginning inventory plus the purchases throughout the period.

$$10 + 12 + 15 + 15 = 52$$

Step 2 is to determine the value of all the goods available for sale during the period by multiplying each group of units by the cost associated with the group and then summing the extensions.

$$10\times 6 = 60$$
$$12\times 8 = 96$$
$$15\times 11 = 165$$
$$15\times 11 = 165$$
$$60 + 96 + 165 + 165 = 486$$

Step 3 divides the result from Step 2, the value of all goods available for sale during the period, by the result from Step 1, the total number of units available for sale during the period, to get the average cost per unit.

$$\frac{486}{52} = 9.35$$

679. $374.00

Calculating the cost of goods sold using the average cost method requires a cost per unit applied to the number of units sold. Calculating cost per unit is a three-step process that results in a weighted average cost per unit. Step 1 is to determine the number of units available for sale during the period. That includes the units in beginning inventory plus the purchases throughout the period.

$$10+12+15+15=52$$

Step 2 is to determine the value of all the goods available for sale during the period by multiplying each group of units by the cost associated with the group and then summing the extensions.

$$10\times6=60$$
$$12\times8=96$$
$$15\times11=165$$
$$15\times11=165$$

$$60+96+165+165=486$$

Step 3 divides the result from Step 2, the value of all goods available for sale during the period, by the result from Step 1, the total number of units available for sale during the period, to get the average cost per unit.

$$\frac{486}{52}=9.35$$

Next, you apply the cost per unit to the number of units sold. If Rich Red had 52 units available for sale during the period and has 12 left in ending inventory, then it must have sold the other 40.

$$52-12=40$$
$$40\times9.35=374$$

680. $112.20

Calculating the value of ending inventory using the average cost method requires a cost per unit applied to the number of units remaining in inventory. Calculating cost per unit is a three-step process that results in a weighted average cost per unit. Step 1 is to determine the number of units available for sale during the period. That includes the units in beginning inventory plus the purchases throughout the period.

$$10+12+15+15=52$$

Step 2 is to determine the value of all the goods available for sale during the period by multiplying each group of units by the cost associated with the group and then summing the extensions.

$$10\times6=60$$
$$12\times8=96$$
$$15\times11=165$$
$$15\times11=165$$

$$60+96+165+165=486$$

Step 3 divides the result from Step 2, the value of all goods available for sale during the period, by the result from Step 1, the total number of units available for sale during the period, to get the average cost per unit.

$$\frac{486}{52} = 9.35$$

Next, you assign the cost per unit to all units in ending inventory.

$$9.35 \times 12 = 112.20$$

681. $10,528.14

Calculating the cost of goods sold using the average cost method requires a cost per unit applied to the number of units sold. Calculating cost per unit is a three-step process that results in a weighted average cost per unit. Step 1 is to determine the number of units available for sale during the period. That includes the units in beginning inventory plus the purchases throughout the period.

$$13 + 20 + 18 + 12 = 63$$

Step 2 is to determine the value of all the goods available for sale during the period by multiplying each group of units by the cost associated with the group and then summing the extensions.

$$13 \times 204 = 2,652$$
$$20 \times 210 = 4,200$$
$$18 \times 220 = 3,960$$
$$12 \times 227 = 2,724$$
$$2,652 + 4,200 + 3,960 + 2,724 = 13,536$$

Step 3 divides the result from Step 2, the value of all goods available for sale during the period, by the result from Step 1, the total number of units available for sale during the period, to get the average cost per unit.

$$\frac{13,536}{63} = 214.86$$

Next, you multiply the average cost per unit by the number of units sold to determine the cost of goods sold. The company had 63 units available for sale, and at the end of the month, it had 14 left. That means it must have sold 49 units.

$$63 - 14 = 49$$
$$214.86 \times 49 = 10,528.14$$

682. $1,994,199.79

Calculating the cost of goods sold using the average cost method requires a cost per unit applied to the number of units sold. Calculating cost per unit is a three-step process that results in a weighted average cost per unit. Step 1 is to determine the number of units available for sale during the period. That includes the units in beginning inventory plus the number of units purchased.

$$43{,}172 + 67{,}000 + 132{,}000 + 125{,}000 + 83{,}000 = 450{,}172$$

Step 2 is to determine the value of all the goods available for sale during the period by multiplying each group of units by the cost associated with the group and then summing the extensions.

$$43{,}172 \times 2 = 86{,}344$$
$$67{,}000 \times 4 = 268{,}000$$
$$132{,}000 \times 5 = 660{,}000$$
$$125{,}000 \times 5 = 625{,}000$$
$$83{,}000 \times 7 = 581{,}000$$
$$86{,}344 + 268{,}000 + 660{,}000 + 625{,}000 + 581{,}000 = 2{,}220{,}344$$

Step 3 divides the result from Step 2, the value of all goods available for sale during the period, by the result from Step 1, the total number of units available for sale during the period, to get the average cost per unit.

$$\frac{2{,}220{,}344}{450{,}172} = 4.93$$

You then multiply the cost per unit is by the number of units sold to determine the cost of goods sold. If 450,172 units were available for sale, and at the end of the period the company still has 45,669 left, then the rest must have been sold.

$$450{,}172 - 45{,}669 = 404{,}503$$

$$4.93 \times 404{,}503 = 1{,}994{,}199.79$$

683. current replacement cost of the product

To apply the lower of cost or market rule when valuing inventory, the company must determine the *market value,* which is defined as the cost to buy the product from the usual suppliers at period's end, the current replacement cost.

684. $4,000

After inventory is valued using a cost flow method such as LIFO or FIFO, the company must compare that cost with the market value of the inventory. The *market value* of the inventory is defined as the cost to buy the item from normal suppliers at the end of the period. Then, the company must value the inventory on the balance sheet at the lower of the cost or the market value. In this problem, the cost of $4,000 is lower than the market value of $4,100, so the balance sheet value is $4,000.

685. $14,552

After inventory is valued using a cost flow method such as LIFO, FIFO, or average cost, the company must compare that value, termed the *cost of the inventory,* with the market value of the inventory. The *market value* of the inventory is defined as the cost to buy the item from normal suppliers at the end of the period. Then, the company must value the inventory at the lower of the cost or the market value. The cost, $14,552, is lower than the market value, $15,039, so the ending inventory is $14,552 on the balance sheet.

686. $0, no adjustment needed

After inventory is valued using a cost flow method such as LIFO, FIFO, or average cost, the company must compare that value, termed the *cost of the inventory,* with the market value of the inventory. The *market value* of the inventory is defined as the cost to buy the item from normal suppliers at the end of the period. Then, the company must value the inventory at the lower of the cost or the market value. In this problem, the cost is lower than the market value, so no adjustment is needed. The value of the inventory is already recorded on the books at $375,800.

687. $0

The cost of the inventory is lower than the market value, defined as the current cost to replace the inventory. The inventory is recorded on the books at cost, so no adjustment is necessary.

688. $100

After inventory is valued using a cost flow method such as LIFO or FIFO, the company must compare that value, termed the *cost of the inventory,* with the market value of the inventory. The *market value* of the inventory is defined as the cost to buy the item from normal suppliers at the end of the period. Then, the company must value the inventory at the lower of the cost or the market value. In this problem, that means the inventory must be on the balance sheet at $4,000, which is $100 less than the value already on the books. The company must reduce the value of the inventory by $100, and that lowers income by the same amount.

689. $359,000

For each category, the company values the inventory at the lower of cost or market. In this problem, the card games are valued at $11,000 rather than $12,000 because $11,000 is lower. The electronic games are valued at $300,000, the cost, not the market value of $310,000 because $300,000 is lower. The board games are valued at $48,000, the market value, because it's lower than the cost of $57,000. Total inventory is the sum of the three.

$$11{,}000 + 300{,}000 + 48{,}000 = 359{,}000$$

690. $9,300 decrease

The cost of the inventory is the average cost per unit for the year times the number of units:

$$12 \times 3,100 = 37,200$$

The market value of the inventory is equal to the year-end replacement cost times the number of units:

$$9 \times 3,100 = 27,900$$

To apply the lower of cost or market rule, the company must compare the cost to the market value and adjust to the lower amount. In this problem, the market value, $27,900, is lower than the cost, $37,200, by $9,300.

$$37,200 - 27,900 = 9,300$$

Inventory is decreased by $9,300, and income is decreased by $9,300.

691. $0

After inventory is valued using a cost flow method such as LIFO or FIFO, the company must compare that value, which is termed the *cost of the inventory,* with the market value of the inventory. The *market value* of the inventory is defined as the cost to buy the item from normal suppliers at the end of the period. Then, the company must value the inventory at the lower of the cost or the market value. In this problem, that means the inventory must be on the balance sheet at $4,000, which is no change from the value already on the books.

692. $487 decrease

The lower of cost or market rule requires companies to value inventory at the value that is lower. The cost is $15,039, so that's the amount at which the inventory is recorded on the books. The market value is lower, $14,552, so the inventory must be decreased to $14,552 from $15,039.

$$15,039 - 14,552 = 487$$

693. to allocate the cost of fixed assets to the periods benefited by their use

Depreciation is the rational, systematic way companies record the expense of using an asset that lasts more than a year. Accounting rules require that all expenses that it takes to produce the revenues be recorded on the same income statement. That matching of revenues and expenses gives users of the financial statements a clearer picture of current-year performance and better predictive information. Imagine a company buying a $2 million machine that will be used in the business for ten years. Without a systematic allocation of the cost to each of the ten years, the year of acquisition would show a $2 million expense, and each of the next nine years would show no expense related to using the machine, even though the revenues earned during those years were dependent on the use of the machine. Depreciation expense is the way a business allocates the cost to all the years that the asset helps to generate revenues.

694. Depreciation expense is higher in the early years of an asset's use than in the last years of use.

Accelerated depreciation methods speed up the recognition of expense by allocating more expense to the first few years of the asset's life.

695. Depreciation expense is $13,000, and book value is $62,000.

Straight-line depreciation evenly allocates the depreciable cost, which is equal to the cost minus the estimated salvage, to the years of use.

$$\frac{75{,}000-10{,}000}{5}=13{,}000$$

Book value is equal to the cost of the asset less the depreciation taken so far, which is only one year.

$$75{,}000-13{,}000=62{,}000$$

696. $12,000

Straight-line depreciation evenly allocates the depreciable cost, which is equal to the cost minus the estimated salvage, to the years of use. Land is not depreciated, so the depreciable cost of the house is $400,000 less the salvage value.

$$400{,}000-100{,}000=300{,}000$$

The depreciable cost is then spread out over the useful life.

$$\frac{300{,}000}{25}=12{,}000$$

697. The desks, computers, printers, and file cabinets.

The company only takes depreciation on assets owned and used in the business. Rented assets are not depreciated because the cost of using them is reflected in the rent expense.

698. $937.50

Although the machine was ordered on June 1, it was not used in the business activities until July 1. Because the machine was only used for half the year, from July 1 to the end of the year, the annual depreciation amount must be adjusted to reflect that. Straight-line depreciation allocates the depreciable cost, cost minus salvage, equally to all periods of the estimated useful life of the asset.

$$\frac{19{,}250-500}{10}\times\frac{6}{12}=937.50$$

699. $1,875

Straight-line depreciation allocates the depreciable cost of the asset, cost minus salvage, equally to all periods of the estimated useful life of the asset.

$$\frac{19,250-500}{10}=1,875$$

700. Depreciation expense is $13,000, and book value is $10,000.

Straight-line depreciation evenly allocates the depreciable cost, which is equal to the cost minus the estimated salvage, to the years of use.

$$\frac{75,000-10,000}{5}=13,000$$

Book value is equal to the cost of the asset less the depreciation taken so far. At the end of the fifth year, 5 years of depreciation would have been recorded for a total of 65,000.

$$5\times13,000=65,000$$

$$75000-65,000=10,000$$

701. $16,437.50

The book value of an asset is equal to the cost less the accumulated depreciation. The accumulated depreciation on an asset is equal to the total of the depreciation expense taken so far on that asset. In this problem, that means the depreciation expense from 2015 plus that in 2016 is deducted from the cost, $19,250. Depreciation in 2015 is for only a half year, 6 of 12 months, because the asset wasn't in use until July 1.

$$\frac{19,250-500}{10}\times\frac{6}{12}=937.50$$

Depreciation in 2016 is for the entire year.

$$\frac{19,250-500}{10}=1,875$$

$$19,250-937.50-1,875=16,437.50$$

702. $32,000

Depreciation expense using the double-declining method is calculated as the book value of the asset at the beginning of the year multiplied by a rate twice that of straight line. Book value is equal to the cost minus the depreciation taken on the asset so far. In the first year of use, the book value is equal to the cost of the building, $400,000. Land is not depreciated. The rate is calculated by dividing 1 by the useful life of the asset and then multiplying that rate by 2.

$$\frac{1}{25}\times2=.08\ or\ 8\%$$

$$400,000\times.08=32,000$$

703. $27,085

Depreciation expense using the double-declining method is calculated as the book value of the asset at the beginning of the year multiplied by a rate twice that of straight line. The rate is calculated by dividing 1 by the useful life and then multiplying that rate by 2.

$$\frac{1}{25} \times 2 = .08 \text{ or } 8\%$$

Book value is equal to the cost minus the depreciation taken on the asset so far. The book value at the beginning of the third year would be equal to the cost of the house, $400,000, less two years of depreciation expense. That means you must calculate the first two years of depreciation expense. The depreciation for the first year is the book value at the beginning of the year times the rate. At the beginning of the first year, the book value is equal to the cost, $400,000, because no depreciation has been taken yet.

Depreciation for the first year:

$$400{,}000 \times .08 = 32{,}000$$

That makes the book value at the beginning of the second year $368,000.

$$400{,}000 - 32{,}000 = 368{,}000$$

Depreciation for the second year equals book value times the rate:

$$368{,}000 \times .08 = 29{,}440$$

That makes the book value at the beginning of the third year $338,560.

$$400{,}000 - 32{,}000 - 29{,}440 = 338{,}560$$

Finally, book value at the beginning of the third year, $338,560, is multiplied by the rate to determine the depreciation expense for the third year:

$$338{,}560 \times .08 = 27{,}085$$

704. Both methods record the same amount of depreciation expense, $300,000, over the useful life of the asset.

Depreciation allocates the cost of the asset to the periods of use. The maximum amount any method can expense equals the cost less the salvage value.

705. $0

The maximum amount any depreciation method can expense equals the cost less the salvage value. Straight-line depreciation would record $13,000 each year:

$$\frac{75{,}000 - 10{,}000}{5} = 13{,}000$$

Five years of recording straight-line depreciation would result in the maximum of $65,000 being allocated to expense.

706. $18,750

The maximum amount of depreciation expense on any asset is equal to the cost of the asset less the estimated salvage value. In this problem, the cost is $19,250, and the salvage is $500.

$$19,250 - 500 = 18,750$$

707. $6,048

The allowance method requires estimating the amount of the bad debts before any accounts have been identified as uncollectible. The company can use any logical method of estimation. A percent of net sales is often used by companies that have historical data to provide input to the estimate. The logic is that the level of bad debts varies with the amount of sales, and if customer creditworthiness remains consistent over time, the percent of bad debts should remain pretty close to the same. The rate is .8%, which is .008 when doing the multiplication.

$$.008 \times 756,000 = 6,048$$

The bad debt expense on the income statement will be $6,048. That is also the amount by which the allowance for bad debts will increase.

708. $8,148

The allowance method requires estimating the amount of the bad debts before any accounts have been identified as uncollectible. The company can use any logical method of estimation. A percent of net sales is often used by companies that have historical data to provide input to the estimate. The logic is that the level of bad debts varies with the amount of sales, and if customer creditworthiness remains consistent over time, the percent of bad debts should remain pretty close to the same. The rate is .8%, which is .008 when doing the multiplication.

$$.008 \times 756,000 = 6,048$$

The bad debt expense on the income statement will be $6,048. That is also the amount by which the allowance for bad debts account will increase. That account has a normal credit balance, and increasing it by the amount of the bad debt expense, $6,048, will result in a balance of $8,148.

$$2,100 + 6,048 = 8,148$$

709. $3,750

The allowance method requires estimating the amount of the bad debts before any accounts have been identified as bad. The company can use any logical method of estimation. A percent of net sales is often used by companies that have historical data to provide input to the estimate. The logic is that the level of bad debts varies with the amount of sales, and if customer creditworthiness remains consistent over time, the percent of bad debts should remain pretty close to the same. The rate is .5%, which is .005 when doing the multiplication. Net sales is equal to sales less any returns, discounts, or allowances.

$$756{,}000 - 6{,}000 = 750{,}000$$

Then, net sales is multiplied by the rate to determine bad debt expense.

$$750{,}000 \times .005 = 3{,}750$$

710. $856,852

On the balance sheet, accounts receivable is presented at the *net realizable value* — what the company expects to collect. That is equal to the gross amount of accounts receivable less an allowance for bad debts. The first step is to calculate the bad debt expense using the allowance method and estimate by a percent of sales.

$$.008 \times 756{,}000 = 6{,}048$$

Step 2 is to calculate the adjusted balance in the allowance for bad debts account. In this case, the account already has a normal balance of $2,100, so the adjusted balance is just the sum of the beginning balance and the expense.

$$2{,}100 + 6{,}048 = 8{,}148$$

Step 3 calculates the balance sheet value for accounts receivable net by deducting the adjusted balance in the allowance for bad debts account from the gross amount of accounts receivable.

$$865{,}000 - 8{,}148 = 856{,}852$$

711. $6,550

The allowance method requires estimating the amount of the bad debts before any accounts have been identified as bad. The company can use any logical method of estimation. Many companies look at the composition of the accounts receivable and estimate the amount that may possibly be uncollectible. That estimate becomes the target balance for the allowance for bad debts account so that on the balance sheet, the net of gross receivables and the allowance account results in *net realizable value* — the amount the company expects to collect. In this problem, the estimate is 1% of gross accounts receivable, or $8,650.

$$865{,}000 \times .01 = 8{,}650$$

But that number is *not* the amount of the bad debt expense. That happens in the next step, which is to calculate the amount of the adjustment necessary to get the balance in the allowance account to be $8,650. The existing balance in the allowance for bad debts is a normal credit balance of $2,100, so the account must be increased by the difference between $2,100 and $8,650.

$$2{,}100 + x = 8{,}650$$
$$x = 6{,}550$$

712. $8,650

The allowance method requires estimating the amount of the bad debts before any accounts have been identified as uncollectible. The company can use any logical method of estimation. Many companies look at the composition of the accounts receivable and estimate the amount that may possibly be uncollectible. That estimate becomes the target balance for the allowance for bad debts account so that on the balance sheet, the net of gross receivables and the allowance account results in *net realizable value* — the amount the company expects to collect. In this problem, the estimate is 1% of gross accounts receivable, or $8,650.

$$865{,}000 \times .01 = 8{,}650$$

713. $856,350

The allowance method requires estimating the amount of the bad debts before any accounts have been identified as uncollectible. The company can use any logical method of estimation. Many companies look at the composition of the accounts receivable and estimate the amount that may possibly be uncollectible. That estimate becomes the target balance for the allowance for bad debts account so that on the balance sheet, the net of gross receivables and the allowance account results in net realizable value — the amount the company expects to collect. In this problem, the estimate is 1% of gross accounts receivable, or $8,650.

$$865{,}000 \times .01 = 8{,}650$$

Accounts receivable, net is equal to the gross accounts receivable less the allowance for bad debts.

$$865{,}000 - 8{,}650 = 856{,}350$$

714. $1,650

The allowance method requires estimating the amount of the bad debts before any accounts have been identified as uncollectible. The company can use any logical method of estimation. A percent of net sales is often used by companies that have historical data to provide input to the estimate. The logic is that the level of bad debts varies with the amount of sales, and if customer creditworthiness remains consistent over time, the percent of bad debts should remain pretty close to the same. The rate is .5%, which is .005 when doing the multiplication. Net sales is equal to sales less any returns, discounts, or allowances.

$$756{,}000 - 6{,}000 = 750{,}000$$

Then, net sales is multiplied by the rate to determine bad debt expense.

$$750{,}000 \times .005 = 3{,}750$$

The bad debt expense on the income statement will be $3,750. That is also the amount that the allowance for bad debts account will increase. That account has a normal credit balance, so if it has a debit balance, it's a negative amount. Adding the amount of the bad debt expense, $3,750, to a –$2,100 would result in a balance of $1,650.

$$-2{,}100 + 3{,}750 = 1{,}650$$

715. $9,020

The allowance method requires estimating the amount of the bad debts before any accounts have been identified as uncollectible. The company can use any logical method of estimation. Many companies look at the composition of the accounts receivable and estimate the amount that may possibly be uncollectible. That estimate becomes the target balance for the allowance for bad debts account. On the balance sheet, the net of gross receivables and the allowance account results in *net realizable value* — the amount the company expects to collect. In this problem, the estimate is .8% of gross accounts receivable, or $6,920.

$$.008 \times 865,000 = 6,920$$

The next step is to determine the increase in the allowance account that will bring the current balance to $6,920. Because the current balance in the allowance for uncollectibles is a debit amount of $2,100, the increase must be greater than $6,920. The $2,100 is a negative amount, so the amount of the expense must get the balance to zero and then get it up to $9,020.

$$-2,100 + x = 6,920$$
$$x = 6,920 + 2,100$$
$$x = 9,020$$

716. $858,080

The allowance method requires estimating the amount of the bad debts before any accounts have been identified as uncollectible. The company can use any logical method of estimation. Many companies look at the composition of the accounts receivable and estimate the amount that may possibly be uncollectible. That estimate becomes the target balance for the allowance for bad debts account. On the balance sheet, the net of gross receivables and the allowance account results in *net realizable value* — the amount the company expects to collect. In this problem, the estimate is .8% of gross accounts receivable, or $9,020.

$$.008 \times 865,000 = 9,020$$

Accounts receivable, net is equal to gross accounts receivable less the allowance for uncollectibles.

$$865,000 - 9,020 = 858,080$$

717. straight line

Declining balance methods are accelerated methods of depreciation, and those methods charge more depreciation in the early years of use. Straight line charges the same amount every year, and when the equipment is new, will have a lower depreciation expense amount.

718. double-declining balance

In the first year of an asset's life, double-declining balance applies a rate equal to twice the straight-line rate to the cost of the asset. This results in the largest depreciation expense.

719. Reduce the estimate of bad debts to 1% of net sales.

The company is trying to find a way to increase earnings by $500,000. The estimate of bad debts is currently $1,000,000 when calculated using 2% as the estimate. If the company used 1% instead, bad debt expense would be decreased to $500,000. That is a $500,000 savings, just the amount needed to meet the forecast.

720. double-declining balance depreciation for new equipment and LIFO when prices are rising

Conservative accounting methods are those that delay the recording of revenue and accelerate the recording of expenses. Double-declining balance depreciation produces the highest expense for new equipment. During a period of rising prices, LIFO uses the newest high costs in cost of goods sold, which makes it higher.

721. double-declining balance and LIFO

To minimize taxes, the company wants the lowest possible income. That means it wants to pick methods that maximize expenses. When equipment is new, double-declining balance will produce the most expense and therefore the lowest income. During a period of rising prices, LIFO will include the newest and therefore the highest prices in cost of goods sold. Higher expenses mean a lower income and lower taxes.

722. FIFO, straight line, and the 1% estimate of bad debts

To produce the highest income, the company wants to choose the methods that will minimize expenses. FIFO produces the lowest cost of goods sold during a period of rising prices because the oldest costs are included in cost of goods sold, and those are the lowest costs. When equipment is new, straight line will result in a lower expense than double-declining balance. The estimate for bad debt expense that uses the smaller percent of sales will produce a lower expense.

723. double-declining balance

In the first year of an asset's life, double-declining applies twice the straight-line rate to the cost of the asset. This results in the highest amount of depreciation expense of all methods.

724. Use double-declining balance for tax purposes and straight line for financial reporting.

When assets are new, double-declining balance will produce the highest expense, so that would achieve the goal of lower income for tax purposes. Straight-line depreciation charges the same amount every year, but in the early years of an asset's life, it will be a lower depreciation expense, achieving the goal of higher income for financial reporting.

725. $18,200

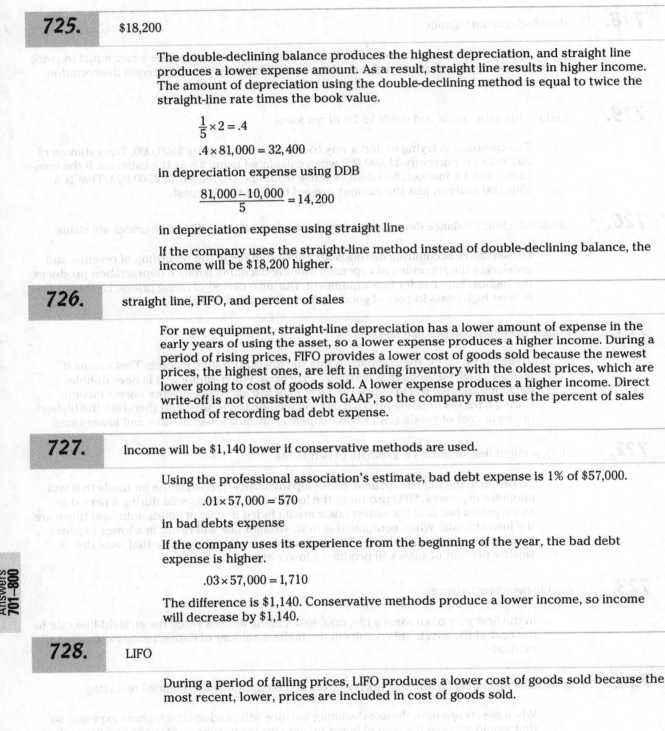

The double-declining balance produces the highest depreciation, and straight line produces a lower expense amount. As a result, straight line results in higher income. The amount of depreciation using the double-declining method is equal to twice the straight-line rate times the book value.

$$\frac{1}{5}\times 2 = .4$$

$$.4\times 81,000 = 32,400$$

in depreciation expense using DDB

$$\frac{81,000-10,000}{5} = 14,200$$

in depreciation expense using straight line

If the company uses the straight-line method instead of double-declining balance, the income will be $18,200 higher.

726. straight line, FIFO, and percent of sales

For new equipment, straight-line depreciation has a lower amount of expense in the early years of using the asset, so a lower expense produces a higher income. During a period of rising prices, FIFO provides a lower cost of goods sold because the newest prices, the highest ones, are left in ending inventory with the oldest prices, which are lower going to cost of goods sold. A lower expense produces a higher income. Direct write-off is not consistent with GAAP, so the company must use the percent of sales method of recording bad debt expense.

727. Income will be $1,140 lower if conservative methods are used.

Using the professional association's estimate, bad debt expense is 1% of $57,000.

$$.01\times 57,000 = 570$$

in bad debts expense

If the company uses its experience from the beginning of the year, the bad debt expense is higher.

$$.03\times 57,000 = 1,710$$

The difference is $1,140. Conservative methods produce a lower income, so income will decrease by $1,140.

728. LIFO

During a period of falling prices, LIFO produces a lower cost of goods sold because the most recent, lower, prices are included in cost of goods sold.

729. $5,000

To find the contribution margin, subtract cost of goods sold and variable costs from sales.

$$10,000 - 3,000 - 2,000 = 5,000$$

730. $7,000

The difference between sales and cost of goods sold is *gross profit,* also called *gross margin.*

$$10,000 - 3,000 = 7,000$$

731. $5,100,978

The difference between sales and cost of goods sold is *gross profit,* sometimes called *gross margin.*

$$7,632,614 - 2,531,636 = 5,100,978$$

732. $1,469,967

Sales revenue less all variable costs, which includes cost of goods sold and other variable costs, equals the contribution margin.

$$7,632,614 - 2,531,636 - 3,631,011 = 1,469,967$$

733. $669,967

Sales revenue less all variable costs and fixed costs equals operating profit. Variable costs include cost of goods sold.

$$7,632,614 - 2,531,636 - 3,631,011 - 800,000 = 669,967$$

734. $500,000

Gross profit is the difference between sales and cost of goods sold. If you know sales and gross profit, you can plug in the cost of goods sold.

$$800,000 - x = 300,000$$
$$x = 500,000$$

735. $100,000

The difference between gross profit and contribution margin is equal to the variable costs.

$$300,000 - x = 200,000$$
$$x = 100,000$$

736. $50,000

Operating profit is equal to the contribution margin less the fixed costs.

$$150{,}000 = 200{,}000 - x$$
$$x = 50{,}000$$

737. $7,576,000

The difference between sales and cost of goods sold is *gross profit,* sometimes called *gross margin*. Sales equal the number of units sold times the selling price.

$$47{,}350 \times 300 = 14{,}205{,}000$$

Cost of goods sold equals the number of units sold times the cost per unit.

$$47{,}350 \times 140 = 6{,}629{,}000$$

Sales minus cost of goods sold:

$$14{,}205{,}000 - 6{,}629{,}000 = 7{,}576{,}000$$

738. $6,155,500

Sales revenue less all variable costs, which includes cost of goods sold and other variable costs, equals the contribution margin. Sales equal the number of units sold times the selling price.

$$47{,}350 \times 300 = 14{,}205{,}000$$

Cost of goods sold equals the number of units sold times the cost per unit.

$$47{,}350 \times 140 = 6{,}629{,}000$$

Total variable costs equal the number of units sold times the variable cost per unit.

$$47{,}350 \times 30 = 1{,}420{,}500$$

Sales less cost of goods sold less total variable costs equals the contribution margin.

$$14{,}205{,}000 - 6{,}629{,}000 - 1{,}420{,}500 = 6{,}155{,}500$$

739. $15

The contribution margin per unit is equal to the selling price less the variable cost per unit.

$$45 - 30 = 15$$

740. $16

The change in total cost reflects the additional variable costs of producing 500 more units. The change in cost is $8,000.

$$35{,}000 - 27{,}000 = 8{,}000$$

That $8,000 produced 500 more units, so dividing the change in cost by the number of the additional units produced will equal an estimate of the variable cost per unit.

$$\frac{8{,}000}{500} = 16$$

741. $11,000

The first step is to estimate the variable cost per unit. The change in total cost reflects the additional variable costs of producing 500 more units. The change in cost is $8,000.

$$35{,}000 - 27{,}000 = 8{,}000$$

That $8,000 produced 500 more units, so dividing the change in cost by the number of the additional units produced will equal an estimate of the variable cost per unit.

$$\frac{8{,}000}{500} = 16$$

Then use that estimate to determine how much of the cost is variable.

$$1{,}000 \times 16 = 16{,}000$$

If $16,000 of the $27,000 is associated with the variable cost, then the remainder is an estimate of the fixed cost.

$$27{,}000 - 16{,}000 = 11{,}000$$

742. $64

The contribution margin per unit is equal to the selling price less the variable cost per unit. The first step is to estimate the variable cost per unit. The change in total cost reflects the additional variable costs of producing 500 more units. The change in cost is $8,000.

$$35{,}000 - 27{,}000 = 8{,}000$$

That $8,000 produced 500 more units, so dividing the change in cost by the number of the additional units produced will equal an estimate of the variable cost per unit.

$$\frac{8{,}000}{500} = 16$$

The second step is to find the difference between the selling price and the variable cost per unit.

$$80 - 16 = 64$$

743. $3,600

Total variable costs are equal to the cost per unit multiplied by the number of units sold. In this problem, total variable cost is $54,000,000, and 15,000 units were sold. So you would divide total cost by units sold to get the cost per unit.

$$54,000,000 = x \times 15,000$$

$$\frac{54,000,000}{15,000} = 3,600$$

744. 76,667

The company must sell enough units so that the total contribution margin covers the fixed costs and produces $1,000,000 in profit. The first step to solve this problem is to calculate the contribution margin per unit. The contribution margin per unit is equal to the selling price less the variable cost per unit.

$$45 - 30 = 15$$

The second step is to calculate the number of units the company must sell to cover an amount to equal the fixed costs plus the desired profit of $1,000,000.

$$\frac{150,000 + 1,000,000}{15} = 76,667$$

745. 10,000

The company must sell enough units so that the total contribution margin covers the fixed costs of $150,000. The first step to solve this problem is to calculate the contribution margin per unit. The contribution margin per unit is equal to the selling price less the variable cost per unit.

$$45 - 30 = 15$$

The second step is to calculate the number of units the company must sell to cover an amount to equal the fixed costs. This number of units will generate a profit of $0.

$$\frac{150,000}{15} = 10,000$$

746. $2,200

Contribution margin per unit is the difference between the selling price and variable cost per unit. You determine the selling price by dividing total revenue by number of units sold.

$$\frac{87{,}000{,}000}{15{,}000} = 5{,}800$$

The variable cost per unit is equal to total variable costs divided by the number of units.

$$\frac{54{,}000{,}000}{15{,}000} = 3{,}600$$

The contribution margin per unit is equal to the selling price per unit minus the variable cost per unit.

$$5{,}800 - 3{,}600 = 2{,}200$$

747. 20,909

Short Elliott wants an operating profit of $26,000,000. That means the contribution margin must cover the desired profit plus the fixed costs, or $46,000,000.

$$26{,}000{,}000 + 20{,}000{,}000 = 46{,}000{,}000$$

Contribution margin equals the contribution margin per unit times the number of units sold. Contribution margin per unit is the difference between the selling price and the variable cost per unit. You determine the selling price by dividing total revenue by number of units sold.

$$\frac{87{,}000{,}000}{15{,}000} = 5{,}800$$

The variable cost per unit is equal to total variable costs divided by the number of units.

$$\frac{54{,}000{,}000}{15{,}000} = 3{,}600$$

The contribution margin per unit is equal to selling price per unit minus variable cost per unit.

$$5{,}800 - 3{,}600 = 2{,}200$$

Dividing desired profit plus fixed costs by the contribution margin per unit results in the necessary number of units sold.

$$\frac{46{,}000{,}000}{2{,}200} = 20{,}909$$

748. 26,818

Short Elliott wants an operating profit of $39,000,000. That means the contribution margin must cover the desired profit plus the fixed costs, or $59,000,000.

$$39,000,000 + 20,000,000 = 59,000,000$$

Contribution margin is equal to the contribution margin per unit times the number of units sold. Contribution margin per unit is the difference between the selling price and the variable cost per unit. You determine the selling price by dividing total revenue by number of units sold.

$$\frac{87,000,000}{15,000} = 5,800$$

The variable cost per unit is equal to total variable costs divided by the number of units.

$$\frac{54,000,000}{15,000} = 3,600$$

The contribution margin per unit is equal to selling price per unit minus variable cost per unit.

$$5,800 - 3,600 = 2,200$$

Dividing the desired profit plus fixed costs by the contribution margin per unit results in the necessary number of units sold.

$$\frac{59,000,000}{2,200} = 26,818$$

749. $365,000

Operating profit is equal to sales revenue less total variable cost and fixed costs. Sales revenue is equal to the number of units sold times the selling price.

$$150,000 \times 10 = 1,500,000$$

Total variable costs are equal to the number of units sold times the variable cost per unit.

$$150,000 \times 4 = 600,000$$

$$1,500,000 - 600,000 - 535,000 = 365,000$$

750. $317,000

Operating profit is equal to sales revenue less total variable cost and fixed costs. Sales revenue is equal to the number of units sold times the selling price.

$$87{,}000 \times 135 = 11{,}745{,}000$$

Total variable costs are equal to the number of units sold times the variable cost per unit.

$$87{,}000 \times 125 = 10{,}875{,}000$$

$$11{,}745{,}000 - 10{,}875{,}000 - 553{,}000 = 317{,}000$$

751. $18,000,000

Operating profit is the difference between total contribution margin and fixed costs. Total contribution margin is equal to the number of units sold multiplied by the contribution margin per unit.

$$2{,}000{,}000 \times 15 = 30{,}000{,}000$$

$$30{,}000{,}000 - 12{,}000{,}000 = 18{,}000{,}000$$

752. $400,000

If each unit sold contributes $4 toward covering fixed costs and generating profit, then deducting the fixed costs from the total contribution margin that results from the sale of 450,000 units will give you the operating profit. The total contribution margin generated from the sale of 450,000 units equals the number of units sold times the contribution margin per unit.

$$450{,}000 \times 4 = 1{,}800{,}000$$

Then deduct the fixed costs from that number to get operating profit.

$$1{,}800{,}000 - 1{,}400{,}000 = 400{,}000$$

753. $17,000

The operating profit is the difference between total contribution margin and fixed costs. Total contribution margin is the number of units sold times the contribution margin per unit. You can calculate the number of units sold by dividing the sales revenue by the selling price per unit.

$$\frac{680{,}000}{40} = 17{,}000$$

Now, you can determine total contribution margin.

$$17{,}000 \times 15 = 255{,}000$$

$$255{,}000 - 238{,}000 = 17{,}000$$

754. $4.55

The contribution margin is the difference between the selling price and the variable cost and the amount each unit contributes to covering the fixed costs and producing profit for the company. The formula to calculate operating profit is number of units sold times the contribution margin minus the fixed costs equals the profit. So the sum of the fixed costs and the profit equals the total amount of contribution margin generated by the sales.

$$3{,}700{,}000 + 850{,}000 = 4{,}550{,}000$$

Dividing the total contribution margin by the units sold equals the contribution margin per unit.

$$\frac{4{,}550{,}000}{1{,}000{,}000} = 4.55$$

755. $300,000

The operating profit is the difference between total contribution margin and fixed costs. The contribution margin is the difference between the selling price per unit and the variable cost per unit.

$$5 - 1 = 4$$

Total contribution margin equals contribution margin per unit times the number of units sold.

$$4 \times 1{,}000{,}000 = 4{,}000{,}000$$

Deducting the fixed costs from the total contribution margin results in the operating profit.

$$4{,}000{,}000 - 3{,}700{,}000 = 300{,}000$$

756. $4,000,000

The contribution margin is the difference between the selling price per unit and the variable cost per unit.

$$5 - 1 = 4$$

Total contribution margin equals contribution margin per unit times the number of units sold.

$$4 \times 1{,}000{,}000 = 4{,}000{,}000$$

757. $4,775,000

The contribution margin must cover the fixed costs and produce a profit. The contribution margin is the difference between the selling price per unit and the variable cost per unit.

$$560 - 130 = 430$$

Each unit sold contributes $430 to covering the fixed costs and generating profit for the company. The total amount of contribution margin available for these purposes is equal to the number of units sold times the contribution margin per unit.

$$37{,}500 \times 430 = 16{,}125{,}000$$

Deducting the fixed costs from the total contribution margin results in the profit.

$$16{,}125{,}000 - 11{,}350{,}000 = 4{,}775{,}000$$

758. $50

The contribution margin is the difference between the selling price and the variable cost. The formula to calculate operating profit is number of units sold times the contribution margin minus the fixed costs equals the profit. So the sum of the fixed costs and the profit equals the total amount of contribution margin generated by the sales.

$$92{,}500 + 373{,}000 = 465{,}500$$

Dividing the total contribution margin by the units sold equals the contribution margin per unit.

$$\frac{465{,}500}{9{,}310} = 50$$

759. $172,000

After the company reaches the break-even sales level, all the contribution margin goes to operating profit. That means that, beginning with vehicle sales 801 through 1,200, each sale earns $430 in operating profit.

$$1200 - 800 = 400$$
$$400 \times 430 = 172{,}000$$

760. $206,000

After the break-even number of sales, each additional sale contributes $103 to operating profit. Every bike sale after 6,000 increases the operating profit by $103.

$$8{,}000 - 6{,}000 = 2000$$
$$2{,}000 \times 103 = 206{,}000$$

761. $1,000

Every sale after 3,800 contributes $5 to operating profit.

$$4,000 - 3,800 = 200$$
$$200 \times 5 = 1,000$$

762. $35,750

The contribution margin is the difference between the selling price per unit and the variable cost per unit. For the breakfast food that is $2.75.

$$6.75 - 4 = 2.75$$

After break-even, the point at which the fixed costs are covered, each unit sold will contribute $2.75 to profit.

$$120,000 - 107,000 = 13,000$$
$$13,000 \times 2.75 = 35,750$$

763. $59,625

Each unit sold after the break-even point of 3,710 fans will produce operating profit equal to the contribution margin per unit. The contribution margin is the difference between the selling price and the variable cost per unit.

$$400 - 175 = 225$$
$$3,975 - 3,710 = 265$$
$$225 \times 265 = 59,625$$

764. $336,000

Each unit sold after the break-even point of 190,000 suits will produce operating profit equal to the contribution margin per unit. The contribution margin is the difference between the selling price and the variable cost per unit. To get the operating profit, you multiply the number of units sold over break-even by the contribution margin per unit.

$$238,000 - 190,000 = 48,000$$
$$80 - 73 = 7$$
$$48,000 \times 7 = 336,000$$

765. $780

After break-even, operating profit increases for every additional unit sold. Splendid Treats sold 260 units over the number needed to break even.

$$1,500 - 1,240 = 260$$

Each unit contributes the difference between the sale price and the variable cost to operating profit.

$$15 - 12 = 3$$

The operating profit is equal to the number of units sold above break-even multiplied by the contribution margin per unit.

$$260 \times 3 = 780$$

766. $76,500

Each sheet sold contributes to operating profit in an amount equal to the difference between the selling price per unit and the variable cost per unit. You calculate the selling price per unit by dividing sales revenue by the number of sheets sold.

$$\frac{560,000}{7,000} = 80$$

$$80 - 35 = 45$$

Each sheet sold after break-even contributes $45 to operating profit. Total operating profit equals the number of sheets sold above 5,300 multiplied by the contribution margin per unit.

$$7,000 - 5,300 = 1,700$$

$$1,700 \times 45 = 76,500$$

767. $48,750

The contribution margin per unit goes to cover fixed costs and to produce operating profit. The contribution margin per unit is equal to the difference between the selling price per unit and the variable cost per unit. Total sales revenue divided by number of units sold results in the selling price per unit.

$$\frac{300,000}{20,000} = 15$$

Total variable cost divided by number of units sold equals the variable cost per unit.

$$\frac{170,000}{20,000} = 8.50$$

$$15 - 8.5 = 6.5$$

Operating profit equals the number of units sold above break-even multiplied by the contribution margin per unit.

$$20{,}000 - 12{,}500 = 7{,}500$$
$$7{,}500 \times 6.5 = 48{,}750$$

768. $112,800

Each app sold contributes to operating profit in an amount equal to the difference between the selling price per unit and the variable cost per unit. You calculate the selling price per unit by dividing sales revenue by the number of apps sold.

$$\frac{960{,}300}{970{,}000} = .99$$
$$.99 - .05 = .94$$

Each app sold after break-even contributes 94¢ to operating profit. Total operating profit equals the number of apps sold above 850,000 multiplied by the contribution margin per unit.

$$970{,}000 - 850{,}000 = 120{,}000$$
$$120{,}000 \times .94 = 112{,}800$$

769. $810,000

If you know the profit per unit, you can calculate operating profit. It is equal to the number of units sold times the profit per unit. Profit per unit is equal to contribution margin per unit less average fixed cost per unit.

$$400 - 220 = 180$$
$$180 \times 4{,}500 = 810{,}000$$

770. $5,000,000

If you know the profit per unit, you can calculate operating profit. Operating profit is equal to the number of units sold times the profit per unit. Profit per unit is equal to contribution margin per unit less average fixed cost per unit.

$$2.75 - 1.50 = 1.25$$
$$4{,}000{,}000 \times 1.25 = 5{,}000{,}000$$

771. $3.50

Average fixed cost per jar is equal to total fixed costs divided by the number of jars sold.

$$\frac{3{,}500{,}000}{1{,}000{,}000} = 3.50$$

772. $461.50

Profit per unit is equal to the selling price per unit less the variable costs per unit less the fixed cost per unit. You determine fixed cost per unit by dividing total fixed costs by the number of units sold.

$$\frac{3{,}500{,}000}{1{,}000{,}000} = 3.50$$

$$500 - 35 - 3.50 = \$461.50$$

773. $9,650

If you know the contribution margin and fixed costs, you can calculate operating profit. Total contribution margin is $47 times 950 boxes sold, which equals $44,650. $44,650 less $35,000 fixed costs equals a $9,650 profit.

774. $667,000

If you know the profit per unit, you can calculate operating profit. Operating profit is equal to the number of units sold times the profit per unit. Profit per unit is equal to contribution margin per unit less fixed cost per unit. Contribution margin per unit is the difference between selling price per unit and variable cost per unit. So, the first step is to calculate contribution margin per unit.

$$350 - 120 = 230$$

Then you can calculate the profit per unit.

$$230 - 85 = 145$$

Finally, calculate operating profit by multiplying the number of units sold times the profit per unit.

$$4{,}600 \times 145 = 667{,}000$$

775. $180,000

Sales decline by 2,000 units (10,000 less 8,000). Contribution margin declines by $180,000 (2,000 units times $90). Total fixed costs do not change. The $180,000 also represents the decline in profit.

776. $150

Profit per unit is equal to the selling price per unit less the variable costs per unit less the average fixed cost per unit. You determine average fixed cost per unit by dividing total fixed costs by the number of units sold.

$$\frac{208{,}000}{2{,}600} = 80$$

$$350 - 120 - 80 = 150$$

777. $92,000

The increase in total contribution margin is the 400 unit increase in sales (4,400 – 4,000) times the $230 contribution margin ($230 times 400 equals $92,000 profit increase). Total fixed costs do not change and do not affect the increase in profit.

778. $545,000

The first 10,000 bags cover the fixed costs, so the additional 500 contribute $90 each to profit. $50 times 10,000 units plus $90 times 500 units equals $545,000.

779. 12%

You calculate return on capital by dividing operating profit by total capital.

$$\frac{120{,}000}{1{,}000{,}000} = .12$$

780. 14%

You determine rate of return on equity by comparing income before taxes to total owners' equity. Income before taxes is equal to operating profit minus interest expense.

$$120{,}000 - 15{,}000 = 105{,}000$$

$$\frac{105{,}000}{750{,}000} = .14$$

781. 27%

Rate of return on capital measures income earned by the company relative to how much capital was used to generate that income. The numerator of the formula is operating profit. The denominator of the formula is the total of interest-bearing debt plus total owners' equity. Companies usually don't pay interest on current liabilities.

$$\frac{27{,}000}{60{,}000 + 40{,}000} = .27$$

782. 60%

You determine rate of return on equity by comparing income before taxes to total owners' equity. Income before taxes is equal to operating profit minus interest expense.

$$27{,}000 - 3{,}000 = 24{,}000$$

$$\frac{24{,}000}{40{,}000} = .60$$

783. 13%

Rate of return on capital measures income earned by the company relative to how much capital was used to generate that income. The numerator of the formula is operating profit. The denominator of the formula is the total of interest-bearing debt plus total owners' equity. Companies usually don't pay interest on current liabilities.

$$\frac{41,600}{200,000+120,000}=.13$$

784. 23%

You determine rate of return on equity by comparing income before taxes to total owners' equity. Income before taxes is equal to operating profit minus interest expense.

$$41,600-14,000=27,600$$

$$\frac{27,600}{120,000}=.23$$

785. 9.6%

Rate of return on capital measures income earned by the company relative to how much capital it took to generate that income. The numerator of the formula is operating profit. The denominator of the formula is the total of interest-bearing debt plus total owners' equity. Companies usually don't pay interest on current liabilities.

$$\frac{37,000}{85,000+300,000}=.096$$

786. 10.1%

You determine rate of return on equity by comparing income before taxes to total owners' equity. Income before taxes is equal to operating profit minus interest expense.

$$37,000-6,800=30,200$$

$$\frac{30,200}{300,000}=.101$$

787. 5.6%

The formula for calculating return on capital compares operating profit to total capital. Total capital is equal to interest-bearing debt plus owners' equity. Companies don't usually pay interest on current liabilities.

$$\frac{32,000}{250,000+320,000}=.056$$

788. 6.5%

The formula for calculating return on equity compares income before tax expense to owners' equity.

$$\frac{20,750}{320,000} = .065$$

789. Operating profit increases by more than 10% because none of the contribution margin of the extra 10 units needs to cover fixed costs.

The company will experience a bigger increase in operating profit than the increase in sales because operating leverage allows better utilization of the fixed costs.

790. operating leverage

The company leverages its operating expenses, using them more efficiently because each of the additional units sold doesn't have to cover any of the fixed costs. That coverage was accomplished at the lower volume, so each new sale adds the entire contribution margin to operating profit.

791. $40,000

The fixed costs are already covered when the company sells 200 treatments. That means that each treatment after that contributes the entire contribution margin to operating profit, up to 300 treatments. The 10% increase in sales from 200 treatments last year translates into 20 more treatments this year. The increase in operating profit is the number of additional units sold multiplied by the contribution margin per unit.

$$20 \times 2,000 = 40,000$$

792. 112.5%

Contribution margin per unit is $185 less $5 equals $180. A 50% sales increase is 100 units times 50% equals 50. 50 units times $180 contribution margin is a $9,000 increase in profit. The original profit was $18,000 contribution margin less $10,000 fixed costs equals $8,000. The increase in profit is $9,000 divided by $8,000, or 112.5%.

793. 16.4%

Contribution margin per unit is $185 less $5 equals $180. A 10% sales decrease is 100 units times 10% equals 10. 10 units times $180 contribution margin is a $1,800 decrease in profit. The original profit was $18,000 contribution margin less $7,000 fixed costs equals $11,000. The decrease in profit is $1,800 divided by $11,000, or 16.4%.

794. Operating profit increases by 35.3%.

The first step is to determine operating profit at each level of sales and figure out the dollar amount of the increase. Operating profit is equal to the contribution margin multiplied by the number of units sold less total fixed costs. Contribution margin is the difference between selling price and variable costs per unit.

$$300 - 200 = 100$$

When sales equal 300 units, operating profit is 17,000.

$$100 \times 300 - 13{,}000 = 17{,}000$$

When sales increase by 20% to 360 units, operating profit is 23,000.

$$100 \times 360 - 13{,}000 = 23{,}000$$

The increase in profit is 6,000.

$$23{,}000 - 17{,}000 = 6{,}000$$

You determine the percent increase by dividing the amount of the increase by the original operating profit.

$$\frac{6{,}000}{17{,}000} = .353$$

795. Operating profit increases by 39%.

The first step is to determine operating profit at each level of sales and figure out the dollar amount of the increase. Operating profit is equal to the contribution margin multiplied by the number of units sold less total fixed costs. Contribution margin is the difference between selling price and variable costs per unit.

$$80 - 15 = 65$$

When sales equal 30,000 units, operating profit is 750,000.

$$(65 \times 30{,}000) - 1{,}200{,}000 = 750{,}000$$

When sales increase by 15% to 34,500 units, operating profit is 1,042,500.

$$(65 \times 34{,}500) - 1{,}200{,}000 = 1{,}042{,}500$$

The increase in profit is 292,500.

$$1{,}042{,}500 - 750{,}000 = 292{,}500$$

You determine the percent increase by dividing the amount of the increase by the original operating profit.

$$\frac{292{,}500}{750{,}000} = .39$$

796. Operating profit decreases by 30.6%.

The first step is to determine operating profit at each level of sales and figure out the dollar amount of the decrease. Operating profit is equal to the contribution margin multiplied by the number of units sold less total fixed costs. Contribution margin is the difference between selling price and variable costs per unit.

$$300 - 200 = 100$$

When sales equal 375 units, operating profit is 24,500.

$$(100 \times 375) - 13{,}000 = 24{,}500$$

When sales decrease by 15% to 300 units, operating profit is 17,000.

$$(100 \times 300) - 13{,}000 = 17{,}000$$

The decrease in profit is 7,500.

$$24{,}500 - 17{,}000 = 7{,}500$$

You determine the percent decrease by dividing the amount of the decrease by the original operating profit.

$$\frac{7{,}500}{24{,}500} = .306$$

797. Operating profit decreases by 30.8%.

The first step is to determine operating profit at each level of sales and figure out the dollar amount of the decrease. Operating profit is equal to the contribution margin multiplied by the number of units sold less total fixed costs. Contribution margin is the difference between selling price and variable costs per unit.

$$80 - 15 = 65$$

When sales equal 36,000 units, operating profit is 1,140,000.

$$(65 \times 36{,}000) - 1{,}200{,}000 = 1{,}140{,}000$$

When sales decrease by 15% to 30,600 units, operating profit is 789,000.

$$(65 \times 30{,}600) - 1{,}200{,}000 = 789{,}000$$

The decrease in profit is 351,000.

$$1{,}140{,}000 - 789{,}000 = 351{,}000$$

You determine the percent decrease by dividing the amount of the decrease by the original operating profit.

$$\frac{351{,}000}{1{,}140{,}000} = .308$$

798. 26.7%

The first step is to determine operating profit at each level of sales and figure out the dollar amount of the increase. Operating profit is equal to the contribution margin multiplied by the number of units sold less total fixed costs. Contribution margin is the difference between selling price and variable costs per unit.

$$4{,}000 - 2{,}000 = 2{,}000$$
$$(2{,}000 \times 200) - 250{,}000 = 150{,}000$$
$$(2{,}000 \times 220) - 250{,}000 = 190{,}000$$
$$190{,}000 - 150{,}000 = 40{,}000$$
$$\frac{40{,}000}{150{,}000} = .267$$

799. Operating profit will increase by a larger percent than the increase in sales.

Each additional sale contributes the entire contribution margin to the operating profit because the fixed costs are already covered by the previous sales. This situation occurs when a company has excess capacity, meaning it can produce and sell more units without increasing fixed costs.

800. the capability of a business to handle sales activity based on all available resources

Many of the costs of doing business are fixed over a certain level of activity. A factory building can produce up to a maximum number of units. If the company wants to increase beyond that maximum number, it must rent or buy another facility to produce those units. It would also have to hire more employees, add delivery trucks, and increase storage for finished goods. The capacity is fixed over a range, and then, when the top of the range is reached, fixed costs increase.

801. $49,000

Because the company can increase sales without increasing fixed costs, the whole contribution margin generates additional operating profit. The increase in operating profit is equal to the number of increased number of sales multiplied by the contribution margin per unit, which is the difference between the selling price and the variable costs per unit.

$$89 - 40 = 49$$
$$1{,}000 \times 49 = 49{,}000$$

802. $30,000,000

Because the company can increase sales without increasing fixed costs, the whole contribution margin generates additional operating profit. The increase in operating profit is equal to the increased number of sales multiplied by the contribution margin per unit.

$$15{,}000 \times 2{,}000 = 30{,}000{,}000$$

803. $80,000

Because the company can increase sales without increasing fixed costs, the entire contribution margin from each additional sale increases the operating profit. You calculate the increase by multiplying the increase in sales by the contribution margin per unit.

$$2,000 \times 40 = 80,000$$

804. $70,000

The increase in operating profit is equal to the increased number of units multiplied by the contribution margin per unit because the company can increase sales without any increase in fixed costs. The contribution margin is equal to the selling price less the variable cost per unit.

$$39 - 25 = 14$$

The increased number of sales is equal to 5,000.

$$100,000 \times .05 = 5,000$$

$$5,000 \times 14 = 70,000$$

805. $15,000,000

Because the company can increase sales without increasing fixed costs, the entire contribution margin from each additional sale increases operating profit. The increase in operating profit is equal to the increased number of sales multiplied by the contribution margin per unit.

Contribution margin is $10,000 less $9,000, which equals $1,000.

Sales increase is 150,000 contracts times 10%, which equals 15,000 units.

Increase in operating profit is $1,000 contribution margin times 15,000 units, which equals $15,000,000.

806. $3,840,000

Because the company can increase sales without increasing fixed costs, the entire contribution margin from each additional sale increases operating profit. The new operating profit based on the increased sales is equal to the old operating profit plus the product of the contribution margin times the additional sales. The additional sales are 14% of 100,000.

$$.14 \times 100,000 = 14,000$$

$$3,000,000 + (60 \times 14,000) = 3,840,000$$

807. $96,000

Because the company can increase sales without increasing fixed costs, the entire contribution margin from each additional sale increases operating profit. The increase in operating profit is equal to the increased number of sales multiplied by the contribution margin. To calculate the increased number of sales, divide the sales revenue by the price per unit. Then multiply that result by 15% to get the additional sales.

$$\frac{1{,}140{,}000}{57} \times .15 = 3{,}000$$

The contribution margin is equal to the selling price less the variable cost per unit.

$$57 - 25 = 32$$

$$3{,}000 \times 32 = 96{,}000$$

808. $1,485,000

Because the company can increase sales without increasing fixed costs, the entire contribution margin from each additional sale increases operating profit. The increase in operating profit is equal to the increased number of sales multiplied by the contribution margin. To calculate the increased number of sales, divide the sales revenue by the price per unit. Then multiply that result is by 10% to get the number of additional sales.

$$\frac{21{,}450{,}000}{650} \times .1 = 3{,}300$$

The contribution margin is equal to the selling price less the variable cost per unit.

$$650 - 200 = 450$$

$$3{,}300 \times 450 = 1{,}485{,}000$$

809. increase selling price and decrease variable cost per unit

Contribution margin is equal to the selling price less the variable cost per unit. That means the only way to increase it is to increase the selling price, decrease the variable cost per unit, or both.

810. 60¢

The dollar amount of the desired increase is equal to 2% of $1,200,000.

$$.02 \times 1{,}200{,}000 = 24{,}000$$

The 24,000 is spread over the 40,000, resulting in a decrease of 60 cents in variable cost per unit.

$$\frac{24{,}000}{40{,}000} = .60$$

811. The change will result in a decrease of $350,000 in operating profit.

The contribution margin will be reduced by $5 if the selling price per bag is reduced by that amount. Operating profit will decrease by $5 for each of the 70,000 bags sold.

$$5 \times 70{,}000 = 350{,}000$$

812. The change will increase break-even by 3,434 units.

Break-even sales volume equals total fixed costs divided by contribution margin. The original break-even level was 56,322 units.

$$\frac{4{,}900{,}000}{87} = 56{,}322$$

The new contribution margin will be $5 less if the selling price is decreased. The new break-even level is 59,756.

$$\frac{4{,}900{,}000}{82} = 59{,}756$$

The difference is an increase of 3,434 units.

$$59{,}756 - 56{,}322 = 3{,}434$$

813. The change will result in an increase of 5,523 units in break-even sales volume.

You calculate break-even sales volume by dividing total fixed costs by the contribution margin. The original contribution margin is equal to selling price less cost of goods sold expense less variable operating expenses per unit, or $112.

$$125 - 8 - 5 = 112$$

The original break-even sales volume is 35,714.

$$\frac{4{,}000{,}000}{112} = 35{,}714$$

The new contribution margin is 97.

$$110 - 8 - 5 = 97$$

The new break-even volume is 41,237, an increase of 5,523.

$$\frac{4{,}000{,}000}{97} = 41{,}237$$

$$41{,}237 - 35{,}714 = 5{,}523$$

814. Operating profit will decrease by $1,500,000.

The change in operating profit is equal to the change in contribution margin times the number of units sold. Contribution margin decreases by $15, from $125 to $110.

$$15 \times 100{,}000 = 1{,}500{,}000$$

815. $300,000

In this scenario, the cost of goods sold expense will decrease by $5.

$$160 - 155 = 5$$

If cost of goods sold expense decreases by $5, then each unit sold will contribute $5 more to operating profit.

$$60{,}000 \times 5 = 300{,}000$$

816. The change decreases operating profit by $480,000.

Each unit sold will contribute $3 less to the operating profit if the cost of goods sold unit increases from $65 to $68 per unit.

$$160{,}000 \times 3 = 480{,}000$$

817. The change will result in an increase in break-even sales volume of 2,472 units.

You calculate break-even sales volume by dividing total fixed costs by the contribution margin per unit. At the original contribution margin per unit, break-even sales volume was 40,385 units.

$$\frac{2{,}100{,}000}{52} = 40{,}385$$

The new contribution margin will be $3 less because of an increase in cost of goods sold expense per unit, from $65 to $68.

$$52 - 3 = 49$$

$$\frac{2{,}100{,}000}{49} = 42{,}857$$

The increase is the difference between the new break-even sales volume and the old one is 2,472.

$$42{,}857 - 40{,}385 = 2{,}472$$

818. The change decreases the break-even sales volume to 27,857 units.

Break-even sales volume is equal to fixed operating costs divided by contribution margin per unit. Originally, break-even sales volume for this company was 30,000 units.

$$\frac{1,950,000}{65} = 30,000$$

If cost of goods sold expense decreases by $5, then contribution margin increases by $5, to $70.

$$\frac{1,950,000}{70} = 27,857$$

819. No, because the contribution margin is decreased by 25%, and sales volume is increased by 12%.

Before the price decrease, the operating profit was 120,000. You multiply the contribution margin per unit by the number of units sold and deduct the fixed costs from that result.

$$(4 \times 80,000 - 200,000) = 120,000$$

With the decreased price, the company will sell 89,600 units if it achieves a 12% increase.

$$80,000 \times 1.12 = 89,600$$

After the price decrease, the operating profit is 68,800.

$$(3 \times 89,600) - 200,000 = 68,800$$

820. 61,539 units

You determine break-even sales volume by dividing fixed costs by the contribution margin per unit. The new contribution margin is equal to the new selling price less the new variable cost per unit.

$$100 \times .05 = 5$$

so the new selling price is $105.

$$105 - 40 = 65$$

is the new contribution margin.

$$\frac{4,000,000}{65} = 61,539$$

821. $233,220,000

The contribution margin from each car must cover the fixed costs of $70,000,000 plus the $980,000 in desired operating profit.

$$\frac{70{,}980{,}000}{7{,}000} = 10{,}140$$

cars must be sold. Each is sold for $23,000.

$$10{,}140 \times 23{,}000 = 233{,}220{,}000$$

in sales revenue, which will produce $980,000 in operating profit.

822. $2,370,000

The new sales volume is 98% of the old one, or 98,000 units. The new selling price is 5% higher than the old one, or $105. The new contribution margin is equal to the new selling price less the new variable cost per unit.

$$105 - 40 = 65$$

Total contribution margin is the per unit amount times the number of units sold, 98,000.

$$65 \times 98{,}000 = 6{,}370{,}000$$

Contribution margin less fixed costs equals the operating profit.

$$6{,}370{,}000 - 4{,}000{,}000 = 2{,}370{,}000$$

823. 10,143 cars

The contribution margin from each car must cover the fixed costs of $70,000,000 plus the $1,000,000 in desired operating profit. The contribution margin is the difference between the selling price and the variable cost per unit, or $7,000.

$$\frac{71{,}000{,}000}{7{,}000} = 10{,}143$$

cars.

824. $1,900,000

The increase in sales would be 10,000 units, which is 10% of 100,000. Each sale would produce an amount equal to the contribution margin toward profit.

$$10{,}000 \times 240 = 2{,}400{,}000$$

in additional profit. However, you must deduct the additional advertising cost.

$$2{,}400{,}000 - 500{,}000 = 1{,}900{,}000$$

increase in operating profit.

825. Operating profit increases by $3,000,000.

Instead of deducting $12,000,000 from the contribution margin, the new fixed costs are $9,000,000, or $3,000,000 lower. Deducting a cost that is $3,000,000 lower results in operating profit increasing by that amount.

826. $15,000

An increase in sales revenue of $25,000 means 2,500 more sandwiches are sold. Each of the sandwiches contributes $6 more in profit.

$$2{,}500 \times 6 = 15{,}000$$

more in operating profit.

827. 106,667 units

Before the price decrease, the operating profit was 120,000. You multiply the contribution margin per unit by the number of units sold and deduct the fixed costs from that result.

$$(4 \times 80{,}000) - 200{,}000 = 120{,}000$$

The new sales volume must cover the fixed costs of 200,000 and produce operating profit of 120,000, a total of 320,000.

You determine the new sales volume by dividing the new contribution margin into 320,000.

$$\frac{320{,}000}{3} = 106{,}667$$

828. Operating profit decreases by $5,700.

Operating profit last year was $16,000.

$$18,000 \times 50 = 900,000$$

in sales revenue.

$$18,000 \times 18 = 324,000$$

in variable cost.

$$900,000 - 324,000 = 576,000$$

in contribution margin.

Deducting fixed costs of $560,000 from the contribution margin results in operating profit of $16,000.

If the price is decreased by 5%, or $2.50, the new selling price is $47.50, and an increase in sales of 30% means the company will sell 23,400 bears.

$$18,000 \times .3 = 5,400$$

more sales.

$$18,000 + 5,400 = 23,400$$

$$23,400 \times 47.50 = 1,111,500$$

in sales revenue.

$$23,400 \times 18 = 421,200$$

in variable cost.

$$1,111,500 - 421,200 = 690,300$$

Deducting fixed costs of $560,000 and the increased advertising of $120,000, the new operating profit is $10,300.

$$690,300 - 560,000 - 120,000 = 10,300$$

The difference between the last year's operating profit of $16,000 and the operating profit resulting from the changes, $10,300, is a decrease of $5,700.

829. bolts of cloth for making shirts

Manufacturing costs are used to determine the product cost for each shirt. The direct materials to produce the product are a manufacturing cost.

830. wages for assemblers who build the kayaks

Manufacturing costs are used to determine the product cost for each kayak. The direct labor to produce the product is a manufacturing cost.

831. raw materials, direct labor, variable overhead, and fixed overhead

Manufacturing costs are the costs of production. The materials, labor, and overhead are all costs of production.

832. $5,657,000

The manufacturing costs are the costs directly associated with production, direct materials, direct labor, variable overhead, and fixed overhead.

$$3,507,000 + 1,200,000 + 700,000 + 250,000 = 5,657,000$$

833. $165,100

The manufacturing costs are the costs directly associated with production, direct materials, direct labor, variable overhead, and fixed overhead. The herbs and the glass jars are direct materials. The electricity to run the drying machines is a variable overhead cost. Depreciation on the drying machine is a fixed overhead cost.

$$137,000 + 8,100 + 5,000 + 15,000 = 165,100$$

834. $1,458,500

The manufacturing costs are the costs directly associated with production, direct materials, direct labor, variable overhead, and fixed overhead. Direct material, the factory workers' wages, the depreciation and insurance on the manufacturing facility, and the utilities at the manufacturing facility are all manufacturing costs. The sales commissions are a selling expense.

$$405,000 + 827,000 + 130,000 + 84,000 + 12,500 = 1,458,500$$

835. $198,400

The manufacturing costs are the costs directly associated with production, direct materials, direct labor, variable overhead, and fixed overhead. The wool, packaging, wages, and depreciation on the factory are manufacturing costs.

$$57,000 + 10,000 + 119,000 + 12,400 = 198,400$$

836. the material used in making a product

The main categories of manufacturing costs are direct materials, direct labor, variable overhead, and fixed overhead. The materials used in production of the products are direct materials.

837. depreciation on the machines that smooth the wood for the tables

Depreciation on factory buildings and production equipment are fixed overhead and are considered a manufacturing cost because the costs are directly associated with making the products.

838. insurance on a factory

Insurance on the factory is a fixed overhead cost which is one of the categories of manufacturing costs. The others are direct materials, direct labor, and variable overhead.

839. $3.10

Cost per unit is equal to total manufacturing costs divided by the number of units produced. Manufacturing costs are direct materials, direct labor, variable overhead, and fixed overhead.

$$\frac{60{,}000+80{,}000+10{,}000+5{,}000}{50{,}000}=3.10$$

840. $840,000

Total manufacturing costs are divided by the number of units produced to get the cost per unit, so you find total manufacturing costs by multiplying the number of units produced by the cost per unit.

$$28{,}000\times 30=840{,}000$$

841. $184

The total of the manufacturing costs per unit equals the product cost per unit. The material, labor, and overhead are the manufacturing costs from the list.

$$95+75+14=184$$

842. $11,446,000

Cost of goods sold expense equals the manufacturing cost per unit multiplied by the number of units sold.

$$118\times 97{,}000=11{,}446{,}000$$

843. $11,800,000

To determine cost per unit, you divide total manufacturing costs by number of units produced. So, to find total manufacturing costs in this problem, multiply the manufacturing cost per unit by the number of units produced.

$$118\times 100{,}000=11{,}800{,}000$$

844. $354,000

The cost of the unsold units is added to inventory. The company produced 100,000 and sold 97,000, so that leaves 3,000 unsold units. The manufacturing cost associated with each unit, $118, is added to ending inventory.

$$3,000 \times 118 = 354,000$$

845. $14.92

The first step is to calculate the total manufacturing costs. Manufacturing costs include the direct material, direct labor, variable overhead, and fixed overhead. The fabric and stuffing are direct materials. The wages for the workers who sew and stuff the animals are direct labor. The utilities associated with the factory and sewing machines are considered variable overhead costs. The depreciation on the machines is a fixed overhead cost.

$$30,000 + 5,000 + 2,500 + 40,000 + 12,000 = 89,500$$

The second step is to divide the total manufacturing costs by the number of units produced to calculate cost per unit.

$$\frac{89,500}{6,000} = 14.92$$

846. $44,160

The first step is to add all the manufacturing costs to get the cost per unit. The materials, labor, and overhead are all manufacturing costs.

$$95 + 75 + 14 = 184$$

The next step is to multiply the cost per unit times the number of units sold to get cost of goods sold expense.

$$184 \times 240 = 44,160$$

847. $291,040

Cost of goods sold expense is equal to the number of units sold multiplied by the product cost per unit. The first step is to calculate the total manufacturing costs. Manufacturing costs include the direct material, direct labor, variable overhead, and fixed overhead. From the list, all the costs except the advertising are manufacturing costs.

$$12,000 + 10,000 + 24,000 + 300 + 20,000 + 100 + 192,000 + 48,000 + 36,000 = 342,400$$

The next step is to divide total manufacturing costs by the number of units produced.

$$\frac{342,400}{10,000} = 34.24$$

The company sold 8,500 units, so cost of goods sold expense equals 291,040.

$$34.24 \times 8,500 = 291,040$$

848. $34.24

The first step is to calculate the total manufacturing costs. Manufacturing costs include the direct material, direct labor, variable overhead, and fixed overhead. From the list, all the costs except the advertising are manufacturing costs.

$$12{,}000+10{,}000+24{,}000+300+20{,}000+100+192{,}000+48{,}000+36{,}000=342{,}400$$

The next step is to divide total manufacturing costs by the number of units produced.

$$\frac{342{,}400}{10{,}000}=34.24$$

849. $45

The first step is to calculate the total manufacturing costs. Manufacturing costs include the direct material, direct labor, variable overhead, and fixed overhead. The materials, wages paid to production workers, factory utilities, and the factory depreciation are the manufacturing costs in the list.

$$150{,}000+50{,}000+15{,}000+10{,}000=225{,}000$$

The next step is to divide the total manufacturing costs of 225,000 by the number of units produced, 5,000.

$$\frac{225{,}000}{5{,}000}=45$$

850. $157,500

The first step is to determine the product cost per unit by dividing the manufacturing costs by the number of units produced. The manufacturing costs are direct materials, direct labor, variable overhead, and fixed overhead.

$$\frac{150{,}000+50{,}000+15{,}000+10{,}000}{5{,}000}=45$$

Then, cost of goods sold expense is equal to the number of units sold times the product cost per unit.

$$3{,}500\times 45=157{,}500$$

851. $67,500

The first step is to determine the product cost per unit by dividing the manufacturing costs by the number of units produced. The manufacturing costs are direct materials, direct labor, variable overhead, and fixed overhead.

$$\frac{150{,}000+50{,}000+15{,}000+10{,}000}{5{,}000}=45$$

Then, the cost of the unsold units is added to inventory. The company produced 5,000 units and sold 3,500, so 1,500 remain unsold.

$$1,500 \times 45 = 67,500$$

852. $51,360

The first step is to determine the product cost per unit by dividing the manufacturing costs by the number of units produced. The manufacturing costs are direct materials, direct labor, variable overhead, and fixed overhead.

$$\frac{12,000 + 10,000 + 24,000 + 300 + 20,000 + 100 + 192,000 + 48,000 + 36,000}{10,000} = 34.24$$

Then, the cost of the unsold units is added to inventory. The company produced 10,000 units and sold 8,500, so 1,500 remain unsold.

$$1,500 \times 34.24 = 51,360$$

853. $1,840

The company produced 250 units but sold 240, so 10 units are left unsold in inventory. To determine the amount, the first step is to figure out the cost per unit by identifying the manufacturing costs. The materials, labor, and overhead are the manufacturing costs, so the sum is the cost per unit, $184.

$$95 + 75 + 14 = 184$$

The amount added to inventory is $184 for each of the 10 tables.

$$184 \times 10 = 1,840$$

854. depreciation on delivery trucks & sales commissions

Period costs are expensed in the period incurred and not matched with product revenue. Selling and administrative expenses are period costs.

855. $344,400

Product costs are all manufacturing costs used to make the product and fall into the broad categories of direct materials, direct labor, variable overhead, and fixed overhead. The indirect materials used in the product are a variable overhead cost. The other product costs are materials used in products, labor costs of assembly line workers, factory supplies used, property taxes on the factory, and factory utilities.

$$6,400 + 120,000 + 110,000 + 24,000 + 45,000 + 39,000 = 344,400$$

Answers 801–900

856. $131,200

Period costs are expensed when incurred, not when the associated product is sold. Selling, general, and administrative expenses are the broad categories of period costs. From the list, depreciation on delivery equipment, gas and oil for delivery trucks, the president's salary, advertising expense, and repairs on office equipment are period costs.

$$10,200+2,200+92,000+25,000+1,800=131,200$$

857. factory workers and the factory manager

Product costs are all the costs associated with producing the product. Direct labor and overhead costs include wages paid to the employees that produce the products. Those employees are the factory workers and the factory manager.

858. chief executive officer, corporate attorney, salespeople, administrative support for executives, and delivery drivers

Period costs are the costs of operating the business that aren't directly associated with production. The costs in selling, general, and administrative salaries are period costs.

859. wages paid to designers of the costumes, fabric used in the costumes, wages paid to sewing machine operators, depreciation on sewing machines, and insurance on the factory building

Product costs are the costs of direct materials, direct labor, and overhead directly associated with the production of the costumes. That would be wages paid to designers of the costumes, fabric used in the costumes, wages paid to sewing machine operators, depreciation on sewing machines, and insurance on the factory building.

860. commissions paid to salespeople, charges for cellphones issued to salespeople, depreciation on delivery vehicles, gas and maintenance on delivery vehicles, insurance on the delivery vehicles, and amounts paid to CPAs who do the accounting and taxes

Period costs are the costs not associated with the actual production of the product but with the sales force and administrative aspect of the company. The items listed are all necessary to run the company but not directly tied to production of the costumes.

861. direct material

The ingredients become part of the product and are considered direct materials.

862. direct labor

The workers are directly involved with producing the trucks, so their wages are considered direct labor, a product cost.

863. overhead

Because the machines are directly involved in producing the product, the depreciation is a product cost. However, it isn't possible to separately identify the cost as direct labor or direct materials, so these costs are classified as overhead.

864. $114,080

The product costs are the direct materials, direct labor, and overhead necessary to build the lofts. The carpenter's wages are direct labor. The wood, nails, and glue are direct materials. The depreciation on the tools and on the costs associated with the truck are all overhead costs.

$$24{,}000+1{,}200+87{,}000+130+250+1{,}500=114{,}080$$

865. period cost

The advertising cost is a selling expense, and selling expenses are period costs.

866. $40,800

Period costs are costs of doing business that aren't directly tied to production. For Dorm Lofts Engineering, the CEO's salary, the salesperson's wages, bank charges, advertising, and accounting services are the period costs. The costs associated with the truck are product costs because the truck is used in the production of the lofts.

$$27{,}000+13{,}000+600+80+120=40{,}800$$

867. Direct materials: wood, nails, and glue

Direct labor: carpenter's wages

Overhead: depreciation on tools, insurance on the truck, depreciation on the truck, and gas and maintenance for the truck

Period costs: CEO's salary, salesperson's wages, bank charges, advertising, and accounting services

The wood, nails, and glue are the direct materials. The carpenter's wages are the direct labor cost. The overhead costs include the depreciation on tools, insurance on the truck, the depreciation on the truck, and the gas and maintenance because the truck is used to produce the lofts. The CEO's salary, salesperson's wages, bank charges, advertising costs, and the cost of accounting services are all period costs.

868. overhead

Utility costs are costs required to run a factory but are not costs that can be directly traced to the manufactured product. Instead, these costs are considered overhead.

869. debit Raw Materials Inventory and credit Accounts Payable

When raw materials are purchased, the Raw Materials Inventory account is increased with a debit, and Accounts Payable is increased with a credit.

870. Work-in-Process Inventory is increased and Raw Materials Inventory is decreased.

As materials are added to production, the Raw Materials Inventory gets smaller, or decreases. The materials are put into production, so Work-in-Process Inventory is increased.

871. debit Raw Materials Inventory and credit Cash

When materials used in production are purchased for cash, the Raw Materials Inventory is increased with a debit, and the Cash account is decreased with a credit.

872. debit Work-in-Process Inventory and credit Accumulated Depreciation

Depreciation on machines used in producing the products is a product cost and is classified as overhead. All product costs are recorded in Work-in-Process and increase that account. The balancing amount is to the contra account, Accumulated Depreciation.

873. debit Work-in-Process Inventory and credit Raw Materials Inventory

The fabric and padding are integral parts of the sneakers and are therefore direct materials. When direct materials are added to production, the Work-in-Process Inventory is increased with a debit and the Raw Materials Inventory is decreased with a credit.

874. $83,800

All manufacturing costs are added to the Work-in-Process Inventory account. That includes direct materials, direct labor, and overhead.

$$45{,}000+30{,}000+2{,}000+3{,}000+1{,}500+200+2{,}100=83{,}800$$

875. Work-in-Process Inventory: $162,500

Cash: $162,500

Selling Expense: $101,000

Cash: $101,000

The product costs are added to the Work-in-Process Inventory. Period costs are added to selling and administrative expenses. The wages paid to salespeople and delivery drivers are selling expenses.

876. $387,300

All product costs, which include direct materials, direct labor, and overhead, are added to Work-in-Process Inventory. When the production process is complete, the costs are moved to the Finished Goods Inventory.

$$157,300+143,000+48,000+3,000+36,000=387,300$$

877. debit Work-in-Process Inventory and credit Cash

Factory workers are direct labor and are therefore a product cost that is added to Work-in-Process Inventory.

878. debit Finished Goods Inventory and credit Work-in-Process Inventory

When products are completed and ready for sale, the costs are moved from Work-in-Process Inventory to Finished Goods Inventory. Inventory accounts are increased with a debit and decreased with a credit.

879. debit Work-in-Process Inventory for $450 and credit Accounts Payable for $450

The items listed are indirect materials and included in the manufacturing costs for the company. That means they must be added to Work-in-Process Inventory when used in the manufacturing process. Work-in-Process Inventory is increased by a debit in the amount of $450, and Accounts Payable is also increased by $450 with a credit.

880. debit Work-in-Process Inventory for $3,000, debit General Expense for $750, and credit Cash for $3,750

The cost of the electricity must be allocated between product cost and period cost. A reasonable allocation is based on percentage of occupancy, with 20% going to General Expenses and 80% going to product cost. The product cost is added to Work-in-Process Inventory with a debit, and the General Expense is also increased by a debit.

$$.2\times 3,750=750$$

General Expense is increased with a debit of $750. Work-in-Process Inventory is increased with a debit of $3,000, and Cash is credited for the total, $3,750.

881. debit General Expense and credit Cash

The legal costs associated with liability are not a product cost. Product costs usually end at the end of production. So, if the legal costs are not product costs, then they are part of General Expenses. Expenses are increased with a debit and Cash is decreased with a credit.

882. Work-in-Process Inventory: $89,350
Payroll Taxes Payable: $89,350
Payroll Tax Expense: $323,400
Payroll Taxes Payable: $323,400

The payroll taxes associated with direct labor are added to Work-in-Process Inventory. The other payroll taxes are period costs and expensed as incurred.

883. debit Finished Goods Inventory for $781,500 and credit Work-in-Process Inventory for $781,500

At the completion of production, the costs are moved from the Work-in-Process Inventory, which is reduced with a credit, to the Finished Goods Inventory, which is increased with a debit.

884. debit Work-in-Process Inventory for $156,000 and credit Raw Materials Inventory for the same amount

As product costs are added to the production process, the Work-in-Process Inventory account is increased with a debit. The cost of the raw materials used in manufacturing the shirts is taken out of the Raw Materials Inventory and added to Work-in-Process Inventory.

885. debit Cost of Goods Sold for $508,250 and credit Finished Goods Inventory for the same amount

The total manufacturing cost in Work-in-Process Inventory is $535,000, consisting of the materials of $156,000, the labor of $298,000, and the overhead of $81,000.

$$156{,}000 + 298{,}000 + 81{,}000 = 535{,}000$$

Because all shirts were completed, that amount was shifted to Finished Goods Inventory. When the shirts are sold, the costs associated with the shirts that were sold are put into Cost of Goods Sold. Ninety-five percent of the shirts were sold, so 95% of the costs are put into Cost of Goods Sold.

$$.95 \times 535{,}000 = 508{,}250$$

886. debit Work-in-Process Inventory and credit Raw Materials Inventory for $42,000

The company would add the cost of the materials put into production to the Work-in-Process Inventory and remove the cost from the Raw Materials Inventory.

887. debit Work-in-Process Inventory for $298,000, credit Cash for $248,000, and credit Payroll Taxes Payable for $50,000

Product costs are added to Work-in-Process Inventory when they are used by the production process. Only the labor necessary to produce the shirts is a product cost, and it includes both the wages and the payroll taxes.

888. debit Work-in-Process Inventory for $81,000, credit Cash for $46,000, and credit Accumulated Depreciation for $35,000

Overhead costs are product costs that are added to Work-in-Process Inventory. The offset for depreciation is the Accumulated Depreciation account.

889. debit Work-in-Process Inventory for $97,000, credit Cash for $80,800, and credit Payroll Taxes Payable for $16,200

The cost of direct labor, including the payroll taxes, is a product cost and is added to Work-in-Process Inventory. Cash is decreased for the amount of wages actually paid, and the payroll tax amount is payable in the future.

890. debit Finished Goods Inventory for $200,000 and credit Work-in-Process Inventory for the same amount

The product costs are put into the Work-in-Process Inventory, and when production is complete, those costs are moved to Finished Goods Inventory. The product costs are direct materials, direct labor, and overhead.

$$42{,}000 + 97{,}000 + 61{,}000 = 200{,}000$$

891. debit Cost of Goods Sold and credit Finished Goods Inventory for $192,000

Only the cost of the 48,000 units sold is moved to Cost of Goods Sold from Finished Goods. The total manufacturing or product costs for 50,000 units are $200,000, the sum of the direct materials, the direct labor, and the overhead.

$$42{,}000 + 97{,}000 + 61{,}000 = 200{,}000$$

That makes cost per unit $4.

$$\frac{200{,}000}{50{,}000} = 4$$

The Cost of Goods Sold is the cost per unit times the number of units sold.

$$4 \times 48{,}000 = 192{,}000$$

892. Work-in-Process Inventory has a zero balance, and Finished Goods Inventory has a balance of $26,750.

The total manufacturing cost in Work-in-Process Inventory is $535,000, consisting of the materials of $156,000, the labor of $298,000, and the overhead of $81,000.

$$156,000 + 298,000 + 81,000 = 535,000$$

Because all shirts were completed, that amount was shifted out of Work-in-Process Inventory and into Finished Goods Inventory, leaving the Work-in-Process Inventory with a zero balance. That makes sense because no work is in process; everything was finished. When the shirts are sold, the costs associated with the shirts that were sold are put into Cost of Goods Sold. Ninety-five percent of the shirts were sold, so 95% of the costs are put into Cost of Goods Sold.

$$.95 \times 535,000 = 508,250$$

That leaves the costs of the unsold shirts in the Finished Goods Inventory.

$$535,000 - 508,250 = 26,750$$

893. debit Finished Goods Inventory for $535,000 and credit Work-in-Process Inventory for $535,000

At the end of production, the costs are moved from Work-in-Process Inventory to Finished Goods Inventory. Finished Goods Inventory is increased with a debit, and Work-in-Process Inventory is decreased with a credit. Only manufacturing or product costs are in Work-in-Process. So, the amount of the journal entry is the sum of the direct materials, the direct labor, and the overhead.

$$156,000 + 298,000 + 81,000 = 535,000$$

894. $2,000

The burden rate is the fixed overhead cost per unit, or $2,000.

$$\frac{300,000}{150} = 2,000$$

895. $3,750,000

Total manufacturing costs for the year are equal to the variable cost per unit times the number of units produced, plus the fixed manufacturing overhead costs.

$$23,000 \times 150 + 300,000 = 3,750,000$$

896. $3,475

The cost per unit is equal to the sum of the variable costs, materials, labor, variable overhead, and fixed manufacturing overhead per unit.

$$800+1,200+100=2,100$$

in variable costs per unit.

Fixed manufacturing overhead per unit is equal to total fixed manufacturing costs divided by the number of units produced.

$$\frac{8,250,000}{6,000}=1,375$$

per unit when 6,000 units are produced.

$$2,100+1,375=3,475$$

is the new cost per unit.

897. $825

The burden rate is the fixed manufacturing cost per unit, which is equal to total fixed manufacturing costs divided by the number of units produced. The new burden rate is calculated using 10,000 units produced.

$$\frac{8,250,000}{10,000}=825$$

898. $23,000

Variable manufacturing cost per unit does not change with increases or decreases in the number of units produced.

899. $1,667

The burden rate is equal to the total fixed manufacturing costs divided by the number of units produced. Total fixed manufacturing costs are equal to the previous number of units produced multiplied by fixed cost per unit.

$$150\times2,000=300,000$$

$$\frac{300,000}{180}=1,667$$

900. $2,925

The cost per unit is made of variable and fixed manufacturing costs. The variable costs per unit stay the same and include the direct materials, direct labor, and variable manufacturing overhead.

$$800 + 1,200 + 100 = 2,100$$

which is the variable cost per unit.

The fixed manufacturing overhead cost per unit is equal to total fixed manufacturing costs divided by the number of units produced.

$$\frac{8,250,000}{10,000} = 825$$

is the new fixed manufacturing overhead cost per unit.

The new cost per unit is the sum of the two overhead costs.

$$2,100 + 825 = 2,925$$

901. $14,500,000

The first step is to calculate the new cost per unit. The cost per unit is made up of variable and fixed manufacturing costs. The variable costs per unit stay the same and include the direct materials, direct labor, and variable manufacturing overhead.

$$800 + 1,200 + 100 = 2,100$$

which is the variable cost per unit.

The fixed manufacturing overhead cost per unit is equal to total fixed manufacturing costs divided by the number of units produced.

$$\frac{8,250,000}{10,000} = 825$$

is the new fixed manufacturing overhead cost per unit.

The new cost per unit is the sum of the two overhead costs.

$$2,100 + 825 = 2,925$$

The next step is to calculate gross margin, which is equal to sales revenue, 10,000 units times the selling price of $6,500, less the cost of goods sold, 10,000 units times the new cost per unit.

$$65,000,000 - 29,250,000 = 35,750,000$$

Next, you deduct variable operating expenses, 10,000 times $1,500, from the gross margin to find the contribution margin.

$$35,750,000 - 15,000,000 = 20,750,000$$

Finally, you deduct fixed operating expenses from the contribution margin to find the new operating profit.

$$20,750,000 - 6,250,000 = 14,500,000$$

902. $24,667

The variable cost per unit will remain the same, but the fixed cost per unit will decrease. Total fixed manufacturing costs are equal to the number of units produced multiplied by fixed cost per unit.

$$150 \times 2{,}000 = 300{,}000$$

That number divided by the new number of coaches produced is the new fixed manufacturing cost per unit.

$$\frac{300{,}000}{180} = 1{,}667$$

The new cost per unit is the sum of the variable cost per unit and the new fixed manufacturing cost per unit.

$$23{,}000 + 1{,}667 = 24{,}667$$

903. $24,500

The variable cost per unit will remain the same at $23,000, but the fixed manufacturing cost per unit will be lower. Fixed manufacturing costs must be $300,000 if the cost per unit was $2,000 when 150 coaches were produced. The new fixed cost per unit is total fixed cost divided by the units produced.

$$\frac{300{,}000}{200} = 1{,}500$$

The new cost per unit will be the sum of the variable manufacturing cost per unit and the new fixed manufacturing cost per unit.

$$23{,}000 + 1{,}500 = 24{,}500$$

904. $1,950

First, calculate the amount of raw materials used in June.

$$500 \times 750 = 375{,}000$$

If about $75,000 was wasted, then the better estimate of the cost of raw materials necessary to produce 500 units is $300,000.

If production of 500 units should have used $300,000, then a better estimate of the cost of raw material per unit is $600.

Then, a more realistic estimate of cost per unit should use $600 as the cost of raw materials.

$$600 + 1{,}200 + 50 + 100 = 1{,}950$$

905. $20,000

If the company could produce 20% more feeders for $100,000, then 20% of the fixed costs are wasted.

$$.20 \times 100,000 = 20,000$$

is the cost of the idle capacity.

906. $1,660

The cost per unit given the records is the sum of the raw materials, the direct labor, and the overhead.

$$500 + 1,200 + 200 = 1,900$$

A more realistic number for the direct material necessary to produce one unit is less. $1200 is 125% of the more realistic cost of direct labor. So to calculate the old labor cost, you divide $1,200 by 1.25.

$$x \times 1.25 = 1,200$$

$$\frac{1,200}{1.25} = 960$$

which is a better reflection of the cost of direct labor.

$$500 + 960 + 200 = 1,660$$

is a more realistic cost per unit.

Then the wasted labor, $240 for each unit produced, can be identified as a cost of wasted labor on the operating profit report.

907. $32,500

Idle capacity is the difference between the maximum level of production, 18,000 units, and the current level, 15,000, or 3,000 units.

$$\frac{3,000}{18,000} = .167$$

which means 16.7% of the capacity is idle.

The fixed manufacturing overhead cost is $195,000, which allows the company to produce, at most, 18,000, and when producing on 15,000, 16.7% of it is wasted.

$$.167 \times 195,000 = 32,500$$

is the cost of the idle capacity.

908. The company should deduct the $14,000,000 from Cost of Goods Sold and deduct it from the Contribution Margin as Wasted Materials Expense.

If $14,000,000 worth of materials were wasted, then the cost per unit is too high by that amount, resulting in an inflated Cost of Goods Sold. To get a better number for Cost of Goods Sold, the company should deduct the $14,000,000. However, it is still a cost of operating during the period, so it still must reduce operating profit. You do that by listing it with the Fixed Operating Expenses.

909. $52,000

The company must repay the principal of $50,000 plus 4% interest.

$$.04 \times 50{,}000 = 2{,}000$$

$$50{,}000 + 2{,}000 = 52{,}000$$

910. $6,500

The interest is equal to the rate times the principal.

$$65{,}000 \times .10 = 6{,}500$$

is the interest that the company will pay at maturity. No interest is paid before maturity.

911. $100,000

The principal amount is the amount borrowed.

912. $25,440

The maturity value of a loan is equal to the amount of cash the borrower must repay. In this case, it's the $24,000 plus the interest for one year.

$$24{,}000 \times .06 = 1{,}440$$

$$24{,}000 + 1{,}440 = 25{,}440$$

913. 5%

The amount of interest is equal to the cash paid at maturity less the cash received at the beginning of the loan.

$$25,200 - 24,000 = 1,200$$

is the interest for one year on $24,000.

$$24,000 \times x = 1,200$$

$$\frac{1,200}{24,000} = .05$$

or 5% is the rate that produces $1,200 of interest for one year.

914. $925

The interest rate is stated as an annual rate, so if the company had the loan outstanding for a year, the interest would be 5% of $37,000, or $1,850. Because the loan will be repaid after only 6 months, the borrower owes half the interest, or $925.

915. debit interest expense and credit interest payable for $18,333

$$.08 \times 275,000 = 22,000$$

is the amount of interest due at repayment. On December 31, the company owes interest for March through December, or 10 months.

$$22,000 \times \frac{10}{12} = 18,333$$

is the amount of interest for 10 months.

However, no payment is required on December 31.

The journal entry will include a debit to interest expense for $18,333 and a credit to interest payable for the same amount.

916. $101,625

The maturity value of the note is equal to the original amount borrowed plus the interest. The company would have to pay $6,500 in interest if the note matured in one year. Instead, it matures in 3 months, which is one quarter of a year. That means the company will have to pay the principal of $100,000 plus one quarter of the annual interest.

$$100,000 + (6,500 \times .25) = 101,625$$

917. The rate is compounded more often than annually.

The 4.5% is the annual rate, but interest may be charged more often, which is called *compounding*. If the interest is compounded, then the effective rate is more than the annual rate.

918. $12,549.19

The interest is compounded more often than annually, so the amount of cash required to repay the loan is equal to the effective rate times the principal plus the principal.

$$(.045766 \times 12,000) + 12,000 = 12,549.19$$

919. $3,709.45

If the interest is compounded quarterly, then interest is charged at the rate of 2% every 3 months. And, the unpaid interest is added to the principal.

First 3 months:

$$.02 \times 45,000 = 900$$

in interest is added to the principal.

Second 3 months:

$$.02 \times 45,900 = 918$$

in interest is added to the principal.

Third 3 months:

$$.02 \times 46,818 = 936.36$$

in interest is added to the principal.

Fourth 3 months:

$$.02 \times 47,754.36 = 955.09$$

in interest is due.

$$900 + 918 + 936.36 + 955.09 = 3,709.45$$

920. 8.243%

The effective rate is equal to the interest actually paid divided by the principal. If the interest is compounded quarterly, then interest is charged at the rate of 2% every 3 months. And, the unpaid interest is added to the principal.

First 3 months:

$$.02 \times 45{,}000 = 900$$

in interest is added to the principal.

Second 3 months:

$$.02 \times 45{,}900 = 918$$

in interest is added to the principal.

Third 3 months:

$$.02 \times 46{,}818 = 936.36$$

in interest is added to the principal.

Fourth 3 months:

$$.02 \times 47{,}754.36 = 955.09$$

in interest is due.

$$900 + 918 + 936.36 + 955.09 = 3{,}709.45$$

total interest paid.

$$\frac{3{,}709.45}{45{,}000} = .08243$$

or 8.243%

921. 6%

The rate is equal to the interest paid divided by the principal, if the term is one year with annual compounding.

$$15{,}000 - 14{,}151 = 849$$

interest paid.

$$\frac{849}{14{,}151} = .06$$

or 6%

922. $123,450

You can solve this problem with a financial calculator or with time value of money tables. The $150,000 is the future value of the amount received today. The rate is 20% annually, but because it's compounded quarterly, the rate per period is 5%. The number of periods is 4 because the interest is compounded 4 times per year. If using the tables, you multiply the $150,000 by the factor you find on the table for the present value of $1. The factor in the table (rounded) is .823.

$$150{,}000 \times .823 = 123{,}450$$

923. $26,700

You can solve this problem with a financial calculator or with time value of money tables. The $30,000 is the future value of the amount received today. The rate is 12% annually, but because it's compounded semiannually, the rate per period is 6%. The number of periods is 2 because the interest is compounded 2 times per year. If using the tables, you multiply the $30,000 by the factor you find on the table for the present value of $1. The factor in the table (rounded) is .890.

$$30{,}000 \times .890 = 26{,}700$$

is the cash received.

924. $52,000

The first step is to determine how much cash the company receives at the signing of the loan. You can solve this problem with a financial calculator or with time value of money tables. The $250,000 is the future value of the amount received today. The rate is 24% annually, but because it's compounded quarterly, the rate per period is 6%. The number of periods is 4 because the interest is compounded 4 times per year. If using the tables, you multiply the $250,000 by the factor you find on the table for the present value of $1. The factor in the table is .792 (rounded).

$$250{,}000 \times .792 = 198{,}000$$

which is the amount of cash received by the company when signing the note.

The next step is to calculate the difference between what is received and what is paid, which is the interest.

$$250{,}000 - 198{,}000 = 52{,}000$$

If you use a financial calculator, you may get a result within a few dollars of this number because of rounding.

925. $24,070

You can solve this problem with a financial calculator or with time value of money tables. The $10,000 gift is the present value, and you're trying to find the future value. The time period is 18 years, and the rate is 5%. No adjustment to the number of periods or rate is necessary because the rate is compounded annually. If using the tables, multiply 10,000 by the factor in the table for the future value of $1. The factor in the table is 2.407 (rounded).

$$10{,}000 \times 2.407 = 24{,}070$$

926. $280,416

You can solve this problem with a financial calculator or with time value of money tables. The $127,000 bonus is the present value, and you're trying to find the future value. The time period is 10 years, and the rate is 8%. However, you need to adjust the rate and years for the quarterly compounding. The number of periods equals the number of years times the number of compounding periods per year.

$$10 \times 4 = 40$$

The rate is the rate per period, which is equal to the annual rate divided by the number of compounding periods per year.

$$\frac{8}{4} = 2$$

Using the tables, multiply 127,000 by the factor in the table for the future value of $1. The factor in the table is 2.208.

$$127{,}000 \times 2.208 = 280{,}416$$

927. $130,350

You can solve this problem with a financial calculator or with time value of money tables. The $6,000 bonus is the present value, and you're trying to find the future value. The time period is 40 years, and the rate is 8%. No adjustment to the number of periods or rate is necessary because the rate is compounded annually. Using the tables, multiply 6,000 by the factor in the table for the future value of $1. The factor in the table is 21.725.

$$6{,}000 \times 21.725 = 130{,}350$$

928. monthly

The monthly compounding option provides the largest future value, which should be the goal. Compounding monthly means that interest is calculated and added to the principal amount calculation more often than the other methods.

929. $n = 2$, $i = 12$

The payments on this loan are annual, so no adjustments to the number of periods or the interest rate are necessary.

930. $11,870.85

Using time value of money tables requires a table that gives factors for the present value of an annuity. You multiply that factor by the payment to determine the present value. In this problem, you know the present value, $50,000. So, if the present value is divided by the factor, the result is the amount of the payment. The factor for 5 periods and 6% is 4.212.

$$x \times 4.212 = 50{,}000$$

where x is the payment amount.

$$\frac{50{,}000}{4.212} = 11{,}870.85$$

931. $n = 240$, $i = .5$

The payments are to be made monthly, so you must adjust both the number of years and the interest rate to reflect that 12 payments are paid per year. The total number of payments is 240 if 12 payments are made each of the 20 years. If the interest rate for the year is 6%, then the interest rate for each month is .5%.

932. $2,012.88

A stream of payments of equal amount made at equal intervals of time, in this case once a year, is called an *annuity.* Use a time value of money table that gives factors for the present value of an annuity. Multiply that factor by the payment to determine the present value. In this problem, you know the present value, $10,000. So, if the present value is divided by the factor, the result is the amount of the payment. The factor for 8 periods and 12% is 4.968.

$$x \times 4.968 = 10{,}000$$

where x is the payment amount.

$$\frac{10{,}000}{4.968} = 2{,}012.88$$

933. The shop in the downtown office building because the ROI is the highest.

The shop with the highest ROI is the best performer.

934. 8%

ROI is equal to operating income divided by average operating assets. Assets at the beginning of the year were $12,000 and at the end of the year were $15,000 because of the purchase.

$$\frac{12,000+15,000}{2}=13,500$$

is the average operating assets.

$$\frac{1,080}{13,500}=.08$$

or 8%

935. The Splint Division is performing the best with an ROI of 9%.

ROI is a good way to compare divisions of different sizes. You calculate ROI as operating profit divided by average assets.

$$\frac{499}{6,238}=.08$$

or 8% ROI for the Booboo Division.

$$\frac{350}{3,889}=.09$$

or 9% ROI for the Splint Division.

$$\frac{570}{9,500}=.06$$

or 6% ROI for the Intensive Care Division.

936. 6.55%

You calculate ROI by dividing operating profit by the average book value of assets. Average assets are the sum of the book values divided by 2. The book value is cost less accumulated depreciation.

Beginning of the year book value:

$$20,000,000-5,000,000=15,000,000$$

End of year book value:

$$20,000,000-(5,000,000+1,000,000)=14,000,000$$

So, the average book value of assets is $14,500,000.

$$\frac{950,000}{14,500,000}=.0655$$

or ROI of 6.55%.

937. 5.88%

Using the DuPont model, ROI is the product of profit margin and asset turnover.

$$3.92\% \times 1.5 = 5.88$$

938. Profit margin is multiplied by asset turnover.

Profit margin measures the relationship between earnings and income. The higher the profit margin, the better the profitability of the organization. But the profit margin doesn't take into account the amount of assets necessary to produce the profit. So, comparing the profit margin of two companies ignores the efficient use of assets. The DuPont model incorporates asset-use efficiency by multiplying the profit margin by *asset turnover,* the relationship between earnings and total assets.

939. Profit margin is 27.9%, asset turnover is 1.5, and ROI is 41.85%.

Profit margin is equal to operating income divided by sales.

$$\frac{98{,}000}{351{,}000} = .279$$

or 27.9%

Asset turnover is equal to sales divided by average assets.

$$\frac{351{,}000}{234{,}000} = 1.5$$

ROI is the product of profit margin and asset turnover.

$$.279 \times 1.5 = .4185$$

or 41.85%

940. Profit margin is 31.7%, asset turnover is .845, and ROI is 26.8%

Profit margin is equal to operating profit divided by sales.

$$\frac{27{,}000}{85{,}300} = .317$$

or 31.7%.

Asset turnover is equal to sales divided by average assets.

$$\frac{85{,}300}{101{,}000} = .845$$

ROI is the product of profit margin and asset turnover.

$$.317 \times .845 = .268$$

or 26.8%

941. $65

The amount of dividends distributed in excess of retained earnings is a return of investment. Because it's the first year of operation, the retained earnings balance starts at zero. It is increased by the net income of $215.

$$280 - 215 = 65$$

of the dividends is a return of investment.

942. $215

There's no beginning balance in retained earnings because this is the firm's first year of operations. Net income is $215. Therefore, the first $215 in dividends is considered income to the shareholders.

943. $255

The amount of dividends distributed up to the amount of retained earnings is income to the shareholders. The retained earnings balance starts at $40. It's increased by the net income of $215, so any dividends payout up to $255 is income to shareholders.

944. $25

The amount of dividends distributed in excess of retained earnings is a return of investment. The retained earnings balance starts at $40. It's increased by the net income of $215, so any dividends payout over $255 is a return of investment.

$$280 - 255 = 25$$

945. 5%

The first step is to find the total return over the time period and convert it to a rate by dividing by the initial investment.

$$\frac{1{,}000 + 2{,}000}{10{,}000} = .30$$

or 30% over the 6 years.

To find the annual return, divide by the holding period of 6 years.

$$\frac{.30}{6} = .05$$

or 5%.

946. 12%

The first step is to find the total return over the time period and convert it to a rate by dividing by the initial investment. The dividends are 2% of the investment of $50,000 for 10 years. The appreciation is the difference between the purchase price and the selling price of the investment.

$$\frac{(.02\times 50{,}000)10+(100{,}000-50{,}000)}{50{,}000}=1.20$$

or 120% over the 10 years.

To find the annual return, divide by the holding period of 10 years.

$$\frac{1.20}{10}=.12$$

or 12% average annual return.

947. 5%

The first step is to find the total return over the holding period of 8 years. In this problem, the total is $8,000 because no increase in the price of the original investment has occurred. If Aaron bought the stock for $20,000 and sold half for exactly half the original investment, the stock price hasn't changed over the 8 years, so there's no return other than the dividends received.

Next, divide the total return by the original investment to get a rate over the entire time the stock was held.

$$\frac{8{,}000}{20{,}000}=.40$$

or 40% over 8 years.

$$\frac{.40}{8}=.05$$

or 5% average annual return.

948. 6%

The total return is equal to the sum of the dividends plus the selling price minus the purchase price.

$$(1+2+2+2+3)1{,}000+(55\times 1{,}000)-(50\times 1{,}000)=$$

$$10{,}000+55{,}000-50{,}000=15{,}000$$

is the total return over the 5 years.

Next, divide the total return by the original investment amount to convert the total return to a rate.

$$\frac{15{,}000}{50{,}000}=.3$$

or 30% over the 5 years.

Divide by the number of years to find the annual rate.

$$\frac{.30}{5}=.06$$

or 6%.

949. 9 years

The rule of 72 gives a rough idea of how long it will take for an investment to double in value given a stable rate of return. Divide 72 by the rate to get the number of years.

$$\frac{72}{8}=9$$

years

950. 4.8 years

The rule of 72 gives a rough idea of how long it will take for an investment to double in value given a stable rate of return. Divide 72 by the rate to get the number of years.

$$\frac{72}{15}=4.8$$

years

951. 7.2 years

The rule of 72 gives a rough idea of how long it will take for an investment to double in value given a stable rate of return. Divide 72 by the rate to get the number of years.

$$\frac{72}{10}=7.2$$

years

952. 7.2%

The rule of 72 gives a rough idea of how long it will take for an investment to double in value given a stable rate of return. The rule solves for the number of years, dividing the number 72 by the rate to get the number of years. In this problem, you know the number of years but not the rate, so dividing 72 by the required rate will result in 10 years needed to double the investment.

$$\frac{72}{x} = 10$$

years

Solving for *x*:

$$\frac{72}{10} = 7.2$$

953. 7%

The process to calculate the weighted average cost of capital is to determine the amount of interest paid on each type of financing and then divide the total interest paid by the total amount of financing.

Principal	Rate	Interest
1,000,000	.06	60,000
1,000,000	.08	80,000
2,000,000		140,000

$$\frac{140,000}{2,000,000} = .07$$

or 7%

954. 9%

The process to calculate the weighted average cost of capital is to determine the amount of interest paid on each type of financing and then divide the total interest paid by the total amount of financing. The line of credit is short-term borrowing, so it's not included in the calculation.

Principal	Rate	Interest
2,000,000	.0625	125,000
1,000,000	.07	70,000
1,500,000	.10	150,000
2,000,000	.12	240,000
6,500,000		585,000

$$\frac{585,000}{6,500,000} = .09$$

or 9%

955. 9.1%

The process to calculate the weighted average cost of capital is to determine the amount of interest paid on each type of financing and then divide the total interest paid by the total amount of financing. The line of credit is short-term borrowing, so it's not included in the calculation.

Principal	Rate	Interest
575,000	.035	20,125
20,000	.07	1,400
150,000	.12	18,000
1,000,000	.12	120,000
1,745,000		159,525

$$\frac{159{,}525}{1{,}745{,}000} = .091$$

or 9.1%

956. 11.6%

The process to calculate the weighted average cost of capital is to determine the amount of interest paid on each type of financing and then divide the total interest paid by the total amount of financing.

Principal	Rate	Interest
2,000,000	.0425	85,000
10,000,000	.05	500,000
150,000	.10	15,000
200,000,000	.12	24,000,000
212,150,000		24,600,000

$$\frac{24{,}600{,}000}{212{,}150{,}000} = .116$$

or 11.6%

957. $25,500

To calculate the NPV, you discount the cash flows using the required rate of return and then compare that to the initial required investment. If the result is positive, the company should invest.

The present value of an annuity of $150,000 discounted at 10% for 4 years is $150,000 multiplied by the factor of 3.17, which equals $475,500.

Comparing the present value of the cash flows with the initial investment:

$$475{,}500 - 450{,}000 = 25{,}500$$

is the NPV.

958. No, because the project has a negative NPV.

The best way to analyze this problem is to compute the net present value, NPV. You discount the cash flows using the required rate of return and then compare that to the initial required investment. If the result is positive, the company should invest.

The present value of an annuity of $200,000 discounted at 10% for 3 years is $497,400.

This amount is less than the cost of the new technology, so the NPV is negative. The company shouldn't invest in a project that has a negative NPV.

959. The company should purchase the first machine because it has a higher NPV.

The best way to analyze this situation is to calculate the net present value, or NPV, for each machine. The highest NPV is the best investment. To calculate the NPV, compare the present value of the cash flows to the initial investment.

For the first machine, the present value of a $15,000 annuity discounted at 10% for 20 years is $15,000 times 8.514, which equals $127,710.

For the second machine, the present value of a $15,000 annuity discounted at 10% for 10 years is $15,000 times 6.145, which equals $92,175.

The NPV is the difference between the present value of the discounted cash flows and the purchase price of the machine.

For machine 1:

$$127{,}710 - 100{,}000 = 27{,}710$$

is the NPV.

For machine 2:

$$92{,}175 - 75{,}000 = 17{,}175$$

is the NPV.

The company should purchase the machine with the higher NPV, machine 1.

960. Yes, because the IRR is 9.6%, which is greater than 8%.

Using a financial calculator, calculate the rate if the payment is $80,000, the present value is $500,000, and the time period is 10 years. The result is 9.6%, which is a higher rate of return than the required 8%.

961. 3.8%

Using a financial calculator, calculate the rate if the payment is $10,000, the present value is $75,000, and the time period is 9 years. The result is 3.8%.

962. current ratio

Liquidity ratios are used to evaluate a company's ability to pay current obligations. The current ratio is the only liquidity ratio in the list.

963. return on equity, return on assets, and earnings per share

All three of these ratios compare income to some other element that measures the profitability for the year.

964. payout ratio

The payout ratio compares the cash dividends declared on common stock to net income. A retiree looking for dividend income will want to invest in a company that has a high payout ratio.

965. The company is collecting its receivables faster this year.

The accounts receivable turnover illustrates how fast a company can convert its receivables to cash. When the number gets bigger, the company is collecting faster.

966. A supplier is trying to determine whether a customer is creditworthy.

Liquidity ratios are used to evaluate a company's ability to pay current obligations. Before extending credit, the supplier will want to analyze the customer's ability to pay.

967. times interest earned, cash debt coverage, and free cash flow

Long-term creditors and stockholders are interested in the company's ability to pay its long-term debt. The times interest earned, cash debt coverage, and free cash flow provide information on repayment ability.

968. asset turnover

You calculate the ratio by dividing net sales by average total assets. The higher the ratio, the more sales are generated per dollar of assets.

969. The company's liquidity is improving.

Last year's ratio means that for every dollar in current liabilities, the company had 87 cents of current assets. The next year, it had 90 cents of current assets for every dollar of current liabilities, so the situation has improved.

970. BebeBanana is less solvent than the average company in the same industry.

You calculate the debt to assets ratio by dividing total liabilities by total assets. A higher ratio indicates more debt in relation to assets, which means solvency is more fragile.

971. No, the solvency ratios are both below the industry average.

A lender would be interested in the borrower's ability to meet interest payment requirements and the amount of leverage existing in the financing of the company's assets. Both of the company's solvency ratios are worse than the industry average, so making the loan would be risky.

972. 5.6

The current ratio is equal to current assets divided by current liabilities. Cash, accounts receivable, and inventory are the current assets. Accounts payable is the only current liability.

$$\frac{150+70+60}{50}=5.6$$

973. 6.92

You calculate accounts receivable turnover by dividing net credit sales by average accounts receivable. To get net credit sales, you deduct returns from the credit sales for the year.

$$\frac{475-25}{(70+60)\times .5}=6.92$$

974. 6.36

Current cash debt coverage assesses the ability of the company to pay its current liabilities. The formula is cash provided by operating activities divided by average current liabilities.

$$\frac{350}{(50+60)\times .5}=6.36$$

975. 4.75

Times interest earned compares earnings before interest and tax to interest expense.

$$\frac{20+8+10}{8}=4.75$$

976. .099; a lower cash debt coverage ratio indicates a company with a weaker solvency position

You calculate cash debt coverage by dividing net cash from operating activities by average total liabilities.

$$\frac{35}{(142+562)\times .5}=.099$$

Closet Queen Organizers has a lower cash debt coverage ratio than its competitor, which suggests weaker solvency.

977. 76

Free cash flow is a measure of solvency and assesses a company's ability to pay dividends and expand. Free cash flow equals net cash from operating activities less capital expenditures less cash dividends.

$$550 - 310 - 164 = 76$$

978. 4.75; because the company has a much lower ratio, it is in a weaker solvency position than the average company in the industry

Times interest earned compares earnings before interest and tax to interest expense.

$$\frac{20 + 8 + 10}{8} = 4.75$$

The company's ratio is much lower than the industry average, indicating that Closet Queen Organizers is less solvent than the average company in the industry.

979. 5.18

You calculate inventory turnover by dividing cost of goods sold by average inventory.

$$\frac{285}{(60 + 50) \times .5} = 5.18$$

980. 52.7

You determine the average collection period by dividing 365, the number of days in a year, by the accounts receivable turnover ratio. You calculate accounts receivable turnover by dividing net credit sales by average accounts receivable. You get net credit sales by deducting returns from the credit sales for the year.

$$\frac{475 - 25}{(70 + 60) \times .5} = 6.92$$

$$\frac{365}{6.92} = 52.7$$

981. 2014: 22.7% and 2015: 62.4%; the increase in the ratio suggests deteriorating solvency

You determine the debt to assets ratio by dividing total liabilities by total assets.

$$\frac{562}{901} = .624$$

or 62.4% in 2015.

$$\frac{142}{625} = .227$$

or 22.7% in 2014.

The debt to assets ratio has increased by nearly 175%. In 2014, the company would have had to sell 22.7% of its assets to pay off the liabilities. In 2015, the company would have to sell 62.4% of the assets. The company's solvency has deteriorated.

982. 18%

ROE is a measure of a company's profitability. Analysts look at the trend over time and compare the company's ratio to the industry average to determine the profitability of the company. ROE is equal to net income divided by common stockholders' equity. Common stockholders' equity is equal to the sum of contributed capital and retained earnings if there is no preferred stock.

$$\frac{970}{5{,}364} = .18$$

or 18%

983. 6.6%

Profit margin or return on sales is a measure of profitability and shows the amount of income resulting from each dollar of sales. You calculate it by dividing net income by net sales.

$$\frac{970}{14{,}727} = .066$$

or 6.6%

984. 97¢

Earnings per share measures the earnings available to common shareholders. The numerator of the ratio is net income reduced by the amount of preferred dividends paid during the year. The denominator is the average number of shares outstanding during the year.

$$\frac{970}{1{,}000} = .97$$

985. 59.3%

You calculate the payout ratio by dividing the cash dividends on common stock by net income.

$$\frac{575}{970} = .593$$

or 59.3%

986. 13%

Return on assets is a profitability measure. You calculate it by dividing net income by average assets during the year.

$$\frac{970}{(8{,}192+6{,}753)\times.5}=\frac{970}{7{,}742.50}=.13$$

or 13%

987. 1.97

Asset turnover is a profitability measure that indicates how well the assets of the company produce sales. You calculate it as net sales divided by average assets.

$$\frac{14{,}727}{(8{,}192+6{,}753)\times.5}=\frac{14{,}727}{7{,}472.50}=1.97$$

988. **Boys Corporation because it distributes less of its income and reinvests more in the company, which contributes to faster growth.**

To grow, a company needs cash. The major source of cash for companies is income, and they can choose to distribute it to shareholders through dividends or retain it in the business to finance growth. Therefore, if a company distributes less of its income as evidenced by a lower dividend payout ratio, it will have more funds available for growth.

989. 23

You calculate the price-earnings ratio by dividing the stock price per share by the earnings per share. You calculate earnings per share by comparing earnings available to common shareholders divided by the average number of shares of common stock outstanding during the year. The numerator of the ratio is net income reduced by the amount of preferred dividends paid during the year. The denominator is the average number of shares outstanding during the year.

$$\frac{970}{1{,}000}=.97$$

is the earnings per share for 2015.

$$\frac{22.31}{.97}=23$$

990. 2014: 6.5% and 2015: 6.6%; indicates a slight improvement in profit margin for the company

Profit margin or return on sales is a measure of profitability and shows the amount of income resulting from each dollar of sales. You calculate it by dividing net income by net sales.

$$\frac{970}{14{,}727} = .066$$

or 6.6% for 2015.

$$\frac{690}{10{,}639} = .065$$

or 6.5% for 2014.

An increasing profit margin is a positive sign and indicates a slight improvement for this company.

991. 2014: 49.9% and 2015: 48.4%; a decreasing gross profit rate indicates the company is less profitable

You calculate gross profit rate by dividing gross profit by net sales.

$$\frac{5{,}305}{10{,}639} = .499$$

or 49.9% for 2014.

$$\frac{7{,}129}{14{,}727} = .484$$

or 48.4% for 2015.

The company is getting weaker because a lower gross profit rate is worse.

992. .64

Current cash debt coverage is a measure of liquidity that is based on cash. The formula is net cash from operating activities divided by average current liabilities.

$$\frac{10{,}900}{17{,}000} = .64$$

993. $18,200

Free cash flow is equal to net cash flows from operating activities less capital expenditures less dividends paid.

$$63{,}500 - 27{,}300 - 8{,}000 - 10{,}000 = 18{,}200$$

994. .15

You calculate cash debt coverage by dividing net cash flows from operating activities by average total liabilities.

$$\frac{101,500}{59,100+600,000}.15$$

995. 1.33

Current cash debt coverage is a measure of liquidity that is based on cash. The formula is net cash from operating activities divided by average current liabilities.

$$\frac{4,000}{(1,000+5,000)\times .5}=1.33$$

996. .727

Cash debt coverage is a solvency ratio that you calculate by dividing net cash from operating activities by average total liabilities.

$$\frac{4,000}{5,500}=.727$$

997. .30

You calculate cash debt coverage by dividing net cash flows from operating activities by average total liabilities.

$$\frac{13,100}{43,000}=.30$$

998. 2.9

Current cash debt coverage is equal to net cash flows from operating activities divided by average current liabilities.

$$\frac{x}{27,000}=3.7$$

Solving for x:

$$3.7\times 27,000=99,900$$

net cash flows from operating activities.

Cash debt coverage is equal to net cash flows from operating activities divided by total liabilities.

$$\frac{99,900}{35,000}=2.9$$

999. –$19,400

You calculate free cash flow by subtracting cash dividends paid and capital expenditures (the purchase of long-term assets) from net cash flows from operating activities.

$$-13{,}100 - 2{,}300 - 4{,}000 = -19{,}400$$

1,000. Travel Nut Luggage is more solvent because it has a higher cash debt coverage than Perfect Bags, Inc.

Higher cash debt coverage indicates better solvency, so Travel Nut Luggage is more solvent.

1,001. –.77

You calculate current cash debt coverage by dividing net cash flows from operating activities by average current liabilities.

$$\frac{-13{,}100}{17{,}000} = -.77$$

Index

• A •

• B •

• R •

• S •

• T •

• U •

• W •

Workspace

Workspace

Workspace

Workspace

Workspace

About the Author

After earning her PhD in accounting at Texas A&M University, **Kate Mooney** began teaching at St. Cloud State University in central Minnesota in 1986 and currently serves as chair of the Accounting Department. In addition to her teaching, she has served on the boards of numerous nonprofit organizations, including chairing the Minnesota Board of Accountancy and chairing the finance committee of a multi-employer health and pension benefit association. In 2010 she was selected to serve on the Pathways Commission. Her publications include three other books and numerous articles and cases. She holds an active CPA license in Minnesota.

Dedication

I'd like to dedicate this book to my family. Heaps of love to Moon, New Moons, Team Chaos, Moonbaums, and Super Baby.

Author's Acknowledgments

This book has been a collective effort. I'd like to thank the team at Wiley, particularly Chrissy Guthrie for guiding me in the ways of *For Dummies*. I'd also like to thank Grace Freedson for connecting me with this opportunity. Finally, I must thank all the students who have taught me so much about the difficulties of learning accounting. Let's hope this book helps you a bit.

Publisher's Acknowledgments

Acquisitions Editor: Stacy Kennedy

Editorial Project Manager: Christina Guthrie

Copy Editor: Todd Lothery

Technical Editor: Ken Boyd

Art Coordinator: Alicia B. South

Project Coordinator: Erin Zeltner

Cover Image: ©iStockphoto.com/cglade

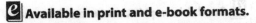